Landmark Essays

Landmark Essays

on
Advanced Composition

Edited by Gary A. Olson and Julie Drew

LEA Hermagoras Press
An Imprint of Lawrence Erlbaum Associates, Publishers

Landmark Essays Volume Ten

Cover design by Kathi Zamminer

Typesetting and camera-ready production by Gary A. Olson

Lawrence Erlbaum Associates, Inc., Publishers
10 Industrial Avenue
Mahwah, New Jersey 07430

Library of Congress Cataloging-in-Publication Data

Landmark essays on advanced composition / edited by Gary A. Olson and
Julie Drew.
    p. cm. --(Landmark essays : 10)
  ISBN 1-880393-25-5 (pbk. : alk. paper)
  1. English language--Rhetoric--Study and teaching. I. Olson,
Gary A., 1954- . II. Drew, Julie. III. Series: Landmark essays :
v. 10.
PE1404.L27 1996
808'.042'07--dc20   95-52237
                                                 CIP

Books published by Lawrence Erlbaum Associates are printed
on acid-free paper, and their bindings are chosen
for strength and durability.

Printed in the United States of America

10 9 8 7 6 5 4 3 2 1

AJM 1572

Acknowledgments

We gratefully acknowledge James J. Murphy for his belief in this project and for his kind encouragement during its completion.

We would also like to thank Sara M. Deats, chair of the department of English at the University of South Florida, for her continuing support and friendship.

Thomas West deserves special recognition for his emotional and editorial assistance, as does Dominique Berrebbi for her help in proofreading. Also thanks to Jeanne Pietrzak of Graphic Gold for her assistance.

Finally, we would like to thank the many compositionists who have dedicated themselves to furthering scholarship and pedagogy in advanced composition, particularly those who appear in this collection.

About the Editors

Gary A. Olson is Coordinator of the Graduate Program in Rhetoric and Composition at the University of South Florida, where he also developed an undergraduate program in Professional and Technical Writing. Presently he serves as President of the Association of Teachers of Advanced Composition. In 1993, the Council of Editors of Learned Journals presented him with an International Award for Distinguished Retiring Editor for his decade of work as editor of the *Journal of Advanced Composition*. His most recent books are *Women Writing Culture* (with Elizabeth Hirsh) and *Composition Theory for the Postmodern Classroom* (with Sidney I. Dobrin), both published by State University of New York Press.

Julie Drew teaches expository writing, professional writing, and advanced technical writing at the University of South Florida. She has published articles and reviews in *Composition Studies*, *Composition Forum*, and *Teaching English in the Two-Year College*. She is currently completing a book in which she examines the role(s) compositionists play in structures of academic authority by examining the disjunctions between the articulated intentions of radical pedagogies found in current scholarship and the profession's actual practices as manifested both within and outside of the academy.

For Nancy Elizabeth Cristiano

and for Philip and Brian

Table of Contents

Part Three: Curricular Content and Emphases

Part Four: Theoretical and Political Issues

Introduction

Landmark Essays on Advanced Composition

by Gary A. Olson and Julie Drew

Landmark Essays on Advanced Composition is a collection of influential essays on the theory and pedagogy of advanced composition. As advanced composition continues to grow as an important sub-area of rhetoric and composition, it becomes increasingly more important for scholars and teachers to have access to key studies produced in the field. *Landmark Essays on Advanced Composition* provides a comprehensive overview of significant work in the field over the last three decades. The collection contains twenty-four essays and articles published in major scholarly books and journals. The bulk of these works were published between 1980 and 1995.

Advanced composition is a difficult term to define, and although many composition scholars have offered definitions, few can agree on what it actually means. Perhaps Lynn Z. Bloom says it best when she writes, "Advanced composition is like love: everybody knows what they mean by the term, few can define it to anyone else's satisfaction, and each practitioner has his or her own way of doing it" (143). While a comprehensive definition is elusive, literally thousands of advanced composition courses are being offered at colleges and universities across the country. Articulating the purpose, content, theoretical bases, and ethics of such courses is becoming increasingly more critical as national discussions of literacy, and education in general, appear more frequently in public as well as academic debate.

In their 1990 article, Ronald Shumaker, Larry Dennis, and Lois Green present research data that illustrate the ubiquity of advanced composition. Shumaker and his colleagues reviewed six hundred institutional catalogues and found that seventy percent of these colleges and universities list advanced composition as an offered course, while the remaining thirty percent list comparable courses under other titles. The authors also present information from one hundred and twenty-four colleges and universities who responded to a questionnaire about the design of their advanced composition courses. (Of these institutions, seventy-seven percent note the absence of a standard syllabus, confirming the difficulty of defining "advanced composition.") Such figures indicate the vast number of composition instructors and administrators who are clearly involved in both classroom and policy decisions regarding the thousands of courses offered in advanced composition. For example, all of the catalogs that Shumaker and his colleagues survey list some sort of advanced composition course. If we consider that there are over 2600 institutions in the United States and assume conservatively that only half of these colleges, universities, and two-year colleges offer advanced writing courses, it becomes clear that many compositionists are involved daily in teaching these courses and administering advanced writing programs. *Landmark Essays on Advanced Composition* serves as a convenient resource for those professionals involved in one way or another in advanced composition.

This collection is divided into four major though sometimes overlapping areas. The six works in Part One, Historical and Institutional Perspectives, explore how individuals and institutions over the last fifteen years have constructed advanced composition courses and programs. Collectively, these essays attempt to "define" advanced composition, but, in doing so, they conclude unanimously that the dizzying array of programs, practices, and pedagogies that fall under the rubric "advanced composition" makes it all but impossible to arrive at anything approaching consensus.

The first essay in this collection, the entry on advanced composition published in the *Encyclopedia of English Studies and Language Arts*, outlines the history and general issues involving advanced composition. Unlike most of the chapters in this collection, this entry suggests that a definitive notion of what advanced composition is and how it should be taught is perhaps neither possible nor desirable.

One of the first surveys of advanced composition was conducted by Michael Hogan in 1980. He surveyed 311 institutions in order to determine what characterized the teaching of advanced composition and found that while various kinds of courses are considered "advanced composition," a rhetorical emphasis seemed to dominate the typical course orientation. Most texts used in these courses were first-year composition texts because few available texts focused specifically on the general advanced composition course—a problem that time has not rectified. There is a political element here as well: Hogan's survey reveals the responses of 311 writing instructors across the country to the 1967 CCCC "Guidelines and Directions for College Courses in Advanced Composition." The consensus was that CCCC's conception of what the advanced composition teacher's qualifications should be was unreasonable and unrealistic.

That same year, Rita Sturm conducted another survey and concluded that advanced composition was experiencing a "renaissance": the course was growing rapidly both in prestige and in appeal to students. She found a dramatic increase in enrollment for such courses, and the students who were enrolling were from a variety of disciplines. Sturm also found that the most frequently articulated problems were related to the level of advanced composition and the lack of consensus in defining the course. The principal difference between Hogan's findings and Sturm's is that Hogan discovered that a large number of instructors stressed improvement in punctuation, grammar, and mechanics as a major objective, while Sturm's respondents rarely mentioned such concerns. Sturm suggests that such differences in their findings might be attributable to dramatic changes in composition theory in general and in this "rapidly developing specialty" in particular. Significantly, both articles were published in the first volume of a scholarly journal devoted exclusively to such issues: the *Journal of Advanced Composition*.

Three years later, Bernice Dicks conducted an extensive study of the field. She identified advanced composition as "a course in expository writing beyond the first-year level" and then reported on survey results and samples to construct a profile of advanced composition as it existed "really" and "ideally." While a bibliographic search revealed many useful pedagogical suggestions, they were so varied in form and purpose that a definition of advanced composition continued to remain elusive. Her samples illustrate the vast array of course offerings across the country that could fall under the rubric of advanced composition. She concluded that advanced composition is needed, as are textbooks that specifically address these needs. Together, the Hogan, Sturm, and Dicks essays are the most cited works on the subject.

A decade after the Hogan and Sturm surveys, Ronald Shumaker, Larry Dennis, and Lois Green published the results of a survey that attempted to determine the state of advanced composition as we entered the 1990s. These researchers note that the trend toward specialized advanced writing courses (Scientific Writing, Business Writing, and so on), in the midst of calls for student empowerment and increased cultural literacy, may be a sign that we are abandoning the essay as a mode of public discourse at the very time when we should be instructing students in advanced exposition so as to enable them to join in that discourse. Similarly, Michael Keene and Ray Wallace, in an essay published in the first book specifically about advanced composition, examine how particular institutions in the various geographical regions of the nation have instituted the advanced course. The authors polled twelve colleges and universities to discover what is happening in advanced composition and to consider the types of advanced composition being taught and its role in English programs.

Essays such as those contained in Part One have proved invaluable in helping compositionists understand exactly how specific instructors and institutions are constructing advanced composition, including what pedagogical approaches they value and what textbooks they require.

The six essays in Part Two, Advanced Writers and Courses, attempt to articulate what distinguishes advanced composition courses, students, and pedagogies from those commonly encountered in first-year composition. The section begins with an official document of the Conference on College Composition and Communication, published in 1967, that sets forth both "guidelines and directions" for advanced composition courses. This position statement attempts to define for the field not only the prerequisites for advanced composition students, but to enumerate various courses under the rubric of "advanced composition," to define the "humane emphasis" of such courses, to specify the ideal qualifications of instructors, and to list the various acceptable modes of instruction. This is the same document that the 311 respondents to Hogan's survey objected to so strongly.

William Covino discusses how scholarship in the history of rhetoric can contribute to a fuller understanding of advanced writing. He draws on works that define "advanced" writers (as opposed to beginners) as tolerant of ambiguity and intolerant of formulaic discourse. He then suggests that dialogic writing—wherein students are encouraged to keep an issue alive through "engaged ignorance" (Plato)—might be the most effective way to teach advanced composition.

For Michael Carter, understanding the concept "advanced" as it applies to writing entails adopting a sophisticated notion of "expertise," since what would distinguish advanced from novice writers is precisely their level of expertise in composing.

Carter believes that advanced composition should be more than just a more difficult first-year course. The problem is that we don't fully understand what comprises expertise in writing. The development of expertise *in writing* is the movement from global writing strategies to sophisticated knowledge of special rhetorical situations. In other words, compositional expertise is a function of specialization. Consequently, there is no such thing as an expert writer *in general*.

One of the most central concerns of any expert rhetor is audience, and Helen Rothschild Ewald examines what we might tell advanced writers about audience given the current state of scholarship. She suggests that advanced composition students should deal with the "constructive reader" as active participant in the making of textual meaning. Attempting to discuss with students how writers should cope with this constructive reader may prove difficult, however. Reading research suggests that the traditional means of coping—assuming the reader through "bottom-up" processing of a writer's cues in a carefully devised text—is "severely limited." A reader-centered approach to the writing process is difficult if not impossible unless students are first grounded in an epistemology that posits meaning as socially and contextually constructed.

Balancing individual and collaborative projects has been an important issue for many compositionists since the advent of the process movement, and Felicia Mitchell contends that such concerns are even more relevant in the advanced class. She designs an advanced composition course that attempts to reconcile the often incommensurate assumptions that writing derives from individual purpose and cognition and that inquiry in writing must begin with a social, cultural, or political awareness. She manages to combine an expressivist approach, wherein students write to discover not only their voices but their relative positions as well, with a socially constructed, critical awareness of the world around them exemplified by the particulars of her writing assignments.

Finally, Ann Kimble Loux and Rebecca Stoddart detail the lengthy road travelled by Saint Mary's College to acceptance of an advanced writing requirement. Through trial-and-error and teacher education, both students and teachers/administrators came to realize the benefits of the requirement. The authors provide a thorough case study that could prove most useful—in terms of long-term encouragement, if nothing else—to a program attempting to adopt a similar requirement.

The third section, Curricular Content and Emphases, contains six essays outlining specific pedagogies for advanced composition. Writing as early as 1969, Richard Larson discusses the value of an advanced composition course for prospective high school English teachers. Gary Olson, writing in the heyday of composition's love affair with sentence combining, argues that such pedagogies should not be relegated to remedial courses and can, in fact, be useful even in the most advanced writing courses. Wilma Clark makes writing for publication the emphasis in her course, while Carol Snyder draws on the work of Michel Foucault to teach advanced writers how to interrogate and analyze the classificatory systems that we ordinarily would perceive as "natural." Russell Rutter incorporates research writing into his course, while Susan Hilligoss focuses on autobiographical writing. This wide range of approaches to advanced composition—from sentence combining to

Foucauldian analysis—vividly demonstrates why those who have attempted to define advanced composition or to illustrate commonality through extensive surveys have exhibited such frustration.

The final section of this collection, Theoretical and Political Issues, explores how scholarship can inform advanced composition and examines several political and ethical issues. Joseph Comprone surveys research in reading and suggests how it may be useful in constructing advanced writing pedagogies. He examines the ways in which fluent readers make "fluent guessers," adept at interpreting textual cues, and he contends that such research suggests a wholly different relationship between writing and reading than now exists at both the first-year and advanced levels. He also claims that expressive writing, common at the first-year level, is the ideal mode of writing for learners and should continue into advanced composition. Comprone believes that advanced writing courses could expand upon a marriage of expressive writing and reading with practice in meeting the rhetorical needs of different audiences.

Katherine Adams discusses how rhetorical theory can inform composition teaching. She points out the recent proliferation in the publication of theory-based texts, which she believes reflects compositionists' desire to teach writing in a way appropriate for advanced students. She contends that while student writing should be the focus of the class, actual research can be a powerful addition to the curriculum. Adams strongly advocates the inclusion of theory—not the application, but theory as such—into conferences, workshops, and discussions of advanced composition.

Kate Ronald suggests that students not try to write *in* the professions but *about* them. She believes it is important for students to explore the rhetoric of professionals in various disciplines—how they characterize themselves and their purposes. The focus of such a course should be on rhetorical invention, on "the *topoi* of the professions: their implied justifications for their subjects and the roles they see themselves playing."

Sandy Moore and Michael Kleine illustrate how the assignments advanced writing instructors give students can have serious consequences, especially when students are instructed to compose on "real world" issues. Do composition instructors have an ethical obligation to protect students from such consequences? Do we have, perhaps, an obligation *not* to assign such public writing?

Richard Coe discusses the skills and proficiency levels of the ideal student in any advanced writing course, and he suggests that the real problem is not in defining what an advanced writing course is, but what *advanced process* is. If advanced composition were to focus on discovering/teaching/learning advanced process, advanced principles of composing, and what advanced writers do that intermediate and beginning writers do not, we could teach students how to analyze and participate in any discourse, without the need of teachers and classrooms. In other words, Coe wants to give students the tools to negotiate any future discourses/communication situations, not just the one(s) they face in any given and immediate classroom situation.

Finally, Julia Gergits and James Schramer discuss how students come to the advanced writing class with twenty years of experience in "collaboration" learned in the family setting. Such experience—often "poorly developed, unfairly exercised, at times even dysfunctional"—has a significant impact on advanced pedagogies that involve collaborative activities. They argue that compositionists would do well to be aware of such dynamics.

The twenty-four essays in *Landmark Essays on Advanced Composition* chronicle composition's struggle to define and construct an appropriate writing course on the advanced level. While these essays have clear historical value—in that together they trace our attempts to come to terms with advanced composition—they also have implications for future work in the area. They suggest how we might continue to draw on scholarship both within and outside of composition to investigate relevant theoretical issues and to construct effective advanced pedagogies.

Works Cited

Bloom, Lynn Z. "Why Don't We Write What We Teach? And Publish It." *Composition Theory for the Postmodern Classroom.* Ed. Gary A. Olson and Sidney I. Dobrin. Albany: State U of New York P, 1995. 143-55.

Original Citations for Essays in this Collection

Adams, Katherine H. "Bringing Rhetorical Theory into the Advanced Composition Class." *Rhetoric Review* 3 (1985): 184-89.

Carter, Michael. "What is *Advanced* about Advanced Composition?: A Theory of Expertise in Writing." *Teaching Advanced Composition: Why and How.* Ed. Katherine H. Adams and John L. Adams. Portsmouth, NH: Boynton, 1991. 59-70.

CCCC. "Guidelines and Directions for College Courses in Advanced Composition." *College Composition and Communication* 18 (1967): 266-68.

Clark, Wilma. "Writing for Publication in an Advanced Course for Undergraduates." *Journal of Advanced Composition* 3 (1982): 24-36.

Coe, Richard M. "Advanced Composition as Fishing Pole: Principles, Processes, Practices." *Teaching Advanced Composition: Why and How.* Portsmouth, NH: Boynton, 1991. 71-88.

Comprone, Joseph J. "Recent Research in Reading and Its Implications for the College Composition Curriculum." *Rhetoric Review* 1 (1983): 122-37.

Covino, William A. "Defining Advanced Composition: Contributions from the History of Rhetoric." *Journal of Advanced Composition* 8 (1988): 113-22.

Dicks, Bernice W. "State of the Art in Advanced Expository Writing: One Genus, Many Species." *Journal of Advanced Composition* 3 (1982): 172-91.

Ewald, Helen Rothschild. "What We Could Tell Advanced Student Writers about Audience." *Journal of Advanced Composition* 11 (1991): 147-58.

Hilligoss, Susan. "Preoccupations: Private Writing and Advanced Composition." *Journal of Advanced Composition* 9 (1989): 124-34.

Hogan, Michael P. "Advanced Composition: A Survey." *Journal of Advanced Composition* 1 (1980): 21-29.

Keene, Michael L., and Ray Wallace. "Advanced Writing Courses and Programs." *Teaching Advanced Composition: Why and How.* Ed. Katherine H. Adams and John L. Adams. Portsmouth, NH: Boynton, 1991. 89-100.

Larson, Richard L. "A Special Course in Advanced Composition for Prospective Teachers." *Journal of Teacher Education* 20 (1969): 168-74.

Loux, Ann Kimble, and Rebecca M. Stoddart. "Denial, Conflagration, Pride: Three Stages in the Development of an Advanced Writing Requirement." *College Composition and Communication* 45 (1994): 521-34.

Mitchell, Felicia. "Balancing Individual Projects and Collaborative Learning in the Advanced Writing Class." *College Composition and Communication* 43 (1992): 393-400.

Moore, Sandy, and Michael Kleine. "Toward an Ethics of Teaching Writing in a Hazardous Context: The University." *Journal of Advanced Composition* 12 (1992): 381-94.

Olson, Gary A. "Advanced Composition." *Encyclopedia of English Studies and Language Arts.* Urbana: NCTE, 1995. 25-26.

_____. "Incorporating Sentencing Combining into the Advanced Composition Class." *Journal of Advanced Composition* 2 (1981): 119-26.

Ronald, Kate. "The Politics of Teaching Professional Writing." *Journal of Advanced Composition* 7 (1987): 23-30.

Rutter, Russell. "Research Writing in Advanced Composition: An Essay in Definition." *Journal of Advanced Composition* 6 (1985-86): 131-38.

Shumaker, Ronald C., Larry Dennis, and Lois Green. "Advanced Exposition: A Survey of Patterns and Problems. *Journal of Advanced Composition* 10 (1990): 136-44.

Snyder, Carol. "Analyzing Classifications: Foucault for Advanced Writing." *College Composition and Communication* 35 (1984): 209-16.

Sturm, Rita. "Advanced Composition, 1980: The State of the Art." *Journal of Advanced Composition* 1 (1980): 37-43.

Part 1:
Historical and Institutional Perspectives

Advanced Composition

by Gary A. Olson

That *advanced composition* defies definition is a trope in the professional literature. Scholarly articles and reviews on the subject traditionally begin by reciting an endless array of approaches and by proclaiming that there is little consensus about what shape the course should take or how it ought to be taught. In its broadest sense, advanced composition refers to all postsecondary writing instruction above the first-year level, including courses in technical, business, and advanced expository writing, as well as classes associated with writing across the curriculum. This broad definition was the one adopted by the *Journal of Advanced Composition* in its early years of publication. However, a good many educators use the term *advanced composition* to refer specifically to a junior- or senior-level composition course concerned more with writing in general than with how writing functions within particular disciplines.

Although various kinds of advanced writing instruction can be detected even in the earliest days of higher education in the United States, the advanced expository course per se probably originated in the last few decades of the nineteenth century and was offered to give advanced instruction in prose style to a "select few." In 1877, A.S. Hill offered Harvard's first advanced composition course, focusing on helping students achieve a "more natural" prose style (Adams and Adams, "Advanced" 7). Hill and others like him constructed such "advanced" courses to meet the specific local needs of their programs and institutions; consequently, a multitude of types of advanced composition courses proliferated, so much so that by the 1950s the CCCC (Conference on College Composition and Communication) began to take measures to clarify the course's identity.

During the 1950s and 1960s, numerous workshops were held at the CCCC conventions to arrive at some kind of consensus, but these sessions only highlighted the confusing diversity of approaches and objectives. Reports chronicling these endeavors were published in *College Composition and Communication* in 1958, 1963, and 1967. Despite this diversity and the concomitant problems with identity, advanced composition courses became extremely popular, so much so that by the 1970s most colleges and universities offered a course under this title. In 1979, a group of dedicated teachers of advanced composition formed the Association of Teachers of Advanced Composition (ATAC)—a special interest group of CCCC—and began publishing the *Journal of Advanced Composition* the following year.

Throughout the 1980s, presentations at the ATAC sessions and articles based on questionnaire/survey research published in *JAC* continued to demonstrate that *advanced composition* could mean practically anything. As late as 1990, research published in *JAC* revealed that the pedagogical focus of such courses could range from autobiographical writing to writing about literature to writing across the curriculum (Shumaker et al.).

Several patterns do emerge from this nearly half century of teaching and research. Many teachers, like A.S. Hill a century before them, treat advanced composition as a course in style, concentrating on producing sophisticated, essayistic prose that exhibits verbal wit and grace. Such courses often have a belletristic flavor, and students read nonfiction essays by noted prose stylists and study one of the popular small style manuals, such as Strunk and White's *Elements of Style*. A competing format emphasizes argumentation and often will revolve around one of the more sophisticated essay anthologies that contain persuasive articles and extensive instructional apparatus on the workings of persuasion. Another popular format emphasizes critical thinking: Students might critique articles in readers or the popular media, or even other elements of popular culture, from a logical or critical/analytical perspective. In fact, as cultural studies and analysis of popular culture become increasingly important areas of study in the academy, these areas are also becoming popular emphases in advanced composition classes. In still other institutions, advanced composition is a course in academic discourse and may or may not be related to a writing-across-the-curriculum program. It would be misleading not to mention, however, that in some institutions advanced composition is a de facto remedial course, designed to assist students who did not reach acceptable levels of writing proficiency in the first-year writing sequence.

Advanced composition's identity crisis is not confined to the dizzying proliferation of approaches. Central to the problem is disagreement over the meaning of the term *advanced*. Does it refer to a level of writing proficiency or the placement of a course in an institution's curriculum? Is it the students who are advanced, or the course itself, or the subject matter? In short, how should we understand the term *advanced*, and, therefore, exactly what distinguishes advanced composition from first-year writing? Michael Carter attempts to answer these questions by proposing a "theory of expertise" in writing. Rejecting the notion that someone can be an expert writer in general, he argues that writers only become expert in specific rhetorical contexts. Carter's theory has implications for all composition instructors, but it specifically lends credence to those who wish to link advanced composition with discipline-specific writing.

It is unlikely that compositionists will ever reach consensus about advanced composition, nor would most teachers want some kind of monologic, universal method and course. What *is* certain is that advanced composition continues to grow in popularity, both among students and instructors, and it remains an active area of scholarship. As *JAC* evolved into a journal of "composition theory," a companion publication, the *Composition Forum*, was formed to publish scholarship on advanced writing pedagogy. In addition, the first book of scholarly articles on advanced composition (Adams and Adams, *Teaching Advanced Composition: How and Why*) was published in 1991. And ATAC continues to sponsor a session annually at the CCCC convention. Clearly, advanced composition will continue to be a vital and evolving sub-area of composition studies for years to come despite, and perhaps even because of, its rich diversity.

Works Cited

Adams, Katherine H., and John L. Adams. *Teaching Advanced Composition: How and Why.* Portsmouth, NH: Boynton, 1991.

Carter, Michael. "What is *Advanced* about Advanced Composition?: A Theory of Expertise in Writing." Adams and Adams 59-70.

Shumaker, Ronald C., et al. "Advanced Exposition: A Survey of Patterns and Problems." *Journal of Advanced Composition* 10 (1990): 136-44.

Advanced Composition: A Survey

by Michael P. Hogan

Although advanced composition courses are offered by most colleges and universities (and even some junior and community colleges),[1] very few articles in the professional journals have been addressed to the issues of theory and pedagogy for these courses. Only in the Guidelines formulated by participants to Invitational Workshops at the 1966 and 1967 College Composition and Communication Conferences has there been a concerted effort to examine how college instructors might design and teach advanced composition courses.[2] Because these Guidelines attempt to set forth a definition for advanced composition, the only one readily available, I used them as the basis for a nation-wide survey in the 1979 spring term to determine what characterizes the teaching of advanced composition courses. The 374 teachers who returned this 21-item questionnaire represent 311 schools.[3] The results show considerable support for the Guidelines but an equal amount of disagreement.

Of the 374 respondents, 29.7 percent endorsed the Guidelines, 28.9 percent criticized one or more topics, and 41.4 percent made no response to the Guidelines portion of the survey. The 1967 Guidelines consisted of six topic entries: (1) Definition of the Course, (2) Variety and Focus, (3) Humane Emphasis, (4) Course Content, (5) Qualifications of Instructors, and (6) Modes of Instruction. I will outline (quoting where possible) each of these topics, discuss the response to them, and relate the relevant questionnaire items to each to reveal current practices in and/or attitudes toward advanced writing courses.

> 1. *Definition*: Advanced composition courses should be "open only to students who have at least passed the freshman course at the same college or who have demonstrated equivalent ability." Such courses "should represent substantial progress beyond the goal of the local freshman course."

This segment of the 1967 Guidelines provides a prerequisite and an alternative but not a definition. And since students progress but courses themselves cannot

Reprinted from the *Journal of Advanced Composition* 1 (1980): 21-29. Reprinted with permission.

[1] Though the survey was intended only for four-year schools, some members of community colleges responded because their names were mixed in with the computerized mailing list purchased from NCTE.

[2] "Guidelines and Directions for College Courses in Advanced Composition," *College Composition and Communication* 18 (1967): 266-68.

[3] For various reasons such as inappropriate recipients, some returned questionnaires were excluded from this analysis.

"represent" progress, how we distinguish advanced writing courses from freshman courses remains unsolved. Many respondents found *advanced composition* similarly a difficult rubric to respond to because so many courses fall into that category or heading. Indeed, one respondent proposed abolishing the term. For the 311 institutions represented in the survey, respondents listed 50 different types of courses under the heading of advanced composition. These courses classify generally as follows: advanced composition/exposition; intermediate composition; genre and techniques of writing; stylistics; research; argument; criticism; teaching composition, theory and practice; creative writing; journalism; technical and professional writing; and business writing.

Regarding prerequisites, several respondents stated that the simple testing out or completion of freshman composition should not qualify students for advanced composition courses. Some schools attempt to ensure qualification by requiring one of the following: freshman composition and literature, 10.2 percent; literature only, less than 1.0 percent; freshman composition and standing above the freshman year, 7.0 percent; senior college standing and instructor permission, less than 1.0 percent. Nevertheless, the majority do require only freshman composition, 54.9 percent, or its equivalent, 2.8 percent. Only 5.7 percent have no prerequisites, accepting students with whatever writing ability they have.[4]

> 2. *Variety and Focus*: "In its general form the advanced course may be viewed as covering the range of the freshman course but in greater depth," with emphasis on "alternative strategies in solving writing problems" and analysis of "the reasons for choosing among verbal forms and theories of rhetoric." Specialized courses "isolate certain kinds of writing problems for intensive examination." Specific course descriptions may be determined by types of writing (forms); writing situations and content; students' goals; modes; or specific problems such as "theories of style or history of English prose style."

In distinguishing general from specific courses, the 1967 Workshop participates recognized that the varieties would depend upon the size of the school, its budget, and its students' needs. Limited size, however, does not preclude specialization. In the 130 schools with a population under 2500, respondents noted 20 types of specialized courses. A few respondents did note that the examples given in Guideline 2 for special problems are "irrelevant except for graduate students and their programs."

Representative responses to Guideline 2 suggest that a definition should concentrate on rhetorical matters. In support of Aristotelian rhetoric, some respondents note that we should concentrate on professional writing or writing external to the classroom, a reader-centered emphasis. Conversely, others make a plea for more emphasis on Platonic rhetorical strategies and less on Aristotelian; thus, the emphasis would be writer-centered, the conceptualization of the thought and the inherent truth of the idea being primary. One respondent vented frustration with

---

[4] Where the percentages do not total 100, the remainder represents no response.

theories of rhetoric as pedagogical tools, saying they are as difficult to use in improving writing as are systems of grammar.

The orientation and the types of assignments noted by the respondents reveal much about the focus of instruction. A rhetorical emphasis does dominate the course orientation, 67.9 percent of the respondents checking this item. In describing what is involved in this emphasis, they broke it down into the following categories: Aristotelian/classical rhetoric (66 citations); new rhetorical theory (21); both (5); forms and structures (58); modes (33); stylistics (22); service to the professional needs of the students (17); and problem-solving (3). Only 6.1 percent of the respondents checked the subject matter item for their course orientation, describing subject matter as ideas (9), thematic issues in fiction (2), or the subject matter in the students' majors (12). Other orientations were noted by 14.4 percent of the respondents: eclectic approaches (9); process orientation (20); McCrorie's free-writing (7); workshops (11); and creative writing (7).

The predominance of certain assignments may indicate that many instructors view their advanced courses as extensions of the freshman course, but the variety indicates efforts to reach beyond its limitation. Respondents listed no fewer than 25 types:

Types	Frequency
analyses	202
personal essays	195
reports	145
research papers	145
articles	132
reviews	129
expository essays	71
argument	47
descriptive essays	43
narrative essays	37
correspondence	33
criticism	27
persuasive essays	22
evaluative essays	15
summaries	14
exploratory essays	13
journals/diaries	12
autobiographies	10
student choice	9
definitions	7
personal narratives	4
classification essays	4
interviews	4
style	3
investigative reports	1

Perhaps the types of assignments are determined in large part by the texts commonly used. The titles of the rhetorics, handbooks, and readers listed by the respondents are far too numerous to list here, but most are those one would find being used in freshman courses. Indeed, one respondent expressed dismay that texts used in freshman composition in her school are used elsewhere in advanced composition courses. Except for highly specialized courses such as business, technical, and professional writing and stylistics, few texts on the market seem to focus on the general advanced writing course. The reason for this sparsity may lie in the lack of a working definition for general writing courses beyond the freshman level. Necessarily, the majority of the instructors, in using "freshman" texts, must rely on their own resources to make the course one of "advanced" focus and status.

The respondents were asked to list their texts according to type. The five most frequently cited texts in each category are listed below in order of frequency:

Rhetorics (123 listed)
Classical Rhetoric for the Modern Student (Corbett)
Style (Eastman)
Rhetoric: Discovery and Change (Young, Becker, and Pike)
Writing Well (Hall)
The New Strategy of Style (Weathers and Winchester)

Handbooks (34 listed)
Elements of Style (Strunk and White)
Harbrace College Handbook
Index to English (Perrin and Ebbitt)
Random House Handbook
The Little English Handbook (Corbett)

Readers (82 listed)
The Norton Reader
Prose Models (Levin)
Reading for Rhetoric (Schrodes, Josephson, and Wilson)
Speaking of Words (McKillop and Cross)
Twenty Questions for the Writer (Berke)

Whether the English major or minor and the English education major are required to take an advanced writing course may reveal something of the focus for the course, but especially departmental attitudes. For these majors and minor, 27.6 percent of the schools do not require the course; 48.3 percent require it of the English major; 52.9 percent require it of the English education major; and 27.9 percent require it of the English minor.

The most common explanations for not requiring an advanced writing course of the English major are that the majors acquire the necessary skills in their literature courses or that the course has low prestige for the English major. But respondents also lamented the literature majors' writing skills. A few respondents gave departmental politics as the reason. Some departments view writing as a program separate from their literature programs, so they offer a writing major but do not require advanced writing courses of their English majors. Such programs are not confined to the large institution; eight respondents representing schools at all levels of enrollment mentioned having a writing major separate from their literature programs.

Respondents were asked to list the types of majors (excluding English majors) electing the course. Responses pertaining to specific courses such as technical and business writing were excluded from the following data:

Major	Frequency
Science	84
Business	78
History	53
Sociology	48
Journalism	47
Political Science	38
Pre-Law	38
Psychology	20
Art	13
Economics	13
Languages	13
Engineering	10
Religion	10
Physical Education	10

The following majors all received fewer than ten citations: home economics, mathematics, industrial arts, music, education, management, and agriculture.

3. *Humane Emphasis*: "Crafts must be mastered, but the goal is understanding how the uses of language define human beings."

Respondents were clearly divided on this Guideline. Those endorsing it asked that it be stressed more heavily; those opposing it asked that it be deleted. No item on the questionnaire addressed this Guideline, though the question of whether the orientation is primarily toward rhetoric or subject matter touched on the issue. One difficulty lies in the dichotomy of goals in Guideline 3, rather than their fusion. Certainly, the crafts to be mastered and the goal of understanding how language "defines" humans could both be addressed under the umbrella of rhetoric.

Another difficulty is the word *humane*. As one respondent noted, "*humane* should mean 'of or pertaining to the humanities,'" expressing the view of several respondents that such emphasis would not reflect their schools' technical, business, legal writing and journalism courses. To this point, a respondent suggested the addition of a scientific emphasis: the use of language to express one's scientific (e.g., chemistry, biology, engineering) perception of reality. Others protested that they could be no more concerned about humane goals in this course than in any other, or that they simply have too much else to accomplish or include to make this emphasis the major goal of the course. Confused about what "humane emphasis" means, respondents found the statement vague and reflective of the times in which it was written, the 1960s.

In understanding the Guideline to mean that defining human beings through language must begin with the writer, one respondent suggested that it be modified to stress that writers use their own written language to understand themselves. Though such an emphasis may not reflect an Aristotelian view of rhetoric, it may fit in quite nicely with the Platonic emphasis on the importance of the conceptualization of ideas.

Perhaps most significantly, one respondent noted that Guidelines 3 and 4 conflict in specifying the goal for advanced writing courses.

> 4. *Course Content*: "The primary content of any advanced course is writing itself. For that reason the insights of modern studies of language, rhetoric, and psychology should be made explicit."

The apparent intent of this Guideline was to fuse writing and theory. However, some respondents criticized the Guideline as too broad and vague. They also took exception to the suggestion that modern studies of psychology could be explicitly applied to writing in such courses. But others suggested placing even more emphasis on the importance of linguistics and psycholinguistics to writing. But warning that composition specialists should beware of pontificating on hobby horses rather than dealing with students' writing, one respondent pointed out the danger in letting side issues become the main focus of the course.

Again, one respondent made a rather strong statement for Platonic rhetoric, asserting that the course content should consist of the "formal university essay of ideas." The purpose is humanistic and liberal in the broadest sense of education. Yet another respondent suggested combining the concern for ideas and the writing itself by emphasizing the relationship between content and style so that the stylistic techniques would emphasize and enhance the ideas.

The formulators of the 1967 Guidelines viewed the course content as deriving from two primary sources: the topics of the students' papers and the "subject" of the writing course; but except for specialized professional courses, they provided no information on what the subject of the course might be. The survey item on course objectives may provide some insight as to what that course content might be and the relative importance respondents attach to each area. Respondents checked five suggested objectives, favoring them in the following order:

Course Objective	Frequency
Develop mature writing style	325
Develop awareness of audience	297
Teach expository forms	234
Teach modes	180
Improve skill in punctuation, grammar, and mechanics	122

In space provided, respondents listed other objectives. Here they are with the frequency listed in parentheses: rhetoric   (25); revision and editing (16); invention (11); develop awareness of thought and language relationships in writing (11); perceiving writing as the discovery of what we know (11); organization (10); research techniques (7); self-discovery (7); analytical skills (6); sentence combining (6); writing as process (5); writing for publication (5); logic (4); helping students overcome fear of writing (4); career writing (2); developing theories of composition (1); appreciating non-fiction prose (1); accumulating a portfolio of an assigned number of pages (1).

The two primary concerns of these teachers, style and audience, are both rhetorical matters.

5. *Qualifications of Instructors*: The teachers of advanced composition should have the following: (1) "special qualifications both as teachers and writers"; (2) "more than ordinary success in teaching freshman composition"; (3) a liberal "academic training"; (4) professional interest in teaching writing, demonstrated by participating in professional societies; (5) "a wide range of extra-academic experience, especially in the areas of professional interest of the students."

Given as the minimum, these qualifications were intended to demonstrate that advanced writing courses should not be taught by "departmental leftovers" but by dedicated teachers as well-trained as those staffing the literature programs. In its field test, the questionnaire had included an item on the training of the respondent for the advanced writing course. In all cases, they cited a literature background and "on-the-job" training in teaching the course. Thus, this item was dropped from the questionnaire. But in the survey, respondents did suggest emphasizing more training in language, rhetoric graduate courses in writing and composition pedagogy so that new teachers can avoid having to "rediscover the wheel" in theory and practices.

Respondents found the Guideline on instructor qualifications unrealistic. In specific criticism, respondents noted that the "emphasis on a wide range of extra-academic experience is impractical, except for teachers of vocational students. An academic career precludes this emphasis for most of us." Others questioned whether extra-academic activities would produce better teaching and complained that such a qualification would prevent them from teaching advanced writing courses. The other qualifications were not so severely criticized, but each was questioned. Respondents remarked on how little time or inclination they have for their own writing—teaching is a full-time job; they questioned how "more than ordinary success" in teaching freshman composition could be determined; they doubted whether participation in professional societies as a demonstration of interest in teaching writing is an adequate criterion for any teacher of composition. For an alternative to Guideline 5, one respondent defined an effective teacher as "one who stimulates students to write well-developed and well-organized and interesting papers."

If promotions indicate anything at all about qualifications, the academic ranks listed by the respondents indicate that the advanced writing courses are not taught by departmental leftovers" as feared by the formulators of the Guidelines. The top three ranks share the advanced writing course nearly equally: Professor (26.7 percent); Associate Professor (28.0 percent); Assistant Professor (33.9 percent); instructors and graduate assistants (8.8 percent).

As for professional affiliation, fully one-third of the respondents are not members of the Conference on College Composition and Communication. But lack of membership in professional societies such as the CCCC may not demonstrate a lack of professional interest so much as failure of such organizations to meet the specific needs of the instructor who teaches the general advanced writing course. In both *College English* and *College Composition and Communication* over the last 16 years, only five articles specifically address advanced composition under that rubric. Of these articles, one promoted Henry James' novels as the basis for a creative writing course, one by Francis Christensen discussed the training of advanced composition teachers, and the rest addressed writing for publication as the basis for the course.

The involvement of these teachers in their advanced writing courses may be demonstrated by the number of sections they teach. For those on the quarter system, 9.0 percent of the respondents teach four sections per year, and 2.0 percent teach eight per year. On the semester system, 26.4 percent teach two sections per year; 6.9 percent one section; 8.2 percent three sections; 5.8 percent four sections; and 2.4 percent from five to eight sections.

> 6. *Modes of Instruction*: The course should have smaller sections than those in freshman composition to allow more time for reading papers and conferring with the writers. The number of assignments would depend on the course. Students' writing should receive "considerable commentary" but grade evaluation should be de-emphasized.

The general evaluation of this Guideline is that it is a statement on workload, not on modes of instruction. Specific responses concern the question of what constitutes a smaller section and whether smaller class size is relevant "because advanced composition students are more mature than freshmen" and require less shepherding. The recommendation pertaining to grade evaluation evokes strong criticism, respondents defending grades because "Students expect to be graded"; "They demand it"; "They work harder when graded"; and "Commentary alone leaves students unclear about their achievements."

In general, class size does not appear to be the crucial issue the Guideline implies it to be. The average class size is 17 students. However, ten respondents, representing institutions ranging from under 2500 to 15,000 students, noted that their class sizes range up to thirty students. Perhaps because of larger budgets and greater student demand for the courses, larger institutions are able to offer smaller classes.

The average number of assignments is 11 per semester. One respondent stated that he makes no assignments but accepts what the students voluntarily turn in, while another requires 30 assignments, noting they are short. Respondents on the quarter system reported the number of assignments ranged from a minimum of 1 to a high of 30, the average being 9 per quarter.

The survey data suggest that the actual modes of instruction are largely traditional. The primary mode of instruction is the lecture, according to 41.7 percent of the respondents. Another 34.2 percent combine lectures with individualized instruction, workshops, discussion, conferences, or peer editing. Only 9.9 percent use individualized instruction as the primary mode; and only 9.3 percent use the workshop, discussion, conference, or seminar as the primary mode.

Summary

Although one respondent lamented the displacement of rhetoric as the focus of advanced composition courses, the survey shows that "traditional" rhetoric still provides the foundation for the majority of the courses as indicated in the objectives, assignments, and texts used (Corbett's *Classical Rhetoric for the Modern Student* dominated the other texts named by respondents). However, the increasing concern for invention has apparently given rise to calls for inclusion of Platonic rhetorical concerns in conceptualization of ideas.

Emphases in the courses appear to be largely traditional and, to a degree, repetitive of those things we do in freshman composition. This point is particularly evident in the predominance of the research paper assignment. A fundamental issue is whether it should play such a major role in the advanced course: are students learning skills in invention, analysis, and synthesis in writing such papers in the advanced course that they have not already acquired in the freshman course (if the research paper was taught there) and their own major courses? Obviously, more research and discussion are needed to examine this issue. Nevertheless, the point about the research paper illustrates the difficulties in defining advanced writing courses and distinguishing them from freshman courses with regard to focus, course content, and modes of instruction.

A definition for the general courses is needed. The specialized courses such as technical writing, creative writing, business writing, and stylistics appear to be well-defined regarding subject, audience, and purpose, as shown by the texts written specifically for the students interested in these areas. But few texts give new teachers and students directions in the general advanced composition courses; some of the respondents, new to the teaching of advanced composition, asked for suggestions about what they might do in designing their courses. Perhaps without a functional definition, the texts are not forthcoming. A second concern is the course requirement for English majors. Whether the literature major is sufficient for preparing students to write and to teach writing is a troubling question. Requiring literature majors to take a course in advanced composition was as vehemently opposed as supported by the respondents in this survey. Such polarization indicates at least the need for discussion.

Much has changed since the Guidelines were issued in 1967. Pedagogical views, goals, and practices in composition have changed. The body of theory for composition has expanded. What is surprising is that amid the great controversy and discussions about freshman composition so little has been said about advanced courses. The 1967 Guidelines provide some foundation for discussion of our goals in the advanced courses, but as the respondents to the survey have shown, they need to be revised. They should be more precise, and they should reflect current practices and the attitudes of those who teach the advanced writing courses.[5]

---

[5] The grants and research funding committee at Southeast Missouri State University provided the funds for this survey, 1979.

Advanced Composition, 1980:
The State of the Art

by Rita Sturm

This review of current trends and concerns in advanced composition is intentionally more impressionistic than analytic and more qualitative than quantitative. I chose an impressionistic approach because I wanted to cover more ground than I could in a controlled analytic study and because I wanted to be free to discuss trends too tentative for quantitative detection. Most of the information was gathered from three sources: the comments, concerns, and topics of interest listed on about 200 membership applications to the Association of Teachers of Advanced Composition (ATAC); more than 300 syllabi, course descriptions, and letters voluntarily contributed to ATAC's information file; and an uncounted number of personal discussions with colleagues throughout the country. Because this information came only from people who chose to contribute, I made no attempt to determine the prevalence of a particular attitude or practice beyond vague indicators such as "a few," "some," and "many." However, since the sample was broad, I treated the information as a reasonably accurate indication of the range of current attitudes and practices.

The first general impression is that advanced composition is growing rapidly in appeal to students and in prestige. In fact, it seems to be experiencing a renaissance. Those who contributed information for this review did so with an unexpected enthusiasm and creative vigor, often reporting that advanced writing has become a more important part of their college curriculum than it has been for decades. Others said that students who for years could neither be tempted nor coerced into advanced writing classes are now begging for a space on a waiting list and that a writing major or concentration is being considered.

The second general impression is not as bright. Many of the fundamental issues that led to the organization of ATAC—most importantly those related to level, goals, and course content—are still unresolved and now need resolution more urgently than before: the growth in enrollment, the increasing number of people teaching advanced writing for the first time, and the proliferation of specialized writing courses.

Enrollments

Many people report steady—sometimes dramatic—increases in enrollment in all upper level writing courses and almost without exception attribute the increase to an

Reprinted from the *Journal of Advanced Composition* 1 (1980): 37-44. Reprinted with permission.

influx of students from disciplines other than English, but no one seems to know the reason for this new interest or why it seems to have developed in some disciplines and not in others. A few correspondents suggest that because of the somber spirit of the times, students are more serious about acquiring marketable skills and have been convinced by the media that writing ability is one of those skills. A few others think the impetus might be coming from faculty in other disciplines who are pressuring students more vigorously than before either because, as advisors, they are worried about their graduates in a tight job market or because they themselves have been influenced by the media and now demand a better quality of written work. A few credit the increased enrollments at their own colleges to some innovative practice unique to them. But although these few correspondents are willing to speculate, far more ask whether anyone knows the reasons, and some express uneasiness.

One correspondent asked that his concern be reported here. He said he is enjoying the new interest in his advanced writing course too much to see the course become, once again, the under-enrolled orphan of the English department. His point is that until we know with certainty what needs are sending students to advanced writing, we are only guessing when we design our courses to include certain topics, forms, and principles rather than others. Our guesses could be right, but they could just as easily be wrong, and if they are wrong, student interest will slacken more quickly than it developed. A different correspondent, prompted by the same uneasiness, suggested an ATAC-coordinated survey of students in advanced writing to determine why they enrolled, what they hope to learn, what disciplines they come from, and why competent writing is important in that discipline.

Level

Problems related to the level of advanced composition are mentioned more often than any other problems. Many ask, "Can we have meaningful dialogue and progress when to one instructor advanced writing means worthy of publication in a national journal and to another it means the ability to write 750 words with no more than six grammatical errors and six awkward passages?" Other questions range as follows:

- How advanced is advanced?

- Are certain writing techniques more advanced than others, and if so, which ones are they?

- Does "advanced" mean greater refinement and skill in a few basic forms of writing or does it mean moderate refinement and skill extended to include a greater variety of forms?

- Is instruction in advanced writing intrinsically different from freshman instruction or does the difference actually lie in the student's improved ability to comprehend instruction?

- Is merely passing a freshman course with a low C or D a sufficient prerequisite for advanced writing?

- How much, if any, of the course work should be devoted to basic concepts of grammar, syntax, diction, and usage?

- What is the purpose of advanced composition?

- Should we be preparing students for undergraduate academic work or career work?

- Should advanced composition precede or follow special-focus advanced writing courses?

- How does an undergraduate advanced composition course differ from a graduate writing course?

Unfortunately, the material available to me reveals little about the level of advanced courses except that most courses so titled make no mention of grammar and punctuation in their syllabi and state either a strong preference or a prerequisite for two semesters of introductory composition plus junior or senior standing. In addition, the courses seem to be staffed most often by full-time faculty (many with associate or full professorships) rather than adjunct faculty or graduate students.

Another indirect indication of level is a marked decline in the number of complaints about remedial students in advanced courses. As many of us remember, it was common practice in the past to recommend advanced composition to students who earned D in freshman composition on the assumption that, despite the title, the advanced course was nothing more than the freshman course all over again at a slower pace. This assumption was supported by the wording of the 1967 "Guidelines and Directions for College Courses in Advanced Composition." In its general form the advanced course may be viewed as covering the range of the freshman course but in greater depth.[1]

Just two years ago many instructors, especially those from schools with a limited composition sequence, complained of their inability to determine and teach an appropriate level because so many of their students were still struggling with basics. In the past year, however, there were far fewer complaints; instead, quite a few people report that both their departments and their administrations have finally begun to differentiate between upper level remediation and advanced writing and now offer some form of sophomore remedial instruction for students who need more preparation before attempting either a competency exam or an advanced writing course. Apparently neither the general faculty nor the students at those schools confuse the two levels of instruction or expect one level to substitute for another.

---

[1] "Guidelines and Directions for College Courses in Advanced Composition," *College Composition and Communication* 18 (1967): 266-68.

If this is a trend (and it continues), we no longer have to consider the entire continuum from functional illiteracy to ready-to-publish when wrestling with the problem of level, but we still have a problem—a problem in urgent need of resolution. Many who teach a general rather than a special-focus advanced writing course described the problem. If the school has a full program of advanced writing courses, those teaching the general course, usually titled "Advanced Composition" or "Advanced Exposition," are not sure where in the sequence their course belongs or what material the course should include. Those whose schools offer only the general course are not sure how much material their course should cover or what its focus should be.

Some of these people say they are currently focusing on principles that govern all writing regardless of the special demands of form or profession and are teaching them as general principles, that is, as tools that can be applied to any specific professional requirement. This practice suggests that although the question of where in a writing sequence advanced composition should be placed has not been resolved—in fact, has not even been clearly addressed—some instructors are beginning to treat the general course as an introduction to professional writing in the same sense that freshman composition is, in theory, an introduction to undergraduate academic writing. One correspondent, in elaborating on the design of her courses, described a sequence similar to the sequencing that seems to be developing at other schools:

Step One: Freshman Composition I and II.

Step Two: Intermediate (Remedial) Composition. (Drill and review for those who need additional work in basics. Some schools offer a remedial lab in lieu of a course.)

Step Three: Advanced Composition. (Heterogeneous classes that teach advanced principles of organization, strategy, and style applicable to all professions and forms.)

Step Four: Specialized Writing. (Special-focus writing courses that apply the general principles to the specific requirements of particular forms—such as proposals, reports, research papers—and professions—such as business, law, science, technology, and journalism.

Content

Discussion of level invariably slides into discussion of focus and content, and for that I had a fair amount of material but a difficult task. No two courses are alike, very few courses are clearly one type or another, and no two instructors use exactly the same descriptive terminology. If I have interpreted the course descriptions correctly, most instructors are designing courses I would call "eclectic" for lack of a better label, that is, innovative mixtures of topics and techniques from rhetoric, psychology, journalism, logic, business, and any other field that offers something that can be used to good effect. Quite a few of those courses stress writing as a process, frequently combined with analytic thinking and problem solving. Interestingly, although very few instructors seem to teach rhetorical theory, quite a few do include communication theory—a practice common in business writing.

Style is the topic stressed most often regardless of the thrust of the course or the forms included. In fact, several courses seem to be devoted almost entirely to aspects of style as are some of the newer texts. The stylistic objective named most often is clarity, and to reach that objective, jargon, inflated diction, and wordiness are most often singled out for attack. Many people listed questions related to style they would like discussed:

- Is there a dominant style today, and if so, what is it?

- In teaching style, how much should we bend to current practice and how much should we defend "correct usage"?

- What style(s) should we stress?

- How far can we go to purge legal and business languages of their stylistic offenses?

- What are the most effective ways to teach style?

- Should we insist on the MLA style sheet or allow students to work from the style sheets appropriate to their major disciplines?

Instructors tend to emphasize either career-related forms of writing or academic forms, that is, either analytic and evaluative reports, articles, and reviews or rhetorically patterned essays, arguments, and research papers, but some include both types and others assign a broad range, such as the personal narrative, popular article, character study, and issue-oriented position statement. A few people even include fiction and poetry writing, while others include letter writing. Most instructors seem to require between six and ten short papers (500 to 1,000 words each) plus a larger project, such as one substantial paper that is developed and polished to publication standards through the course of the semester. Practically everyone stresses revision and professional-looking papers. I recall only one person who permitted handwritten out-of-class papers, and I remember (with admiration and awe) one who settles for nothing less than "letter perfect copy." That instructor's syllabus states clearly that not a single error in mechanics or transcription will be tolerated.

Format and Texts

Very few course descriptions indicate format, but from what I could infer, most instructors include some workshop sessions focused on student-generated material, and some rely on this format entirely. Several think the workshop format is essential because it dramatizes audience awareness and develops critical editing skills.

Most instructors also include individual conferences, but while some make conferences an integral part of the weekly schedule, others confer with students individually only once or twice in the semester. Several whose courses serve pre-professionals from a variety of disciplines use conferences as small group meetings in order to tailor the general instruction to the student's professional needs.

The lack of textbooks designed specifically for advanced composition continues to be a common complaint, but this problem seems to be easing. The publishers have become aware of the growing interest in advanced writing, and I know several are planning to issue the type of texts needed. One person suggested that *JAC* publish an annotated bibliography of recommended texts and include in each issue descriptive reviews of appropriate texts as they are published.

Writing Programs

Perhaps the strongest evidence that advanced writing is growing in both strength and complexity is the increasing number of colleges which have recently introduced, are about to introduce, or are thinking about a non-fiction writing concentration for both English majors and students from other disciplines. Unfortunately, I have very little to report since most of my correspondence was from people requesting information rather than from those with experience to share. However, a summary of the questions asked most often gives some idea of the topics that need discussion:

- What courses should a writing concentration require, and what other courses should it offer?

- What should the developmental order be?

- What disciplines have a career market for professional writers trained in both the discipline and writing?

- How much rhetorical theory and/or communication theory should be included?

- Should advanced grammar and/or linguistics be included, and if so how much and on what level?

- Should the history of the English language be included, and if so, should it be required of pre-professionals as well as English majors?

- Can the same program serve the English major preparing for secondary school teaching or graduate school and the non-English major preparing to write for a profession?

- What credentials should advanced writing faculty have?

Can regular English faculty with expertise in composition teach pre-professional courses, such as pre-law or science writing, without special training in the discipline?

- If not, where and how can established faculty retrain themselves?

Judging by the tone of several of the letters, those who are designing programs often have to act quickly; therefore, it seems to me that many of these questions should have priority in our discussions and research efforts.

Conclusion

The inferences I drew from my sources differ from the findings reported in Michael Hogan's 1979 survey in several minor but only a few significant details. Hogan's study, a controlled, analytic survey of 374 teachers of advanced composition showed that only seven percent require both Freshman Composition and advanced standing as prerequisite for advanced writing courses, while many of the course descriptions I received listed both as either a preference or a prerequisite. Hogan's survey also found that about twenty-five percent stressed improvement in punctuation, grammar, and mechanics as a major objective, while very few of my sources even mentioned these basics.[2]

These differences may be entirely the result of the differences in the types of materials used in the two reviews and the ways in which Hogan and I evaluated our materials. Hogan's survey was focused on specific questions and, therefore, the responses could be quantified. In contrast, my material was wide ranging, and since it covered only what each contributor chose to send, the responses had to be interpreted and estimated. In addition, Hogan used objective analysis to arrive at his findings, while I allowed myself the luxury of unscientific impressionism. This last difference alone could account for the differences in our findings.

On the other hand, the differences might also be the result of dramatic change in a rapidly developing specialty. If growth and maturation are at least part of the explanation, the prognosis for advanced composition is bright. We may have more questions than answers at the moment and some pressing fundamental problems to resolve, but we seem to be surprisingly unified in our developing trends, in our perception of the problems, and in our notions of what solutions should be sought first. We need dialogue and research in many areas, but most urgently we need to address the following:

- An updated set of guidelines.

- A sharper delineation of the level of writing implied by the title "advanced."

- The sequencing of writing courses.

---

[2] "Advanced Composition: A Survey," *Journal of Advanced Composition* 1 (1980): 21-29.

- The reasons for the new student interest in advanced writing.

- The curricula most likely to prepare students for the writing requirements in specific professions.

- The career writing opportunities in specific professions.

- The components of a sound writing program.

- The problems of training new faculty and, above all, retraining established faculty.

Some of these concerns are projects that should be undertaken by ATAC, but others are topics that individuals can address through articles submitted to *JAC*.

State of the Art in Advanced Expository Writing: One Genus, Many Species

by Bernice W. Dicks

The survey and samples that follow are subject to two limitations and one assumption that I have applied in approaching the identity of the advanced composition course as it exists really and ideally. First, two limitations: I have not included material or ideas for "Honors" courses for first-year students, nor have I given much attention to "advanced" courses required for prospective teachers. Second, I have assumed that most freshman composition courses, no matter what they are called, have essentially the same characteristics: they are either "straight" writing courses, or they are literature-based courses with some emphasis on writing. The prevailing general description of advanced composition applies throughout: a course in expository writing beyond the first-year level.

A bibliography search (the *Humanities Index*, the *College English* index, and the *College Composition and Communication* index, mainly) revealed that over the last twelve years there have not been many articles on the subject of advanced composition. Even the thirty volumes of *CCC* yield few items. This is not to say, however, that the CCCC has ignored the matter: all along, workshops of the conference have been devoted to the problem of defining the species "advanced composition" and, in 1966-67, to establishing guidelines, an abstract of which was distributed in 1979 at the ATAC organization meeting.

In October 1954, *CCC* reported on the "Composition Career (of All Students) after the Freshman Year": the participants concluded that "a required advanced course in composition is desirable, but difficulties in scheduling such courses were recognized. It was felt that an advanced course in writing in the last two years has a good chance of success because the student is more mature, has more information, can integrate his information better, has more motivation for improving his writing, and merits more attention."[1] A year later, the workshop participants were "unanimous in [their] opinion that advanced courses in composition are necessary for all students beyond the freshman year."[2] Also in 1955, there was a workshop in "Imaginative Writing in Advanced Composition" that came to eight conclusions about "creative writing" courses; the phrase "advanced composition" does not appear in the body of

---

Reprinted from the *Journal of Advanced Composition* 3 (1982): 172-91. Reprinted with permission.

[1] "Composition Career (of All Students) after the Freshman Year,"*College Composition and Communication* 5 (1954): 114. Hereafter, the journal title will be given as*CCC*. NB: I have made no attempt to alter the use of pronouns in quotations from my sources; to do so would have been unwieldy and confusing.

[2] "Composition Career (of All Students) after the Freshman Year,"*CCC* 6 (1955): 146.

the report.[3] I mention this oddity only to indicate the confusion that seems to have
prevailed in discussion of the subject from the beginning.

The February 1956 issue of *CCC* carried two brief items that dealt with advanced writing courses: in "Metaphor and Exposition," Harry R. Garvin described
his attempts to deal with "his role of rhetorician, the teacher of vivid writing," through
the use of student writing to illustrate "vivid and dead metaphor" and "warmed-over
and fresh diction." In "College and the Writer," J. Donald Adams urged the reader
to break loose from fiction-based, poetry-analyzing courses for writing students. In
neither article is there help in defining what advanced composition should be.[4]

In 1958, CCCC discussed "The Advanced Course in Expository Writing: Aims,
Texts, and Methods."[5] After summarizing the descriptions given by participants of
existing advanced courses, the variety of practices regarding texts (predictably,
"both a rhetoric and a book of readings [or] a rhetoric only [or] a book of readings
or current magazines only [or] no text at all"), the workshop report ends as follows:
"The course is difficult to describe because it is actually several courses: a multiple-
section required course on some campuses, a small elective course on others; occasionally a course oriented to a particular vocational goal, such as teaching; and,
rarely, a remedial course." With a certain degree of pride, the writer adds that advanced writing courses are "currently gaining ground. . . ." The workshop recommended that the 1959 CCCC offer two workshops, one for the required version of
advanced composition and one for the elective version. However, CCCC apparently did not act positively on the recommendation.

In 1960 and 1961, the emphasis changed to the "Gifted Student"—meaning freshmen, actually, and not addressed to the question of the upper-level students who
have already taken the first-year course and who want (and probably need) more
work in writing.[6]

In 1962, there was a workshop on "Teaching Advanced Composition for Teachers" that yielded three descriptions of courses of this variety: Virginia Burke gave
details of a "required advanced course at Wisconsin [that] involves the reading and
close rhetorical analysis of classic and modern essays, the writing of twelve one-
thousand word themes, a study of various semantic problems and techniques, and
thorough practice in the evaluation of student writing." Francis Christensen reported
that "after a semester of systematic grammar [his students] turn their attention to composition. . . ." He stated that "he teaches control of the structure of a sentence plus
the careful arrangement of sentences in a paragraph. . . . In addition to twenty assignments, many brief 'finger exercises' further illustrate how a writer may use
words to control the ebb and flow of an idea." And Jane Lynch described a course
built on "many examples of literature-based expository writing. Prospective teachers
are expected to show original observation based upon the literary text. Consider

---

[3] "Imaginative Writing in Advanced Composition," *CCC* 6 (1955): 153-55.
[4] "[Advanced Writing Courses] College and the Writer," *CCC* 7 (1956): 28-29, 5-7.
[5] "The Advanced Course in Expository Writing: Aims, Texts, Methods," *CCC* 9 (1958): 165-67.
[6] "The Composition/Communication Course for the Gifted Student," *CCC* 11 (1960): 168-70; "Motivating the
Gifted Student in the Composition/Communication Program," *CCC* 12 (1961): 149-51.

able attention to theory is blended with the writing experiences, but the research paper and 'creative' writing are ruled out. . . ."[7] The comments provide some models that might be useful to a teacher confronted with developing an advanced composition course.

In 1963 a workshop took up "The Undergraduate Advanced Composition Course" only to report—predictably—that there was no agreement on "what Advanced Composition should be, or is" or the "objectives, . . . the content, the order of topics, the number or length of essays, the emphasis various factors in composition should get, or what related material to bring in." Nor was there agreement "about the sorts of topics to assign, or whether to assign topics . . . about in-class versus outside writing, examinations, and certainly not about criteria for grading [or about the] optimum size of effective texts."[8]

At the CCCC meeting in 1963, there was a discussion of "The Graduate Course for Training College Teachers" that reported such recommendations as these: the "content" of the course should include "rhetoric, logic, structural linguistics, psychology of learning, evaluation of student and professional writing, and criticism of composition textbooks"; the students should read "CCCC and NCTE journals and books dealing with the art of teaching and the profession of English."[9]

A workshop on "Composition Aims in Advanced Writing Courses" in 1964 suggested that such courses have "objectives of two basic types: functional objectives, which aim at making students more skillful writers, and objectives which aim at improving the individual himself, his sensitivity, his reading, his self-knowledge, and his critical ability . . . the student's style, his sensitivity to language, to pace, tone, and rhythm, and his command of rhetoric resources such as the elements of argumentation."[10] A discussion of the "Content of the Advanced Composition Course" (1965) addressed itself to definition of the course as well as to its purpose, content, population, selection of students, size and "teacher load." The participants stressed quality of writing as the primary focus of the course and recommended flexibility "in material and methods," but with "a basic organizational plan." They went so far as to propose the format for an advanced composition course: it should focus "on discursive prose," precise and appropriate language usage, "special writing problems," and the study of "*smaller* units of composition (the paragraph and sentence)"; it should also feature both free choice of topics and "personal supervision . . . so close as to amount almost to tutorial help" within small classes. Finally, the advanced composition teachers should have a light teaching load to make time for these pursuits.[11]

The questions of guidelines and training for advanced composition teachers were the meat of the "Invitational Workshop on Advanced Composition" in 1967, which was one of the two meetings that produced the "Guidelines and Directions for College Courses in Advanced Composition" published in *CCC* in December of that year, a statement to which I shall return later in another connection.

---

[7] "Teaching Advanced Composition for Teachers,"*CCC* 13 (1962): 77-78.
[8] "The Undergraduate Advanced Composition Course,"*CCC* 14 (1963): 190.
[9] "The Graduate Course for Training College Teachers,"*CCC* 14 (1963): 192.
[10] "Composition Aims in Advanced Writing Courses," *CCC* 15 (1964): 190-91.
[11] "Content of the Advanced Composition Course," *CCC* 16 (1965): 197.

At this point, let me digress slightly and quote the recommendation about the "training" that an advanced composition teacher should have: "Master of Arts in English, with an emphasis in composition which would provide minimal academic training plus a period of 'internship'. . . . Three specific subject matter courses were viewed as basic: modern grammars and rhetoric; history of the English language; analysis of prose styles." The future advanced composition teacher should write constantly and widely "under close supervision," should be "a competent and disciplined writer," have "a strong liberal arts background," be "familiar with a variety of ideas and experiences, preferably through direct encounter," be "interested in what other people are interested in so that he can actively participate in what he is reading and editing," and be "dumb like a fox." Finally, this paragon of an instructor should publish "at least some of his own work"—for all which accomplishments, the report concludes, the teacher should have "rank and salary commensurate with his special competence. . . ."[12] I must pause and wonder: if we can ever define advanced composition, will we ever be able to staff it?

The repetitiveness of the materials suggests not only that advanced composition people were repeating themselves but also that much of what they were saying is applicable to the situation of any writing teacher. When, in 1969, yet another workshop set out to answer the obvious question, "What is *advanced composition*?" it concluded—hardly surprisingly—that "*Advanced composition* eludes abstract definition" and then went on to summarize the participants' versions of courses under that title.

"The label," the writer continued, in terms that still apply, usually refers to an undergraduate level course ostensibly designed for a progression in writing experiences of students who have met or waived the requirements of a preceding college course in written composition, required of freshmen. In one institution that has offered a major in composition for approximately fifty years the advanced composition major may elect advanced composition as one of his required number of courses in advanced writing. In another institution the course provides professional writers the opportunity to prepare their manuscripts for publication. In a small college all students are required to take six hours of advanced composition, but of two varieties— advanced writing for the English major, but a continuation of basic writing skills for the non-major. In an institution that has a large enrollment in the technical fields, teachers and students are expressing a preference for advanced composition over technical writing. Most of the institutions represented offer a required three- or six-hour advanced composition course for English majors, particularly the major qualifying for teachers certification, and offer also a parallel elective course in advanced composition for students who elect it and meet its prerequisite requirements.[13]

It was interesting that this was the first report to address itself also to the identity of most practicing advanced composition teachers: "scholars in another area of specialization associated with language and literature, who by circumstances or inclination, or both, subsequently developed professional competence and stature in the teaching of composition, mainly by teaching it." And it was in this workshop that

---

[12] "Invitational Workshop on Advanced Composition," *CCC* 18 (1965): 199-200.
[13] "Advanced Composition Courses," *CCC* 20 (1969): 254-55.

substantial mention was made[14] of a technique that has since become fairly common in advanced composition courses for non-professional writers: "the requirement of specific pieces of writing slanted toward a publication audience and further controlled by the demands of a publisher's market" as a motivational device.[15] Indeed, some instructors based the grade for the course on the fact of acceptance for publication—a practice that struck me as punitive; later I shall present course descriptions that call for the students to show proof of an attempt to publish, which seems less harsh.[16]

The 1970 version of the advanced composition workshop dwelt upon three "Issues": "the nature of an advanced composition course"; "grading practices"; and "revision techniques." Advanced composition here is "merely a continuation and extension of Freshman English, differing in that it had a more highly motivated student, in that it presented a more structured treatment of style, and in that it offered a variety of writing experiences."[17] The use of "merely" is curious in light of earlier treatments of the subject in which advanced composition was intended to be much more than a sequel to the freshman course.

In the last report of a workshop (1971) in the run of *CCC*, I found a prettily alliterated statement of purpose for advanced composition courses: "The attainment of a conscious, careful, concentrated, calculated craftsmanship."[18]

My reaction to the experience of reading through the workshop reports was nicely summed up by Duane C. Nichols in an article in *CCC* in December 1970: he confessed to have no idea of "what [advanced composition] is now"; "beyond the fact that advanced composition is a non-fiction writing course for which freshman English is a prerequisite, few generalizations can be made."[19] What, then, can teachers do when confronted with the task of designing an advanced composition course, whether they are asked to do so by students or by administrators? After all, most of us come into the field, as Nichols put it, "by accident and despite the general failure of graduate English Departments to recognize the need for training in composition or rhetoric," and because advanced composition is a course that "thrives . . . because it gives interested students a chance to write about the things that matter and to receive intelligent comment about that writing."[20] In other words, many teachers may well have to devise an advanced writing course of some sort as it becomes more difficult for freshman English to correct the short-comings of grade- and high-school education and as concern over the writing ability of our students accelerates across the campus, bringing departments other than English to the realization that "something must be done"—preferably by the English Department.[21]

---

[14] *Ibid.*
[15] *Ibid.*
[16] Letter from Frances Teague, Department of English, Univ. of Georgia, November 1, 1979; Michael P. Orth, "An Advanced Composition Course Aimed at Publication," *CCC* 27 (1976): 210-12.
[17] "The Advanced Composition Course," *CCC* 21 (1970): 289-90.
[18] "Advanced Composition: What Is It?" *CCC* 22 (1971): 291-92.
[19] Duane C. Nichols, "To New-Found Methods and to Compounds Strange," *CCC* 21 (1970): 391.
[20] *Ibid.* 392.
[21] *Ibid.* 393-94, where Nichols addresses these points at length.

There are some articles bearing useful suggestions. Writing in *College English* in October 1963, Donald M. Murray describes advanced composition as "that course which typically appears as a requirement for the English major in his junior year. It is called Advanced Composition, Junior Composition, or Creative Writing, and it tries to improve the student's writing ability beyond the point to which freshman composition and the preparation of term papers have taken him. It is the course which usually gives him a chance to experiment in the writing of short stories or poems or essays or plays."[22] What Murray proposes is the use of Henry James' "The Art of Fiction" as the entrée to writing prose fiction: he recommends that the course begin with discussion of the contents of James' essay and with suggestions for application of James' precepts: "fiction is a serious affair, dealing with the life one has really felt"; "keep a notebook and cultivate perceptiveness. 'Try to be one of the people on whom nothing is lost!'"; "fidelity to life"; "the need for selection"; "a specific, fundamental idea to start with (a donnée) and some plan for execution"; an "angle of narration."[23] The hope for the course is "that the students who have gone to school to James will write stories that are both more honest and better controlled than when they began." Professor Murray concludes with the observation that "Probably any author who is both standard fare in the literature courses and articulate on the subject of his art might" serve as the focal figure in this species of advanced composition course: Hemingway, for one, and Ezra Pound, via his letters, for "the poetry phase of the course."[24]

In October 1970, Paul Briand described his advanced course in an article entitled "Turned On: Multi-Media and Advanced Composition." Briand undertook to solve what he saw as the main problems in any writing course: "subjects for theme writing," "theme discussion in class," "the teaching of theme writing," and "theme reading." He graded the papers by means of tape recordings: the students wrote and recorded their papers and turned in both forms; Briand commented in writing on the mechanics and recorded his responses to "larger more abstract matters." For class discussion, he showed video-tape recordings of himself commenting on representative themes; he also edited a paper (using an overhead projector) as the class watched. To deal with "the teaching of theme writing," he lectured for twenty minutes on a given principle, using three slide projectors and three screens to list the principles and to produce a theme from thesis through the revising and editing processes. To generate topics, he produced "six idea-saturation programs" using the three-screens-and-slides approach as well as film clips. The course was expensive—between three and four thousand dollars—and therefore hardly practical for most teachers whose departments are strapped for Xerox money.[25]

In the May 1974 issue of CCC, Donald C. Stewart presented his version of "An Advanced Composition Course That Works." His scheme was to offer the students "four options":

---

[22] Donald M. Murray, "Henry James in the Advanced Composition Course,"*College English* 25 (1963): 26.
[23] Murray 27-29.
[24] Murray 30.
[25] Paul Briand, "Turned On: Multi-Media and Advanced Composition," *CCC* 21 (1971): 267-69.

1. "for students who are insecure about their writing abilities . . . prescribed assignments which progress from explanations of the ways they acquired their attitudes toward writing to extended analogies and meditations."

2. "for the student who would rather react to the prescribed writing assignments, some point made in the reading, or a position generated by class
discussion," six individual papers due on the same schedule as the "prescribed" themes.

3. "for the aspiring professional writer[s] . . . papers on various topics of
their own choosing" with the "goal [of] publication of their work in acceptable popular, scholarly, or technical publications."

4. for the student who preferred a large undertaking, "a semester-long
project" that generated "a series of papers" intended for publication.

Students were permitted to shift options "on any writing occasion"; class time was
devoted to "lectures, readings, and responses" on such topics as the "history and
growth of English departments and composition courses" and the connections between composition and literature, composition and rhetoric, and composition and linguistics as discussed by Corbett and Tate.[26]

A version of Stewart's third option constitutes the core of Michael P. Orth's advanced composition course as described in *CCC* in May 1976. "In a ten-week quarter, I lead students through six papers, culminating in a carefully planned article
aimed at a specific audience and market. I mail the final papers to the newspapers
and magazines the students designate, and twenty percent of them are published."
The papers are between one and two thousand words in length and must be "honest . . . full of digested facts presented to make some point." Class time is distributed
among workshop situations, in-class writing, and lectures on "the concept and elements of style; . . . my notions of the proper process of writing as process," and the
avoidance of "jargon and doublespeak." Workshops include a student editorial
board that reviews articles and "group writing" on an "argument paper."[27]

Donald C. Stewart returned to *CCC* in 1980 with other ideas for advanced composition, suggesting that writing "for publication" is a practical task that might engage
students' interest particularly when combined with any "real" writing task: "writing a
letter to the student paper, preparing a job application statement for a real job that
the student wants, preparing revisions in the constitution of an organization to which
the student belongs." In Kansas, where Stewart teaches, advanced composition "is a
requirement for certification of the secondary English teacher": for that reason, he
was concerned with the problem of sharpening their "evaluative capabilities," so he
arranged to have them "read, evaluate, and *grade* [his] freshman papers." He discovered that the cooperation of the two groups developed "audience conscious-

---

[26] Donald C. Stewart, "An Advanced Composition Course That Works"*CCC* 25 (1974): 197-200.
[27] Michael P. Orth, "An Advanced Composition Course Aimed at Publication,"*CCC* 27 (1976): 210-12.

ness" in both and made student selection of topics somewhat easier: the freshmen addressed campus issues with which the upper-level students were conversant. The method was relatively simple: "one person in the [advanced] class [acted as] scribe for each paper. That person made marginal notations and wrote the terminal comment offered by the class." Secret ballots for grades assured "consensus" and defused potential hassles. On the whole, Stewart found the system both workable and valuable for the students.[28] Obviously, only instructors who teach both first-year and advanced courses at the same time can take advantage of the suggestions.

So much for articles in *CCC* and *CE* specifically addressed by title to advanced composition. Obviously, the hypothetical neophyte in the advanced composition business could adapt any of the models for freshman English or the less numerous formats for "advanced" courses to the needs of "advanced" students (which all too often means only farther along in their college careers than year one). They could simply use the same format they developed for first-year courses, requiring a "harder" textbook, more writing, and increased one-on-one attention. For example, when I first taught advanced composition, I was using Donald Hall's *Writing Well* with my first-year students; I assigned Peter Canavan's *Rhetoric and Literature* for the advanced class. In subsequent incarnations of the course, I have moved up to Winterowd's *The Contemporary Writer* and D'Angelo's *Process and Thought in Composition*. But before I get into the question of textbooks, let me report on some models I collected by the simple expedient of writing and asking for them.

Of the sixty responses I received, most fall into what is apparently a standard pattern for advanced—and most other—composition courses: there is a writing textbook, sometimes teamed with a reader and a handbook. Students write and revise anywhere from five to twelve papers during the course, frequently involving a conference with the teacher over the rough draft or the revision (or both). Occasionally the teacher will include a limited amount of fiction: for example, Anne Warner at Agnes Scott includes a literary criticism component in her advanced course and assigns James' *The Turn of the Screw*; class discussion includes "interpretation, review, character analysis, technical analysis, comparative, contextual, [and] psychological."[29]

In the fall semester of 1979-80, Indiana University offered a total of five versions of "Advanced Expository Writing": two of the sections listed no texts and indicated the use of student papers for discussion. Two required that tried and true friend, *Elements of Style*. One assigned Lattimore's translation of Homer's *Odyssey* for "a community of interest" and "the writing and revising of three brief papers."[30]

At some institutions, advanced composition or advanced expository writing is only one dish in a smorgasbord of writing options after the first year. Charles Davis, Director of Composition at the University of Arizona, sent me materials describing the writing courses for the spring: "Sophomore Composition" (four sections), assigning variously *Writing Well* and *A Writer's Reader*; *Popular Writing in*

---

[28] Donald C. Stewart, "Practical Work for Advanced Composition Students," *CCC* 31 (1980): 81-83.
[29] Letter from Anne B. Warner, Department of English, Agnes Scott College, n.d.
[30] Materials from Michael C. Flanigan, Director of Composition, Indiana Univ., October 25, 1979.

America; and *A Writer's Reader* and *Elements of Style*. "Advanced Composition" (two sections) emphasizes "expository and argumentative writing" for "already competent writers who plan to enter graduate and professional schools or who will do a great deal of writing in their careers"; the text is Corbett's *Classical Rhetoric for the Modern Student*. (The remaining courses include six sections of technical writing, five of business writing, one of business report writing, one of advanced scientific and technical writing, and one of advanced English composition for international graduate students.)[31] Indeed, in some schools, such courses as technical writing and creative writing are the advanced composition courses—as at Denison University, for example, where a creative writing advanced course appears alongside a course called "Expository Writing" designed for "students who have completed or passed the proficiency exam for English 101" and another course, English 236, entitled "Writing for Science and Social Science Majors," in which the texts are *The Lives of a Cell*, *Social Problems 79/80*, and *Focus: Biology*.[32]

Auburn University offers three versions of "Advanced Composition"; the University of Rochester lists four "Advanced Writing" courses: "The Essay" comes in three essentially similar formats based on an essay anthology, student essays, a writing text and a handbook in one combination or another. The fourth is "Preparation of Scientific Papers," which combines "extensive reading and analysis of exemplary papers in the literature of biology or some other science" with writing articles, reviews, abstracts, and research-grant proposals.[33]

The University of Maine at Orono offers "Advanced Professional Exposition," which is designed "to help students improve their writing skills in preparation for careers and professions" and is offered "primarily [to] juniors and seniors in business, scientific, technical, and professional disciplines who have mastered the fundamentals of standard written English." Assignments include definition *per se*, definition of problems, informal proposals, researching information, letters of inquiry, technical descriptions, formal proposals, abstracts and summaries, and progress reports.[34] "Advanced Writing," which has as prerequisites "the semester freshman course" and "Descriptive and Narrative Writing," was "planned . . . as a series of experiments of freedom and discipline . . . for 'good writers.'" Virginia Steinhoff, allowing the class to create the course as they went, required as texts Walker Gibson's *Persona* and the Christensens' *Notes Toward a New Rhetoric*; she recommended Didion's *Slouching Toward Bethlehem*, Thomas' *Lives of a Cell* and White's *Essays*.[35]

Brown University offers poetry-writing, fiction, and journalism courses under the "advanced" rubric as well as "English Composition, Advanced Course," which asks students "to develop and bring to completion an original work or series of works in prose, verse or drama"; it is open only to seniors and graduate students.[36]

---

[31] Materials from Charles E. Davis, Director of Composition, Univ. of Arizona, November 5, 1979.
[32] Materials from Tommy R. Burkett, Chair, Department of English, Denison Univ., n.d.
[33] Materials from the Department of English, Auburn Univ., n.d.; from Rowland L. Collins, Chair, Department of English, the Univ. of Rochester, January 14, 1980.
[34] Materials from Richard T. Brucher, Eh 17 Course Chair, Department of English, Univ. of Maine at Orono, December 6, 1979.
[35] Materials from Virginia Steinhoff, Department of English, Univ. of Maine at Orono, October 29, 1979.
[36] Materials from Ruth Oppenheim, Coordinator, Department of English, Brown Univ., October 17, 1979.

The "Advanced Writing" course at Newcomb College, Tulane University, is specifically patterned upon John Trimble's precepts, and perhaps even on his syllabus for "Advanced Expository Writing" at the University of Texas—Austin. Both courses require a good deal of writing—10 and 12 papers respectively—as well as in-class discussion of student work and a heavy emphasis on editing, not to mention a good amount of reading in such texts as *Contexts for Composition*, *Writing with Style*, and *Revising Prose*. The clientele is intended to be, in Trimble's words, "17-20 people eager to polish their style, increase their fluency, learn how to edit, and receive maximum feedback on their writing," some of which feedback occurs in required conferences.[37]

I acquired two examples of what I call the "intense" advanced course (I owe the adjective to my own advanced composition students). One is offered by Sam Watson at the University of North Carolina at Charlotte: "Advanced Expository Writing." The reading list is formidable: *Writing Without Teachers*, Plato's *Gorgias* and *Phaedrus*, *Readings in Classical Rhetoric*, *Zen and the Art of Motorcycle Maintenance*, *Teaching Composition: Ten Bibliographical Essays*, *The Contemporary Writer*, *Contemporary Rhetoric*, and *Measuring Growth in English*. Then comes a list of journals of which the students should be "aware": *Philosophy and Rhetoric*, *Rhetoric Society Quarterly*, six specialized journals of the Speech Communication Association, and the obvious English and composition journals. To sum up, Watson teaches a rhetoric course of considerable density that bears similarities to his course, "Rhetorical Theory," the syllabus of which he sent to me. In his comments to the students, Watson defends what may seem to be a thorny path to writing better: "'Rhetoric' is the discipline which underlies composition pedagogy, and we will begin with a survey of classical rhetorical theory and doctrine. Frankly, I will be unconcerned if our work in this area seems immediately to have little relevance to current classroom concerns. The stuff is interesting in its own right, and I think its relevance will become clear as the course progresses.[38]

The other example of an "intense" course came from Ohio Wesleyan University, where there is a writing major: "Advanced Composition" appears under both the "Creative" and "Non-Fiction" listings; the syllabus sent to me by Ülle E. Lewes is for English 50, the "non-fiction" version. The texts are Hirsch's *The Philosophy of Composition*, Lanham's *Style: An Anti Textbook*, and Miller's *Word, Self, Reality*—yoked, for what struck me as a relenting of the pressure, with Newman's *Strictly Speaking* and *Elements of Style*. Class time is devoted to discussing the "various—and sometimes conflicting—theories" and to "some sort of experiment in writing." "Members of the class will also be assigned a longer or more complex writing task to do at home every week."[39]

Just briefly, here are a few more unusual versions. At Queens College, Charlotte, NC, "Advanced Composition" is a course in reading and then writing descrip-

---

[37]Materials from John C. Schafer, Newcomb College, Tulane Univ., November 5, 1979; from John Trimble's appearance at *CCCC*, Minneapolis, April, 1979.

[38] Materials from Sam Watson, Department of English, Univ. of North Carolina at Charlotte, October 22, 1979.

[39] Materials from Ülle E. Lewes, Department of English, Ohio Wesleyan Univ., October 24, 1979.

tions, poems, short stories, personal essays, caricature, a children's story, a choice of a play or an article, and satire, which may be poetry or prose or "a short scene from a play."[40] At Florida State, there is an "Advanced Article and Essay Workshop" in which there is no assigned text but a great deal of writing and discussion of student work, which should be slanted toward publication, and frequent conferences.[41] North Texas State University provides two upper-level courses: "Specialized Expository Writing" is limited at present to "Legal Writing," but is planned eventually to deal separately with "Medical Writing," "Business Writing," and others. The university's "Advanced Expository Writing" course is taught on a tutorial basis and focuses on "logical and rhetorical principles" as well as "analyzing [and] criticizing models."[42]

I have received three descriptions of advanced courses that were geared to the students' academic and professional interests—the students' papers must address subjects in their major fields. At the University of Southwestern Louisiana and at the University of Tennessee at Chattanooga, the students are encouraged to write with the intention of submitting at least some of their work for publication. Hence, the courses spend a fair amount of time considering the question of audience as well as of logic and organization. At Baylor University, the approach is rhetorical and practical, including work on interviewing and job researching.[43]

To sum up as briefly as possible: the models I collected, thanks to the generosity of those who sent them, as well as the literature I found elsewhere, indicate that there is a multitude of species available to teachers of advanced expository writing: we can invent, imitate, cull, combine. Unfortunately, the wealth of models suggests again that advanced composition may well prove impossible to define once and for all: if, as Peter Dowell at Emory wrote to me, "the content is at the discretion (or whim) of the individual instructor," then we really are no farther along toward a statement about the course than we were when CCCC started out in 1954 to pin the creature to the wall.[44] Maybe a sentence from a letter from R.W. Daniel at Kenyon points out part of our problem: "The course has not proved to be very advanced, because most of the students are not."[45] In the midst of the materials scattered across the study and office as I worked, it occurred to me to wonder if we aren't beginning at the wrong end: perhaps we should first define the true advanced composition student. Or perhaps an observation from Mary Dobbie, Senior Lecturer at Columbia University, might give us a notion of what will both attract students and help them along: "I am giving a 'Workshop in Advanced Grammar' this term, and I find my students are taking it to improve their writing."[46] Perhaps what the students really want

---

[40] Materials from Paul B. Newman, English Department, Queens College, Charlotte, North Carolina, n.d.

[41] Materials from David Kirby, Director of Writing Programs, Florida State Univ., October 24, 1979.

[42] Materials from James T.F. Tanner, Chair, Schedule Committee, Department of English, North Texas State Univ., November 12, 1979.

[43] Materials from the Department of English, the Univ. of Southwestern Louisiana, October 26, 1979; from T.C. Ware, Head, Department of English, Univ. of Tennessee at Chattanooga, November 29, 1979; from Darrel Thomas Hanks, Department of English, Baylor Univ., October 3, 1979.

[44] Letter from Peter Dowell, Department of English, Emory Univ., October 22, 1979.

[45] Letter from R.W. Daniel, Department of English, Kenyon College, November 15, 1979.

[46] Letter from Mary Dobbie, Department of English, Columbia Univ., October 29, 1979.

is to back up, in effect, and start over with smaller units.

I turn to an attempt at indicating the range of texts available to teachers of advanced composition. One way for me to deal with the matter is simply to refer you to the expanded version of the responses to a 1979 survey (by Michael P. Hogan) of teachers of advanced composition: here is a collection of readers, rhetorics, handbooks, research-paper guides and assorted other books that are in use around the country in "our" course. The range and variety are enormous—like those of the course itself.

There is also the more-than-obvious recourse of reading reviews of composition texts in the February *CCC*; in Larsen's now abandoned "Selected Bibliography of Research and Writing about the Teaching of Composition" in the May *CCC*; in *College English, English Journal, English Studies, CEA Critic, PMLA* (occasionally), and the *Chronicle of Higher Education*. We might keep an eye on the semi-annual bibliographies in *Research in the Teaching of English* and consider some of the state journals such as *Arizona English Bulletin, Kansas English*, the *Journal of English Teaching Techniques*, the *Journal of Basic Writing*, and *CEA Forum*. Perhaps at some time an article like Karen Steiner's "A Selected Bibliography of Individualized Approaches to College Composition" might inspire an advanced composition teacher to try something that has worked in a freshman or other writing course.[47]

There are almost too many obvious possibilities: we all receive dozens of ads for textbooks, new and revised; we all talk to publishers' representatives (we should badger the publishers through their field personnel about advanced composition textbooks—that is, if we're not ready to write them ourselves). I am just faintly surprised that the representatives who come to see me seem non-plussed by my interest in an "advanced" text: the representative from Oxford University Press simply pointed at my copy of Mina Shaughnessy's *Errors and Expectations*.

Now, of course, there is the *Journal of Advanced Composition*. We can work for the best in this venture to provide the articles, critical reviews and bibliographies that we all need to continue to do our jobs in a course that, as so many workshops and writers have insisted, is indeed badly needed—even though we may continue to struggle for awhile with its shape and content.

---

[47] Karen Steiner, "A Selected Bibliography of Individualized Approaches to College Composition,"*CCC*, 28 (1977): 232-34.

Advanced Exposition: A Survey of Patterns and Problems

by Ronald C. Shumaker, Larry Dennis, Lois Green

Recent developments in English studies suggest a renewed interest in reading and teaching expository essays. The work of Chris Anderson, John Warnock, and others has produced articles and books directing professional attention to "literary nonfiction." New anthologies seek to engage students with classic essays as well as current essays by influential contemporary writers. Generating much of this work is an awareness that the essay is a powerful modern genre, a major vehicle for public discourse. Paradoxically, however, this public respect for the expository essay does not seem to be shared in university English departments. As Anderson has asked, "Why has the essay as a form declined in the academic world even as it has gained in popularity outside the academic world" (300)?

Although Anderson's question refers to the reluctance of English scholars to write and teach the essay, it raises a related issue for teachers of writing. In our experience, the advanced composition course traditionally has asked students to write expository essays aimed at public discourse and to strive for the style and sophistication of accomplished essayists. It may be, however, that the last several years have taken advanced writing instruction away from that expository, public focus. The proliferation of new courses in advanced writing is healthy and laudable, but the very titles of such courses often suggest narrowly defined audiences: Scientific Writing, Technical Writing, Business Writing, Writing for the Professions, Writing in the Disciplines. The specialized skills and voices these courses engender may come at the expense of a broader advanced writing course. Moreover, this specializing trend comes in the midst of calls for student empowerment and increased cultural literacy. If the profession is at last recognizing the power of the essay as a mode of public discourse, are we, paradoxically, abandoning the kind of instruction in advanced exposition that might enable our students to join in that discourse?

As teachers of advanced composition, we share the impression that this paradoxical development is indeed taking place. Few textbooks exist for general courses in advanced writing. Little of the professional literature on composition theory addresses itself to such courses. Even a cursory examination of catalog course descriptions indicates extremely diverse visions of what such a course should do. Discussions with colleagues at other institutions reveal uncertainties like ours

Reprinted from the *Journal of Advanced Composition* 10 (1990): 136-44. Reprinted with permission.

about the nature and content of advanced writing instruction. Suspecting that the place of advanced expository writing courses is increasingly problematic, we conducted a survey to examine the current institutional situation of courses named "advanced composition."

Advanced Composition: A Survey

First, we examined more than 600 institutional catalogs to cull descriptions of courses labeled "advanced composition" or what appeared to be its equivalent. Then we prepared and mailed questionnaires to 300 representative institutions across the country. The questionnaire covered four areas: organization of courses, instructors, pedagogy, and theory. A fifth section invited respondents to volunteer comments on issues of concern. Under "Organization," we asked about the existence and form of advanced composition courses, their size, student populations, prerequisites, and definition of acceptable performance. The section about "Instructors" asked who assigned instructors to the course and the qualifications required of those who teach it. The section on "Pedagogy" asked about texts, numbers and types of writing assignments, instructional modes, and course focus (such as, research writing, writing for publication, writing about literature). The section on "Theory" examined the theoretical base of the course as well as the theorists who have shaped the thinking of instructors. This section also asked about the place of the course in relation to writing-across-the-curriculum programs.

Of the 300 institutions queried, 124 returned the questionnaire. Our findings represent 42 states, the District of Columbia, and Puerto Rico. Responding schools included 68 public institutions and 47 private. Nine were two-year institutions. Of 115 four-year plus schools, 59 were large multipurpose universities, 54 were predominately undergraduate schools, and two were military academies. Our respondents, then, represent a relatively broad range of institutions.

Like many similar studies, this survey raises as many questions as it answers. On the other hand, it indicates some clear patterns and problems important to colleagues who teach advanced composition courses and who face the uncertainties and program configurations sketched above. In this article, therefore, we offer first some statistical highlights and then some consideration of the implications of responses. Together, the patterns and problems suggest disarray in courses identified as "advanced composition." Such courses seem not to have benefited fully from the paradigm shift that has fundamentally altered our approach to developmental and freshman writing in the university.

Two surveys of advanced composition from earlier in this decade provide a background against which to measure the results of our study. The first, published by Bernice Dicks in the *Journal of Advanced Composition*, expresses cautious optimism about the national situation of courses in advanced writing. Dicks' title, "State of the Art in Advanced Expository Writing: One Genus, Many Species," suggests both the optimism and the caution. While "one genus" finds a core of commonality among such courses, "many species" conveys some uneasiness about the Protean nature of the surface forms taken by them. Dicks' report reaches a carefully measured conclusion:

> To sum up as briefly as possible: the models I collected . . . indicate that there is a multitude of species available to teachers of advanced expository writing: we can invent, imitate, cull, combine. . . . Unfortunately, the wealth of models suggests again that advanced composition may well prove impossible to define once and for all. (186)

The second survey, conducted by Priscilla Tate, reaches a more optimistic conclusion. In an unpublished summary, Tate notes the increasing use of contemporary theory and pedagogy among her 115 respondents and concludes, "I believe that this segment of our discipline is in good hands" (2).

So long as we look at the individual responses to the questionnaire, we concur in Tate's optimism. Many of our respondents provided thorough accounts of their course, based on clear theoretical convictions and pedagogical justifications. When, on the other hand, we try to place the various responses against each other, to draw some composite image of courses in advanced exposition, we find our position closer to Dicks' ambivalent summation. Finally, when we reflect on the implications of the data we collected, we are inclined to a rather sober assessment.

The Shape of Advanced Composition

Approximately 70% of the institutions have a course titled "advanced composition" among their listings. The remaining 30% have a comparable course under other titles. The course is typically upper division, for majors in English, Communications, English Education, or Education. It appears that the course does not reach a heterogeneous audience within the academic community. This may be cause for concern. Where do other student writers receive the advanced training in public discourse that the traditional course in advanced composition offers?

In about 90% of the institutions, advanced composition has prerequisites. In 50% of the cases, a single composition course is required; in 33% of the cases, two prior composition courses are required (7% indicated some prerequisite but did not specify its nature). At nearly two-thirds of the institutions, the course is strictly elective. This finding suggests that even many English majors are not required to take advanced writing, corroborating the recent *MLA Newsletter* assertion that only 31% of English major programs require advanced composition.

Class size is limited to twenty students in 53% of the institutions, to twenty-one to twenty-five at 28% of the schools, and to more than twenty-five at 19% of the schools. In 88% of the institutions, grades determine acceptable performance; at 12% portfolios or publishable articles do so.

Our selection of institutions came from the Writing Program Administrators membership rolls. However, teaching assignments for advanced composition were made by the Director of Writing at only 9% of the schools. Department chairs assigned staff at 56% of the institutions, with the remaining respondents indicating alternative methods of selecting staff. Our findings seem to suggest that the leadership role of Directors of Writing rarely extends to advanced composition.

At 82% of the institutions, graduate assistants are not involved in the teaching of advanced writing courses. At 9% they serve as instructors, and at another 9% they work as aides. With so little involvement by graduate students, where do future teachers of advanced composition receive training?

At 72% of the schools, instructors work independently of one another, while 25% indicate coordination among teachers of the course. A broad coordination with considerable flexibility was noted by 3%. These findings parallel the absence of a standard syllabus at 77% of the institutions.

Textbooks are used by 65% of the respondents. Almost half use a reader; nearly a third use a rhetoric; a fifth use a handbook (other respondents indicated that a text is required but did not define the type). Of those respondents who use a text, two-thirds expressed dissatisfaction with current choices. Those who do not use a book employ student writings and instructor handouts.

Nearly 37% of respondents require six to eight papers in the advanced course; 33% require one to five papers; 30% require more than eight papers. More than half of the respondents see two or more revisions of each paper, while more than half also require a journal or portfolio.

Nearly 60% of the institutions incorporate peer groups into advanced writing instruction. Lecturing or workshops are cited by more than a third as primary instructional approaches.

Respondents indicate many different points of focus for advanced courses, ranging from research writing to writing for publication, and from argumentation to autobiography. It seems to be impossible to predict the content of a course named "advanced composition."

Nearly half of the institutions have writing-across-the-curriculum programs, and nearly 80% of those without current programs are considering their implementation. Writing across the curriculum has increased demand for advanced writing courses at 24% of the schools where it exists and has decreased demand at only 4%. Other institutions report no significant impact.

Problems with Advanced Composition

The fifth section of the questionnaire gave respondents the opportunity to comment freely on the issues facing advanced exposition courses. From these and other comments scattered throughout their responses arose some of the most interesting and disturbing implications of the study. These implications recurred in several patterns, enabling us to construct a view of the attitudes and worries of many of us who teach advanced courses, and of some who administer them. The remainder of this article considers those implications.

First, a number of respondents indicated doubt about the future of general courses in advanced exposition at their institutions. Noting that the course is offered irregularly, the English department chair of a private university in New England commented on the few students who enroll, even in the occasional section offered: "Usually they are a handful of students majoring in English with a concentration in writing for whom the course is required." At a public university in the midwest, similar enrollment problems prompted the department chair to say that because the course has "virtually no population . . . we are going to stop offering it. Last time offered there were four students in it." He continued, in a vein shared by some other responses, "We are not going to offer the course any more. No students take it. It has no purpose. Our upper-division and graduate writing courses (tech writing, creative writing, professional writing) have large enrollments and seem to fill a need; advanced composition doesn't."

That ominous prospect has already arrived at a few schools. The writing director at a major university made the simple notation that there is no longer a course in advanced composition at that school. A well-known military institution indicated the same situation, as did a private university in the midwest. This is not to say that those institutions do not offer advanced writing courses, usually in a configuration that includes technical and scientific writing, business writing, and writing across the curriculum. It does mean, however, that they have dropped the traditional course in advanced expository writing.

Some respondents expressed directly their disillusionment with advanced expository courses. The writing director at a university in one of the plains states mused, "I do think that one advanced composition course is less desirable than a breakdown. Such a course exists only in academia, whereas reports, arguments, and personal essays go beyond the academy."

At some institutions, then, the general advanced composition course is already gone or is on its way out of its traditional place in the curricula. Poignant testimony to this came in a mystifying response from the writing director of a large eastern university whose answers were usually question marks or the word " yes" followed by a question mark. The mystery vanished when, at the end of the questionnaire, we found this laconic comment: "We have advanced comp. on our books. To my knowledge it has never been offered."

Certainly the picture, as our statistics indicate, is not everywhere so negative. Many institutions reported a stable population for advanced composition courses, and a few reported burgeoning enrollments. In many cases, however, these are institutions in which the expository emphasis has already disappeared in favor of sequences of courses in technical, business, disciplinary, or personal writing. The situation is sufficiently confused to make it necessary, it seems to us, that we as a profession develop some clearer sense of what we mean when we label a course by the general title "advanced composition."

That necessity underscores a second problem indicated by the research: the variety of course contents and points of focus in the courses described by respondents. Anything that can serve as the matter of a writing course appeared somewhere among the responses. Several clusters were evident. Writing for publication appeared frequently, as did research writing. Personal or autobiographical writing of some sort formed still another cluster. Writing about a theme or problem which differs with each offering of the course recurred, along with writing about literature. While most responses fit one or another of these clusters, a bewildering variety of other points of focus surfaced, enough to make one cautious about accepting in transfer a course named "advanced composition" at another institution.

For example, several responses indicated that traditional grammar is the focus of the course; others concentrate on the writing of "family histories." One description emphasized the "basic paragraph" as the central feature. Another, from a private college in the west, evoked echoes of an earlier era in the teaching of writing:

"Study of the sentence; correctness in the use of parts of speech, punctuation, capitalization, syntax, and idiom." Some instructors indicated that the work of a single essayist forms the subject of the course. One response even indicated that the work is conducted individually, by mail and by telephone conferences.

Indicative of the uncertainty about what constitutes advanced composition were a number of responses which expressed, sometimes wistfully, sometimes tartly, the disagreements among instructors of advanced composition in the same program. One such comment was especially revealing. After indicating the contemporary approach of the respondent's own classes, the informant added: "The other primary instructor of advanced expository writing approaches the course in a totally different way. It is a grammar/literature course using a literary anthology and a freshman handbook." This comment suggests how very different might be the experience of two advanced writing students at the same university in the south.

We do not mean to challenge any of these approaches as invalid or unjustifiable. Our concern is with the impossibility of identifying what advanced composition means, given the threats and confusions noted earlier in this report. A student, an advisor, or an administrator examining a program could legitimately ask what common experience will be shared by students in different sections of such courses.

A third problem emerging from the study discloses the theoretical divisions among those who teach advanced courses. One of the questions asked for an assessment of the effect of process theory on the respondent's teaching. Responses reflected the theoretical divergences which mark the current professional discourse on writing theory. Some clearly thought the question simply unnecessary. One writing director asserted, "I can't recall teaching any other way." Another replied, "I've been using process since 1968." Still another huffed that process theory had influenced her teaching, "vastly, obviously." The tone of such answers bespoke the conviction that we all agree, that the question hardly need be asked.

Other responses, by contrast, dramatized our reasons for asking the question and the theoretical cleavage noted above. One respondent expressed deep concern about the assumptions of the question: "Your question about process-oriented theory alarms me. Do not try to pour human clay into ceramic molds." Another attacked process theorists: "Process people are arrogant and simple-minded." Still another condemned the products of process teaching: "Process-trained students turn out feeble, emotional junk, not well-reasoned and stylish essays. The content of their essays is pathetic." An experienced instructor passed summary judgment on two decades of work on process theory:

> I have been dismayed at the practical results of the process orientation
> over the past fifteen or so years. It simply has not produced better writers.
> We need to return to a writing-centered, not student-centered pedagogy.

Another response left us chastened: "The 'process' people, not well trained in literature and classical rhetoric, should be kept out if possible. They are subjective, romantic, anti-intellectual, and arrogant, as a rule." Two other responses indicate the problems still facing this twenty year-old "new" pedagogy. The first answered the question about process theory succinctly: "Can't answer. Don't know what you mean." The second was even more economical: "What is 'process-oriented' theory?"

While many responses to questions about theory grow from current debates and competing ideas about rhetoric and pedagogy, others betray the impatience of writing directors who are prevented from staffing advanced courses with instructors trained in *any* contemporary theory. Some respondents noted the tendency in their departments to give advanced courses to senior faculty averse to teaching freshman writing. Asked what changes they would like to see in the teaching of advanced writing in their departments, several directors gave answers typified by this comment from a western state university: "I would like to see it put entirely in the hands of the rhet/comp faculty."

Whatever view one takes of the complex and delicate politics of assignment of staff, several responses attest to the benefits of contemporary pedagogy in advanced courses. A director at a public university in New England adopted a "textless, tutorial, revision-centered" method eight years ago. Since then, "students fill every section we offer; other departments send their majors to us for final polish. Faculty *like* to teach it." Clearly, advanced composition courses thrive at that institution.

Areas of Agreement

Despite the problems we have indicated, broad areas of agreement emerge from responses to the questionnaire. First, the relationship between writing across the curriculum (WAC) and advanced exposition is generally perceived as positive. Some do see a conflict, as does a respondent from a private college in New England who mused, "I think there is room for advanced composition courses distinct from WAC courses. I realize this is increasingly coming to be a minority position." Two other comments, on the other hand, are more representative. A western director saw WAC as "broadening the base, not subsuming our courses." A chairperson from a midwestern institution argued, "Surprisingly there is an even greater demand for advanced composition courses than before WAC." This relationship requires more investigation. Asked if a special area remains for traditional courses in advanced exposition as WAC programs develop, many respondents answered affirmatively but declined to define that special area.

Another frequent area of agreement urges the inclusion of rhetorical theory, ancient and modern, in the student's encounter with advanced exposition. Undeniably, as previous quotations illustrate, there is some resistance to theory in any of its contemporary manifestations. One instructor at a private college in the south denounced our survey and the recent direction of the profession for this injection of theory: "Your excessive concern with 'theory' is symptomatic of turning away from writing to ephemeral ideas *about* writing." More frequently, however, respondents said that they already introduce their advanced students to formal writing theory.

A third emerging consensus stresses the need for advanced composition faculty trained in contemporary and classical theory. One director yearned for "more informed faculty." A western university requires that *all* instructors in advanced composition classes be composition specialists. Still other institutions require that advanced writing instructors themselves be published writers. Such comments suggest a trend toward using trained and experienced writers, as opposed to faculty for whom advanced courses are rewards for long service or high rank. One director, for example, noting that the course is taught by a senior American literature specialist, hastened to point out that the professor is also a good writer who has published on more than just his academic specialization.

Finally, many respondents admitted their uncertainties about what constitutes "advanced" writing. Several mused thoughtfully about that designation. An instructor at a California school wrote, "Advanced might mean much fuller engagement with processes, or more experienced in the composing role, or able to participate more fully in a writing community, or even able to engage in a writing community that continues past the class." An instructor from the midwest would emphasize "what Flower calls 'reader-based prose' over 'writer-based prose.'" Some stressed attention to style and grace as the hallmark of an advanced course. Others regarded the turn to argumentation as the demarcation between freshman writing and advanced discourse. A recurrent emphasis was the development of audience-awareness as the central feature of advanced instruction. A writing director from Missouri, for example, granted that her course shares the "amorphous quality of its ilk across the nation," but decided that "the role of audience and purpose becomes crucial."

Clearly, our survey unearthed a variety of problems and patterns in advanced general writing courses. It also uncovered little genuine conviction about what these courses should do. While we recognize that what we have gathered is more often opinion than hard data about classroom performance, we can see in these survey responses a series of major issues calling for more professional dialogue. Among those issues is the very survival of the advanced exposition course which aims itself not at the specific audiences of specialized advanced courses but at the broad audience necessary to public discourse in a democratic society. Truly empowered students speak and write not only within a discipline but within a public forum, to a myriad of issues. Writing in *College English*, Chris Anderson has argued that in the expository essay, "we can accomplish at least the pleasure of discourse on important ideas" (307). We concur. The advanced exposition course should continue to enable students to join that discourse and to enhance their pleasure in doing so.

Works Cited

Anderson, Chris. "Hearsay Evidence and Second-Class Citizenship." *College English* 50 (1988): 300-08.
Dicks, Bernice. "State of the Art in Advanced Expository Writing: One Genus, Many Species." *Journal of Advanced Composition* 3 (1982): 173-87.
"Survey of Requirements in English." *MLA Newsletter* 21 (1989): 24-25.
Tate, Priscilla. "Survey of Advanced Writing Programs." Unpublished report, 1985.

Advanced Writing Courses and Programs

by Michael L. Keene and Ray Wallace

If you read the literature being published today about writing, or if you talk with people at the CCCC convention, what kind of writing do you hear about other than freshman composition? Usually technical writing, writing across the curriculum, and creative writing, and maybe a little about ESL and writing centers. What else could there be? In our experience, a subject that *doesn't* often come up is advanced composition. Where is it, and what is it? Is there any set curriculum or sequence? Do people major in it? Minor in it? How does the generic title relate to technical writing and other specific course labels?

To posit an answer to these questions, and thus to consider the types of advanced composition being taught and its role in writing and English programs we conducted a poll of 12 colleges and universities. The schools were selected for geographic distribution, for a mix of large and small schools, and for inclusion of both public and private institutions. We asked each school's representative the same set of questions concerning their course offerings and their successes and problems, but we also allowed ourselves the freedom to stray from our pre-arranged script whenever the situation seemed to merit it. We were especially concerned about what we called the *fourth-quadrant*, courses in exposition and persuasion or advanced workshops that might come under the advanced composition label. Our questions are given here.

Series One: The Setting

> What size is the school?
> What is the mix of rural and urban students?
> What are the number and type of writing faculty
>   (professional, tenure-track, or tenured)?
> What percent of the whole faculty teaches freshman composition?
> What percent teaches any other writing courses?
> Do literature majors have to take any writing course beyond
>   the freshman level?
> Is there a major or minor in writing?

Reprinted from *Teaching Advanced Composition: Why and How*, Ed. Katherine H. Adams and John Adams, Portsmouth, NH: Boynton/Cook, 1991. Reprinted with permission.

Series Two: Writing Beyond the Freshman Level: About Technical Writing, Creative Writing, and Writing Across the Curriculum

> How many different courses and sections are there?
> How many faculty teach those courses?
> How many students take this in one calendar year?

Series Three: The Fourth Quadrant (everyone else's "other" category)

> How many different (other) writing courses do you have—and how
>   many sections—that are not covered in the three
>   previously mentioned areas?
> How do these courses articulate (as, for example, part of a writing
>   major or minor) with the other kinds of writing courses?
> What are the *core* textbooks for these courses?
> How is this course not just "more of the same"—different
>   from freshman composition?
> Do you have a writing center that advanced composition students *can* use?
> Do they? Is it remedial help?
> Is there a writing fellows program?
> What's the biggest problem with advanced composition at your school?
> May we call you back if we have further questions?

Part One of this essay summarizes the results of our phone discussions. Part Two offers our thoughts on the larger significance of the results of that survey.

Part One: Results

The Northeast

College A has 5,100 students; because of national recruitment and a prestigious reputation, the students come from many locations. There are 53 professorial English faculty: 22 tenured and 31 nontenured. All the nontenured faculty and a few tenured faculty teach freshman composition. The English department only offers a literature major. There is no major or minor in writing.

College A doesn't offer technical writing courses, but it does have eight or nine creative writing courses, a total of 10 or 12 sections per year. Four or five faculty teach these classes, which enroll fewer than 18 students per section.

College A has a university-wide expository writing program, with a tutorial program for students and with writing-intensive sections in most fields. Faculty in other disciplines who teach the writing-intensive courses are assisted by subject-qualified teaching fellows who are also trained in teaching writing. Quite a few of these courses are generically titled The Writing of . . . (Social Science, History, or whatever). This program is run by a campus-wide Committee on Expository Writing.

The English department has three of the fourth-quadrant type of courses. Each year, it offers 10 sections of a modern prose course, usually filled with AP freshmen and other students from all departments. The second course, prose traditions, is usually offered in three sections of around 15 students. It differs from the first one by considering an expanded historical range of authors. The third course is a senior-level nonfiction prose writing workshop (one section, 15 students), taught each year by a different well-known author.

According to the faculty member we interviewed, the biggest problem is that the other departments in the university don't pay enough attention to writing; only in a class specifically devoted to writing does a student receive writing instruction and practice. In other words, the biggest problem is maintaining and improving the very good skills the freshman program develops. In the English department, because it is primarily literature-oriented, convincing faculty to teach or develop advanced writing courses is difficult.

The East

College B has 30,000 students, from rural and urban areas. The English department has 55 faculty members, with 13 in creative writing and 10 in other kinds of writing. None of the other faculty teaches any writing courses beyond the freshman level, but all College B students have to take at least one advanced writing course. The literature majors usually satisfy that requirement by taking creative writing. The only writing major is in creative writing.

College B offers two technical writing courses, with 80 sections of one (1800 students) and 10 of the other (180 students) each year. These courses are taught mostly by adjunct faculty, plus a few of the professorial staff. The department also offers 12 creative writing courses each year, totalling 75 sections, involving 1500 students. There are no writing-across-the-curriculum courses in the English department, but several dozen in other departments.

College B has one advanced composition course (the text is Hairston's *Successful Writing*), plus a course in peer tutoring taken mostly by students who plan to go into teaching. There is a writing center that the advanced composition students can use, but they are much more likely to be working there, especially after taking the peer tutoring course.

The college offers 10 sections of the advanced composition course each year; of the peer tutoring course, three. There is a determined curricular effort to make the advanced composition course different from freshman composition. The advanced course focuses more on invention, arrangement, and style. It is more sophisticated analytically and stylistically. It was described as a "genuinely wired-up course," complete with detailed attention to audience analysis. The biggest problem with advanced composition at College B is finding staff to teach the courses.

The Southeast

College C has 17,000 students, a rural/urban mix. The English department has 35 faculty members, of whom seven are writing specialists. Most of the faculty teach freshman composition, but (other than the writing specialists) none teaches any other writing courses. No literature majors take expository writing beyond the freshman level, but there is a minor in creative writing. College C offers one technical writing course, taught by one faculty member and one adjunct. It enrolls 22 students per section. Many sections of the seven creative writing courses are taught by four or five faculty, with 15 students per section. This school has no writing-across-the-curriculum program, although there is a legal writing course and a social work writing course. There is one advanced composition course (the text is either Hairston or nothing), with four sections per year. The course differs from freshman composition in that the students have ample freedom to write what they want to write. No literature majors take it. Some of the advanced composition students use the school's writing center, mostly for remedial help. The biggest problem with the advanced composition course is that, because of a lack of publicity and a lack of faculty, "the good word hasn't gotten out."

The South

College D enrolls just under 10,000 students and offers degrees from the B.A. to the doctorate. The students are 60 percent rural and 40 percent urban. The English department has 60 faculty members, 40 of whom are either tenured or tenure-track. The department offers a B.A. in English and American Literature and a minor in literature. All of the faculty teach freshman composition, and five faculty teach advanced writing courses. No advanced writing courses are required of English majors.

Technical writing is taught four times per year by two faculty members, reaching 66 students. Creative writing is taught twice a year by two faculty, reaching 30 students. Writing across the curriculum has been developed under an NEH grant, and all new instructors across the campus have to teach writing in all classes. (The program is not governed by the English department.)

The only advanced composition course is expository and narrative writing, an elective for English majors that has not been taught since 1983. There are two writing centers, but both are perceived as remedial and are not used by advanced writers.

The writing expert there said the advanced composition course had become obsolete because other courses taught the same thing: "Writing across the curriculum reaches all the students each semester. Technical, creative, and business writing courses reach smaller groups. English majors are not seen to need an advanced writing course because the major is in literature: 'writing courses are perceived as unnecessary for them.'"

College E enrolls 25,000 students from a rural/urban mix. There are 48 professorial faculty members. Many graduate students and lecturers currently hold teaching positions. The professorial staff includes five creative writing teachers, four technical writing teachers, and four rhetoric/composition teachers. There is no writing-across-the-curriculum program, although some departments have "writing intensive" courses. Most freshman composition sections (about 90 percent) are taught by instructors or graduate students.

The English department offers either a traditional literature or a writing (technical or creative) undergraduate degree. A writing minor (on either the B.A. or M.A. level) is also available. Students are now beginning to be interested in pursuing a rhetoric Ph.D. The writing center is expanding but is still mostly remedial. Students may use eight computer labs on the campus.

Undergraduate literature majors are required to take one writing course beyond the freshman sequence, while undergraduate writing majors take four or five. The technical writing courses are the most popular (four or more sections of advanced technical writing per semester, plus three other technical writing courses once a year), both with the English majors and with students from other disciplines, producing a demand the department cannot satisfy. Creative writing (poetry, fiction, screen writing) courses are offered in four sections a semester. Two sections of an expository writing course and one or two of a persuasive writing course, taken by English and business majors, are also offered each term.

The major problem with advanced composition at College E is that the faculty most interested in teaching it are spread too thin, having to teach other writing courses (as well as graduate-level courses) where the demand, both from English majors and students from other departments, is more pressing. In addition, they feel somewhat uncertain as to just what the advanced courses are designed to accomplish, and the students who take the courses tend to have widely differing skill levels and expectations.

The Midwest

College F enrolls between 3,000 and 3,500 students per academic year, offers degrees from the associate level to the masters, and has a student body described as 90 percent rural. In the English department, there are 20 faculty members, only five of whom are tenured or on tenure-track lines. The rest of the faculty are part-time instructors. All faculty teach freshman composition, but no writing major or minor is offered. College F does not have a writing center, and the only undergraduate degree is literature-based. However, advanced expository writing is required for all English majors, the only writing course these students must take after the freshman level. Only one section of this course is offered each semester. Additionally, one technical writing and one creative writing course are taught each year. A few experimental writing-across-the-curriculum courses have been recently created.

In terms of advanced composition, two faculty take turns teaching this course, but neither has composition or rhetoric training, and the course is described as a responding-to-literature course. Interestingly enough, the two faculty who *are* trained in rhetoric/composition are not allowed to teach the course because it is considered upper division and—as untenured faculty—they cannot teach upper division. These two faculty members cannot see much pedagogical difference between their freshman composition classes and this advanced class; to them, standing admittedly on the outside, it seems to be just more of the same.

College G enrolls 10,000 students and offers both undergraduate and graduate degrees to the specialist rank. The student body is described as 50 percent rural and 50 percent urban. The English department has 53 faculty, 34 of whom are either tenured or tenure-track. A writing expert at this school claimed 98 percent of the faculty teach freshman composition and that the department has developed a very successful writing center. At the undergraduate level, the English department offers both a B.A. (without teaching certification) and two writing minors (in either professional or creative writing). At present, the literature majors must take one writing course beyond the freshman level, but this requirement is regularly opposed at each curriculum meeting. The department offers two courses in advanced document design each semester, reaching 80 students per year. There are three creative writing courses (beginning, intermediate, and advanced) after the freshman level; six sections are taught each year, reaching 150 students. This institution is in the process of implementing a writing-across-the-curriculum project.

In advanced composition, the English department offers a junior-level writing class in six sections each semester. It is required of English, special education, and professional writing minors. In the past two years, 12 different faculty members have taught it. A writing expert there noted that Hairston's text was the usual one and that this course differs from freshman composition in that it involves more work on heuristics and discussion of rhetorical theory.

The biggest problems with the advanced composition course at College G were these: the faculty were uneven in their preparation for teaching composition (only one had any formal rhetoric/composition training); and since students only needed a *C* in freshman composition to enter the class, their abilities varied drastically.

College H enrolls 23,000 students and offers degrees from the B.A. to the doctorate level. The English department has 70 members, of whom 45 are tenure-track. The student body at this university consists of 20 percent rural, 40 percent suburban, and 40 percent urban. The English department offers both a B.A. and B.S., as well as minors in writing and ESL. Very few tenured or tenure-track faculty teach freshman composition; this "chore" is left to graduate assistants enrolled in masters and doctoral programs and to the instructors who are not tenure-track. However, about 10 percent of the faculty do teach upper-division writing classes. To graduate, English majors must take one advanced writing course after the freshman sequence.

At this institution all the writing courses are taught on computers (both IBM-compatible and Macintosh). The two undergraduate technical writing courses are taught by six faculty members, and they serve 150 students each year. The three creative writing courses are taught by five faculty members and reach 160 students. The writing-across-the-curriculum courses, which reach 500 students per year, are not taught by English faculty.

Three courses seem to fall into the category of advanced composition: an advanced grammar and usage course for writers, an advanced composition course, and a writing seminar course. The grammar course is exactly what its name implies. The advanced exposition course is designed "to add sophistication to the writer's style." In it, content is stressed over form. The writing seminar stresses writing for publication, with each student working on three projects over the semester. There is a writing center that the advanced composition students do in fact use, mostly to get reactions and opinions from a skilled reader.

The writing expert there claimed that the major problem with advanced composition in this institution was that the expectations of the faculty and the students do not match. The advanced composition teachers often feel that students are ill prepared for advanced work and, in fact, still need remediation. An associated problem is that the freshman composition course lacks a core structure; thus the students' writing backgrounds are quite varied when they arrive in the advanced exposition course.

The Southwest

College I has 50,000 students, with a mix of rural and urban backgrounds. The English department has 85 faculty members, of whom six are writing specialists. There is no major or minor in writing: the literature majors take no writing courses beyond the freshman level.

College I does not offer technical writing courses, but it does have 8 or 10 creative writing courses comprising 10 or 15 sections. These classes are taught by five or six people. A handful of writing-across-the-curriculum courses, designated as "substantial writing component" courses, are taught in other departments.

The only other course is advanced expository writing. Three sections are offered each year. The students are juniors and seniors; none are English majors. The course focuses on explanatory and persuasive writing and includes some oral presentations. The main problem with the course is that there aren't enough sections or faculty members willing to teach it.

The Northwest

College J has about 11,000 students, mostly from a rural background. There are 22 faculty members in the English department, with one writing specialist. About a third of the faculty teach freshman composition, and two or three teach other writing courses. There is no major or minor in writing, but a writing course beyond the freshman level is strongly recommended for English majors.

College J has a technical writing course (25 sections per year, with 22 students per section) that can substitute for second semester freshman composition. It is taught by three regular faculty members. There are two creative writing courses (eight sections) taught by four faculty members. The creative writing classes have 15 students per section. There is no writing-across-the-curriculum course at College J.

College J has two other writing courses, totalling four sections. Both courses are referred to as advanced composition. These two courses don't articulate with the other writing courses at all. Their core texts are various essay collections, and the courses differ from freshman composition mostly in that they involve more peer instruction. Education majors take one of the courses, and English majors take the other. While there is a writing center, the advanced composition students do not use it (it is mostly remedial). The biggest problem with advanced composition at College J is that no one knows what it is. The courses cannot be very advanced because the students who take them think they need more basic instruction, and, in fact, they do.

The West

College K enrolls 12,000 students, and the English department offers degrees at the bachelor's and master's levels. The English department has 23 professorial faculty, of whom six are writing specialists. Students at the college are mostly from an urban background. About 20 to 30 percent of the whole faculty teach freshman composition, and 50 or 60 percent of the non-writing faculty teach the other writing courses. The college has both a major and minor in writing, as well as a cross-disciplinary major shared with the journalism department. Literature majors do not have to take any writing courses beyond the freshman level.

The department offers two technical writing courses, plus a special projects course and a co-op course. These add up to 15 sections per year. Seven faculty teach these courses, which enroll about 140 students per year. The special projects and co-op courses happen only occasionally and involve only a few students when they do. There are no writing-across-the-curriculum courses.

Creative writing offerings in College K include 9 or 10 different courses, a total of about 12 sections per year. Two regular faculty teach these courses, which serve about 200 students.

The courses that concern us most here are expository writing, advanced expository writing, persuasive writing, and advanced persuasive writing—for a total of 10 or 12 sections per year, with 15 to 20 students in each section. Students from all over the college, including writing majors and minors, often take one of these courses. These classes use many different texts, or no textbook at all. The courses differ from freshman composition in that they are not just about "how to succeed in college," but more specifically about "getting to be a writer." Students in the advanced composition courses use the department's writing center, both for help with their writing and for its computer work stations.

The biggest problem with advanced composition at College K, according to the writing specialist we interviewed, is the wide mix of students in the classes. Some students are in the classes just to "fill out their schedules," and others are there to become professional writers. Lack of staffing contributes to the problem since only a handful of these courses can be taught each year, so that the more basic and the more advanced writers get mixed in together in both the exposition and persuasion classes.

College L has 3,000 students, from a rural/urban mix, with a large percentage (20 percent) of ESL students, most of whom are recent immigrants to the area. The English faculty consists of 10 professorial staff and two lecturers. Each semester, all faculty teach at least one section (and sometimes two) of either the traditional freshman composition course or an ESL composition course. All English majors are considered to be literature majors, and they are required to take one other writing course after the freshman composition course. There is no major or minor in writing at College L.

College L has no creative writing courses, but each semester the English department offers two sections of advanced technical writing and business writing. In addition, one section of advanced composition is offered once each year. A university-wide writing proficiency exam is given to all students at the end of the junior year. The pass rate on this exam is low, about 45 percent on the first attempt. Students are advised (but not forced) to take one of the post-freshman writing courses to prepare for the exam; they cannot retake freshman composition to brush up on their skills. Despite this advice, most students rely instead on simply taking the exam again and again.

There is not an active writing-across-the-curriculum program. The writing center is not equipped to deal with advanced composition students, but there is a computer-assisted composition lab with staff to help the advanced students.

The advanced composition course is not the most popular writing option for either English majors or those other majors (business, education, and science) who must also take a writing course. Most students prefer to take the technical writing course; if it is not available, they try for the business writing course. The advanced composition course is taken mainly by English majors; faculty generally teach it as a responding-to-literature course.

The biggest problem with advanced composition at College L, according to the person we interviewed, is that no one really wants to teach it, in large part because no one is really certain what it is supposed to achieve. The course most often turns into a harder section of freshman composition.

Part Two: What Does It Mean?

Of course, a survey of 12 schools of varying size across the nation can have only limited validity when used as the basis for generalizing about nationwide phenomena. But we did note startling similarities among these randomly selected institutions, regardless of size and location.

Today, with more and more underprepared students being admitted to all types of colleges and universities across the country, a variety of methods are needed to help them improve as writers throughout college. Although advanced composition courses historically had the major role in satisfying this need, students today can choose among writing-across-the-curriculum, technical writing, business writing, creative writing, and ESL courses, among others. These writing courses—both inside and outside the English department—have been quite responsive to what students perceive to be their needs as writers in academic settings and as future professionals. Also, when institutions look at the nature and role of writing instruction campuswide, they frequently start writing-across-the-curriculum programs, often sited outside the English department. This increases the number of students (other than English majors) who look to their own departments for advanced writing instruction. While some students take an advanced composition course followed by, say, technical writing, instances of students who are not English majors taking more than one advanced writing course seem quite rare. (For that matter, instances when English majors take more than one such writing course are also quite rare.) Thus, the population that takes advanced composition seems often to be restricted to English majors. The only way to alter that situation would involve a fundamental change in the basic philosophical nature of advanced composition itself.

Other problems lessen the popularity of advanced composition courses: they are very difficult to staff, and there is no real consensus about what they should cover or what approach(es) they should take. At some institutions, advanced composition is not very popular with the faculty—including the few writing specialists who may be stressing other kinds of writing experiences, perhaps in literature-based courses or subject-specialized writing courses. The writing faculty's energies are also taken up by designing graduate curricula.

The course's identity is perhaps a more crucial problem than is staffing. What we saw, in our limited survey, was that no one was quite sure what the course was supposed to be. There were often significant differences in expectations about the course's identity—even within the faculty at an institution, and certainly from institution to institution—and faculty expectations frequently differed from those of the students. The students themselves had such varied backgrounds that addressing their needs seemed to require an impossible variety of approaches. And while individual faculty members could often explain the pedagogical rationale for their own advanced composition course, we could neither adequately locate such specific courses on any kind of spectrum, nor begin to discover how any kind of consensus might evolve among writing faculty. For example, while a number of professionals seem to feel the course needs to teach *higher order* rhetorical skills, these skills never seem to be the same from college to college. Beyond that, an alarming number of people told us that there was not a great deal of difference, in fact, between freshman composition and advanced composition; generally, what we saw as the most common difference was that the latter requires longer papers. In a worst-case scenario, advanced composition seems to mean an ill-defined, badly organized writing experience that repeats (or covers for the first time) the elements of instruction our profession might be more likely to expect to see in freshman composition.

We are left feeling that advanced composition will follow one of three paths. Down one path, the course will simply fade away—either because it is seen as redundant in light of the existence of other advanced writing options, or because it is simply seen as unnecessary in and of itself. Down another path, the course will continue muddling along, needing more definition, occasionally spinning off discipline-specific courses. Down the third path there is what we see to be a brighter future, one that involves people who specialize in rhetoric and composition finding an identity for advanced composition and persuading our colleagues and students of its importance—that this course offers something significant the other advanced writing courses do not (perhaps the skills students need to succeed in careers regardless of discipline, perhaps advanced thinking skills, perhaps lifetime writing skills that are not directly career-related). This double task—that of finding an identity for advanced composition courses and convincing our colleagues and students of the course's usefulness—is well within our individual intellectual abilities, but may be beyond our collective will. If so, it would be ironic in the extreme: imagine a profession coming into being through teaching writing to freshmen, and then subsequently, in effect, abandoning those same students at the next level because we cannot, or will not, come to a consensus as to what that next level should contain.

Part 2:
Advanced Writers and Courses

Guidelines and Directions for College Courses in Advanced Composition

A Report of Invitational Workshops at the Annual Meetings of the College Conference on Composition and Communication

Denver, March 26, 1966—Louisville, April 8, 1967

1. **Definition**: An advanced composition course should be a composition course open only to students who have at least passed the freshman course at the same college or who have demonstrated equivalent ability. This relative and operational definition admits that the freshman course at one college may be more advanced than the advanced course at another one. Even an "A" student from a weak college might not be ready for the advanced course at a strong one. Although at some colleges the title is a euphemism to flatter the junior or senior who didn't really master his freshman work, the advanced course should represent substantial progress beyond the goal of the local freshman course. When remedial programs are needed, they should be offered as clinics, workshops, or courses properly labeled. If the student from a weak college transfers to a strong one, he might have to take the regular freshman course. On the other hand, advanced courses may on occasion include some material which might be called "remedial," if such material is brief and incidental in response to an individual's need.

2. **Variety and Focus**: Advanced composition courses emphasize the possibility of alternative strategies in solving writing problems. Examination of the reasons for choosing among verbal forms and theories of rhetoric are the substance of the courses. In its general form the advanced course may be viewed as covering the range of the freshman course but in greater depth. Many advanced courses, however, represent efforts to isolate certain kinds of writing problems for intensive examination. Courses may be described in terms of forms examined (e.g., report writing, verse writing), in terms of typical situation and content (e.g., technical writing, business writing), in terms of the students electing the courses (e.g., composition for teachers), in terms of mode (e.g., discursive writing, persuasive writing), or in terms of special problems (e.g., theories of style or history of English prose style). These specialized courses allow the teacher to concentrate in great depth upon a limited range of possible kinds of expression.

From *College Composition and Communication* 28 (1967): 266-68. © 1967 by NCTE. Reprinted with permission.

The apparent arbitrariness of classification of courses can perhaps better be understood as developing out of the freshman course. The advanced expository course (which usually covers more than exposition) is the most direct descendant of the freshman program; it may well be the only advanced course offered in smaller schools. At one extreme from this central course are the courses in the writing of poetry, fiction, or drama. Although working with language in order to reach an audience is still the object of these courses, the emphases are much different from those in the usual expository course. In some ways the "creative" writing course is closely akin to literary criticism. The special courses for future teachers lie between these creative writing courses and the expository courses, for teachers must be especially concerned with problems of analyzing and evaluating writing of all kinds and probably need to be more sensitive than most people to the nuances of writing which are expected in literary prose. At the other extreme are the rigorously factual courses in technical writing. Here prose which accurately and explicitly represents the world of ordinary affairs is stressed. Other courses for students with clearly defined professional objectives—"useful" is their emphasis—probably come closer to the expository writing course in their allowances for a variety of audiences and audience appeals.

How many different courses can be offered at one college depends both upon matters of budget and the number and kinds of students needing advanced work. Whatever courses are offered, the chief justification lies not in the preparation for work in other college courses, but in mastering writing for its own sake or in acquiring skills for post-collegiate years.

3. **Humane Emphasis**: Despite the practical goals of most of the advanced writing courses, the ultimate justification of the close study of expression in language is humane. The advanced courses tend to view writing as a process rather than an object, to see language as a reflection of relationships among humans and objects. Crafts must be mastered, but the goal is understanding how the uses of language define human beings.

4. **Course Content**: The primary content of any advanced course is writing itself. For that reason the insights of modern studies of language, rhetoric, and psychology should be made explicit. Where professional content seems to dominate, as in courses in business or technical writing, the naming of the professional area describes the orientation of the student audience; the teacher then chooses his own rhetorical appeals on the basis of having a relatively homogeneous student audience. One ought not confuse the subject of the students' papers, which should always be very important to them, with the subject of the course. Where the students share professional interests other than writing, their interests tend to select the kinds of writing given particular study, but the purpose of the course is still to learn about writing. In many courses no text will be necessary, other than the writing produced in the class itself. The student's formulation of experience will enforce attitudes of discovery and tentativeness of judgment by allowing a chance for testing the reactions of larger audiences. Teachers who wish models will find many collections both

contemporary or historical in orientation or may choose to deal with samples culled from current practice in the world of affairs. Literature may also offer examples. But the serious problem with any collections of writings is that the subjects may entice the teacher and student away from the process of writing, and the apparatus of well-meaning editors may interfere with the unprejudiced joint exploration of the text by students and teachers.

5. **Qualifications of Instructors**: The teachers of advanced composition should have special qualifications both as teachers and writers. They usually should be people who have had more than ordinary success in teaching freshman composition or its equivalent. Probably they should have had a course in the teaching of composition or should have experienced a good supervised in-service training program, although extensive practical experience as a teacher or as an editor or writer might well serve the same purpose.

The academic training of the teacher of advanced composition must be liberal. He is the teacher of an art which is essential to any of the separate disciplines of human learning, so he must be versed in the ways of humanity as well as in particular subjects. His art, however, is language broadly defined, so he should have studied linguistics, rhetoric, and literature, with particular emphasis upon how these studies show language formulating human knowledge and experience. He should be aware of the history of the language, of systems for describing languages, of the processes of verbal learning, of style and systems for describing style, and of rhetorical theory. The facts of academic life suggest that he will have had to learn much of this outside of courses, but the fortunate teacher will have undertaken graduate study where appropriate courses are available. The teacher should give evidence of professional interest in teaching writing by participation in professional societies (e.g., CCCC, STWP), by editorial and consulting work, and by the constant practice of writing of the kind he teaches. A teacher of fiction writing might be writing stories, a teacher of science writing might be editing articles, a teacher of expository writing might be preparing proposals for curricular change to the college faculty. Although his writing may be unpretentious and for a local audience, it should be constantly available to the scrutiny of colleagues.

The teacher of advanced composition ought to have a wide range of extra-academic experience, especially in the areas of professional interest of the students. Prospective technical writers deserve a teacher who at least tries to keep informed of current work in the sciences; prospective high school teachers deserve a teacher who is informed about the work in secondary schools. The writer need not be a specialist in the area of the students' interests, but he must be receptive to new ideas, and he must be unusually sensitive to human relationships so that he can correctly assess rhetorical situations. The ivory tower is merely a base for his excursions into the light and dark places of the world.

These suggestions for the minimum qualifications of teachers should make clear that advanced composition is not a course for departmental leftovers. Not even every good professor of English is automatically qualified to teach advanced composition; the fully qualified teacher may indeed be rare and so should be honored in rank and salary along with others who are noted for professional excellence. If advanced composition courses are to be worth a student's investment, they must be staffed with at least the same care used to staff the advanced courses in literature.

6. **Modes of Instruction**: Because the papers are more subtly done than are freshman papers, more time is required for teachers to read papers and confer with students. As a result, the sections generally should be smaller than those in the freshman course. Efforts to have courses taught by professionals of other disciplines, e.g., historians teaching history majors, are limited by the limits of the instructor, who may write exceedingly well for his own purposes and yet may not know enough about the principles of writing to generalize for his students. He may be very helpful teaching in a team with an English professor, but there seems little reason to believe that the Department of English can really escape its responsibility of providing people especially competent to teach writing.

The amount of writing required in the course may vary according to the nature of the assignments. A large number of short assignments—especially if designed sequentially and cumulatively—may fit one course, and a few intricate assignments which encourage revision and alternative versions may fit another. Either way the course itself should have a progression and point of its own. One expects considerable commentary about the writing of the students, but the frequent issuing of grades may be inappropriate for the kind of interest these students should be presumed to have. Although a student should not be led to believe he is writing well when he is writing badly and regular progress reports are needed, probably the negative effect of being classified by a grade inhibits some students from experimenting with language.

Jacquelin Berke, Drew University
Mary C. Bromage, University of Michigan
John Butler, Wichita State University
Francis Christensen, University of Southern California
Donald Emery, University of Washington
Hubert English, University of Michigan
John Folsom, Boston University
William Gillis, Bradley University
Alan B. Howes, University of Michigan
Billie Pyle Kuydendall, University of Tennessee
Glenn Leggett, Grinnell College
John Lindberg, University of Northern Iowa
John McKiernan, College of St. Thomas
Fred MacIntosh, University of North Carolina at Chapel Hill
Margaret Neville, DePaul University
Robert Slack, Carnegie Institute of Technology
Darwin Turner, North Carolina A and T College
Laura Weddle, University of Kentucky
Richard Lloyd-Jones, University of Iowa, Chairman

Defining Advanced Composition: Contributions from the History of Rhetoric

by William A. Covino

> But that use of wit and knowledge is to be allowed, which laboureth to make doubtful things certain, and not those which labour to make certain things doubtful.
>
> So then that knowledge is worthiest which is charged with least multiplicity.
>
> Francis Bacon, *Advancement of Learning*

Francis Bacon ushers in the Enlightenment when in 1605 he equates *advanced* knowledge with uniformity and universal principles, with certainty, with the schematization of diverse phenomena under the rubric of "simple Forms or differences of things, which are few in number" (2.7: 96). Later in the seventeenth century, the Royal Society of London for Improving Natural Knowledge would reaffirm the importance of reducing and containing the diversity of the world, reinforcing the prevailing belief that intellectual maturity coincides with order, perspicuity, and closure, and calling for a reform of language that would "reject all amplifications, digressions, and swellings of style, [and] return back to the primitive purity, and shortness, when men delivered so many *things*, in an almost equal number of *words*" (Sprat 113). In general, these and other influential post-Cartesians associate less advanced intellection with "kalendars of doubts" not yet "thoroughly sifted and brought to resolution" (Bacon 2.7: 103), and they associate advanced intellection with statements of manifest unity and coherence expressed in precisely controlled language.[1]

This post-Cartesian conception of advanced knowledge remains dominant today and informs our definitions of advanced composition. An advanced composition course often differs from a beginning course in that the former emphasizes reading, research, and topics of greater breadth, difficulty, and complexity, and it demands greater rigor in managing and reducing the complex; advanced students, that is, must demonstrate mastery of closure and conventions, from the arrangement of a formal

---

Reprinted from the *Journal of Advanced Composition* 8 (1988): 113-22. Reprinted with permission.
[1] I present some of the points in this essay more extensively in *The Art of Wondering*.

argument to the small particulars of MLA style and documentation. In departments outside English, advanced composition is often the label for upper-division practice in a schematic professional or academic genre; the advanced composition course for business majors, for example, might be an internship in report writing. And sometimes, advanced composition courses merely emphasize theme-writing of the sort required by graduate competency tests or graduate-school hurdles like the LSAT, drilling students in the prototypical Introduction + Examples + Conclusion formula.[2] In short, the products of advanced writers are expected to be more "finished" and "polished" than those of beginners. Thus, advanced composition pedagogy seems to mirror Bacon's notion that intellectual maturity is connected to consistency, coherence, unity, certainty, and resolution. I intend to propose a definition of advanced composition that calls into question these virtues of closure, a definition which can be drawn from the works of rhetoricians since Antiquity. For example, Plato, Aristotle, and Cicero distinguish "advanced" from "beginning" rhetors by associating the former with tolerance for ambiguity and intolerance for formulaic discourse and its precepts. All three rhetoricians identify their worst students with obedient mastery of stock forms and formulae, and the very form of their own rhetorical theories—wandering prose that frustrates students who want their rhetoric quick and easy—questions the virtue of single-mindedness. However, these rhetoricians' conceptions of advanced rhetoric have been largely ignored, and the history of rhetoric has presented these thinkers as advocates rather than opponents of homogenized, rule-managed writing.[3] Looking to Plato's *Phaedrus*, Aristotle's *Rhetoric*, and Cicero's *De Oratore*, we can define advanced composition as *the open intellectual play of multiple perspectives*, a definition later reaffirmed by Montaigne, Vico, and De Quincey, who follow in the tradition of the Ancients by emphasizing discursive license and continuing to define advanced composition as endless wondering.

Classical Perspectives on Advanced Composition

Plato's *Phaedrus* and Cicero's *De Oratore* both posit the mature rhetor as a lover of dialogue and persistent questioning who demonstrates inconclusiveness and uncertainty. In both works, this mature rhetor is counterpoised with the students who want clear instructions and prefer summary to speculation. The Phaedrus of Plato's dialogue, for instance, craves unambiguous advice about discourse. He is confused by Socrates' two speeches (critiques of Lysias's speech on love) that extend and complicate the nature of both love and rhetoric:

> **Socrates**: Would you like, then, to take that speech of Lysias you have with you and the ones I delivered and examine them for points which illustrate what we may call art and the lack of it?

---

[2] In the California State University system, for example, upper-division writing proficiency is required for graduation and has been measured by either a timed theme-writing test or in courses in formulaic composition. In either case, advanced writing proficiency is identified with efficient, regimented thinking.

[3] Knoblauch and Brannon present the classical tradition as many commentators throughout the centuries have portrayed it: as a collection of narrow, long-irrelevant rules and procedures. (See especially Chapter 2.)

> **Phaedrus**: Oh yes, that would be splendid! For what we are saying now is too abstract. We need some workable examples.

> **Socrates**: And by some special stroke of good fortune it looks as though the two speeches offer an illustration of how a man who knows the truth may play with words and lead his audience astray. It's the local divinities, Phaedrus, that I judge to be the cause of this; or perhaps the Muses' prophets, singing overhead, may have breathed their inspiration into us; for I, at any rate, have no gift of speech.

> **Phaedrus**: All right, as you please. Just tell me what you mean! (262)

As Socrates continues to discuss the speeches on love, the responses of Phaedrus portray a student less interested in thinking things over than in merely assenting, whether he understands or not: "Yes"; "Of course"; "We certainly do"; "That's the way it is"; "Why, of course" (262-63). Phaedrus feigns complete understanding at every turn, revealing his strong desire for packaged knowledge and his impatience with being "led astray" from quick understanding by the intellectual play of Socrates, who knows that truth is broad and complex and can only be pursued through continual, irresolute dialogue. Further, Phaedrus is all too eager to admire the "outstanding quality" of Lysias's completeness: "Of all the points of the subject worthy to be enumerated, [Lysias] has neglected not one." But Socrates defines complete understanding as a worthy but impossible goal, approachable only through successive definition and division, in discourse that is always changing and that is "exactly attuned to every changing mood of the complicated soul." Truth is not reducible to summary; the investigation of truth is foreclosed by thinking, speaking, and writing that convert complexity and ambiguity to doctrine, that "lay down laws in written form." Writing that does not exploit the persistent curiosity (so striking in Socrates and so absent in Phaedrus) which defines philosophy "is a disgrace to the writer" (277).

Cicero echoes this theme in *De Oratore*, a dialogue that identifies intellectual accomplishment with the "knowledge of a vast number of things" refracted through a number of perspectives (1.5: 10). The mature orators Crassus and Antonius fill hours and days speculating on "the perfect orator," thereby demonstrating that this topic cannot be reduced to a system of precepts, and exasperating the students who are listening. By constructing his most inclusive work on rhetoric and eloquence as a dialogic drama of viewpoints, Cicero associates the accomplished rhetor—himself—with incessant, inconclusive discourse; and he dissociates himself from the younger Cicero who had written the formulaic *De Inventione* (1.2: 7), and from Sulpicius and Cotta, students who, like Plato's Phaedrus, want teachers to offer schematic advice amenable to efficient obedience.

Early in the dialogue, following Crassus's initial argument that the perfect orator must constantly pursue wide-ranging knowledge ("the reason and nature of every thing and of all sciences"), Antonius begins to respond that such a philosophical life is impractical: life is too short to occupy oneself with study, reflection, *and* action (1.18: 26). However, Antonius counters Crassus by demonstrating the breadth of his own intellect and experience and the power of his memory, thereby joining Crassus as one disinclined to take the efficient way to a conclusion. For five excursive pages, Antonius reconstructs a past excursion to Athens, where he talked with "most learned men" who themselves recalled earlier generations of philosophers, reaching back to the origination of rhetoric with Corax and Tisias (1.18-21: 26-31). Thus, Antonius responds to Crassus in a dialogue recollecting another dialogue containing still further recollections of still other dialogues. Antonius's response is finally inconclusive and circular, ending where it had begun, with tribute to Crassus as the perfect orator.

The student Sulpicius protests that Crassus and Antonius should so "insensibly glide into a discourse of this kind" and asks to be taught "something worthy to be remembered . . . fully and exactly" (1.21: 30-31). When Crassus responds by further insisting that the accomplished rhetor must continually pursue unlimited knowledge, he is met with silence. Asked later to speak on the principles of style, Crassus digresses to a survey of Greek philosophy only to be met with another student demand for stock information, "the ordinary knowledge of common affairs" (3.36: 234). Through such conflicts between teachers and students, Cicero repeatedly associates "beginners" with a reductive view of rhetoric as an absolute system of set forms founded on "ordinary knowledge," and he associates "advanced" rhetors with a playful refusal to ossify thought and language.

A response to Plato and a source book for Cicero, Aristotle's *Rhetoric* does not exploit dialogue as a genre but does make dialectical thinking a requirement for the rhetor who claims more than preceptive knowledge of the art. In his conclusion to the *Rhetoric*—"I have done; you all have heard; you have the facts; give your judgment" (1420b)—Aristotle suggests with a "textbook" peroration that rhetoric and judgment are simple matters of fact, adopting the very technique that orators find useful for closing debate and calling for an absolute verdict. Clearly, the attitude toward language and knowledge mimicked in this peroration is the same one we have seen in Phaedrus, Sulpicius, and Cotta, but it is an attitude that Aristotle refutes through the meandering irresolution that defines rhetoric in the *Rhetoric*. Aristotle's peroration leaves the dull novice with the comfortable illusion of closure and invites the more alert and curious to reconsider equating mastery with final pronouncements. The *Rhetoric* identifies rhetoric with inquiry: the function of rhetoric is "not so much to persuade, as to find out in each case the existing means of persuasion" (1355b). Sustained questioning—that habit of mind that contends with Aristotle's neat peroration—defines the style and substance of rhetoric:

> The question whether a thing has or has not happened must be considered from the following points of view. . . . If a man was able and wished to do a thing, he has done it; for all men do a thing, when they are able and resolve to do it, for nothing hinders them. Further, if a man wished to do it and there was no external obstacle; if he was able to do it and was in a state of anger; if he was able and desired to do it; for men as a rule, whenever they can, do those things which they long for, the vicious owing to want of self-control, the virtuous because they desire what is good. (1392b)

For Aristotle, we can do no better than to require that students persist in raising questions and practice "knowing" as inquiry. With a commentary that itself resists system and closure—full of always irresolute and incomplete lists of perspectives—Aristotle dissociates the aim, or "end," of rhetoric from final judgments.

Assaults on the Classical Perspective

Despite the Ancients' warning mockery of eager decisiveness in their students, that quality receives continued emphasis in the formulary rhetoric and pedagogy that extend from the Hellenistic revisions of Aristotle's *Rhetoric* through the schools of imperial Rome and the medieval Church.[4] And the preference for language that maintains *established* knowledge gains popularity from the late Renaissance onward with the aggressive containment of philosophy and science. Peter Ramus's *Dialectic* (1546) is one of his influential assaults against broad and complex classical explications of rhetoric and logic. In response to a philosophical rhetoric whose "method" exploits the instability of knowledge, Ramus defines method in simple, absolute terms: "method is . . . the arrangement of various things brought down from universal and general principles to the underlying singular parts, by which arrangement the whole matter can be more easily taught and comprehended" (Murphy 17).

In *The Advancement of Learning* (1605), Bacon refuses the strictly binary schemata that inform Ramus's construction of knowledge, but he echoes the call for an organized, methodized learning of truths that can be weighed, measured, and subordinated to universal and mechanical laws. Bacon associates immature learning with entertaining multiple truths: "Children at the first will call every woman mother, but afterward they come to distinguish according to truth, so experience, if it be in childhood, will call every philosophy mother, but when it cometh to ripeness, it will discern the true mother" (2.8:104). Similarly, in *Discourse on Method* (1637), Descartes associates intellectual growth with the ability to reach uncontestable conclusions.

Ramus, Bacon, and Descartes are founders of a powerful epistemology, adopted by the French Academy and the British Royal Society and leading to the association of ambiguity in thought and language with children and primitives. Hugh Blair supports this view in his tremendously popular *Lectures on Rhetoric and Belles-Lettres* (1783):

> The Progress of Language . . . resembles the progress of age in man. The imagination is most vigorous and predominant in youth; with advancing years, the imagination cools, and the understanding ripens. Thus Language, proceeding from sterility to copiousness, hath, at the same time, proceeded from vivacity to accuracy; from fire and enthusiasm, to coolness and precision [and to] simple style, plain arrangement. Language is become, in modern times, more correct, indeed, and accurate. (1.6: 124)

---

[4] The pseudo-Ciceronian *Ad Herennium*, which identifies composition and oratory with strict arrangement, was the prototypical rhetoric throughout the Middle Ages.

Sustaining a "Renegade" Tradition

While classical emphases on open discourse as the sign of intellectual maturity still go unrecognized as civilization "advances," the equation of closure with ignorance has been pressed on by thinkers whose influence on education is, unfortunately, negligible. Following Ramus and preceding Bacon, Michel de Montaigne in *Essays* (composed and revised from 1572 through 1588, and first translated into English in 1603) continues the classical parody of the Phaedruses among us, who associate intellectual progress with patterned language:

> They keep us four or five years learning to understand words and stitch them into sentences; as many more, to mold them into a great body, extending into four or five parts; and another five, at least, learning how to mix and interweave them briefly in some subtle way. (1.26: 124-25)

Writing here in "Of the Education of Children," Montaigne identifies the typical student of advanced composition as the master of a formula, as one whose education culminates in the facile rearrangement of standard rhetorical parts. Montaigne's own "development" culminates in insistent uncertainty, reiterated throughout his final essay, "Of Experience": "the inference that we try to draw from the resemblance of events is uncertain, because they are always dissimilar: there is no quality so universal in this aspect of things as diversity and variety" (3.13: 815). Diversity of experiences and ideas makes all assertions uncertain and fragile; further, positing any inference as more advanced or correct insists that language accommodates certainty. For Montaigne, language mocks certainty:

> I ask what is "nature," "pleasure," "circle," "substitution." The question is one of words, and is answered in the same way. "A stone is a body." But if you pressed on: "And what is a body?"—"Substance."—"And what is substance?" and so on, you would finally drive the respondent to the end of his lexicon. We exchange one word for another word, often more unknown. . . . To satisfy one doubt, they give me three; it is the Hydra's head. (818-19)

Rejecting the language of disciplined judgments as fraudulent, Montaigne allies the strongest intellect with the endless generation of new perspectives:

> It is only personal weakness that makes us content with what others or we ourselves have found out in this hunt for knowledge. An abler man will not rest content with it. . . . It is a sign of contraction of the mind when it is content, or of weariness. A spirited mind never stops within itself; it is always aspiring and going beyond its strength; it has impulses beyond its powers of achievement. . . . It is an irregular, perpetual motion, without model and without aim. Its inventions excite, pursue, and produce one another. (817-18)

Celebrating generative, variegated, unsystematic writing, Montaigne offers an implicit rebuttal of Ramus and rejects in advance Bacon's valorization of coherent knowledge.

At the beginning of the eighteenth century, Giambattista Vico begins a direct and explicit critique of Descartes. As Professor of Rhetoric at the University of Naples, Vico delivers a speech, *On the Study Methods of Our Time* (1708), in which he cautions against the prevalence of Cartesian analytics, whose mastery he associates with adolescents whose narrow minds keep them from mature, copious discourse. Emphasizing the importance of topical invention (14), Vico proposes that students immersed in "the totality of sciences and arts" and aware that "probabilities are many" can contribute vitality to an intellectual community. Like the Ancients' students that he describes, Vico's ideal students would not practice the insolent ignorance or obedient silence typical of those controlled by formulaic knowledge:

> They would not feel the impulse to step rashly into discussions while they are still in the process of learning; nor would they, with pedestrian slavishness, refuse to accept any viewpoint unless it has been sanctioned by a teacher. . . .

> A five-year period of silence was enjoined upon all of Pythagoras' students. After that time, they were allowed to maintain what they had learned, but had to ground their reasons only upon the authority of their master. "He said it," was their motto. The chief duty of a student of philosophy was to listen. (19-20)

Identifying Descartes with Pythagorean learning and himself with the topical imagination exploited by Aristotle, Vico proposes that the conflict between ambitious ignorance and the art of wondering is not new, and he yearns for teachers and students who define intellectual progress as an ever-widening sense of complexity, aware that "nature and life are full of incertitude" (15).

By the early nineteenth century, when advanced education in rhetoric was identified with the "perspicuity and precision" stressed continually in Blair's *Lectures*, Thomas De Quincey eulogizes the "renegade" tradition I have surveyed here:

> The rhetorician's art in its glory and power has silently faded away before the stern tendencies of the age; and, if, by any peculiarity of taste or strong determination of the intellect, a rhetorician *en grande costume* were again to appear amongst us, it is certain that he would have no better welcome than a stare of surprise as a posturemaker or balancer, not more elevated in the general estimate, but far less amusing, than the acrobat, or funambulist, or equestrian gymnast. No; the age of Rhetoric, like that of Chivalry, has passed among forgotten things. (97)

De Quincey's own prose demonstrates the "inversions, evolutions, and harlequin changes" that define the lost art of rhetoric as he admits the futility of making or finding those rhetors whom Plato, Aristotle, Cicero, Montaigne, and Vico would call masters of the art—rhetors for whom composition is "progress and motion, everlasting motion" (129). De Quincey looks into the nineteenth century of industry and science—and beyond, to the reign of bureaucracy and technology today—when he concludes that the "urgency of public business" makes virtues of efficiency and conviction and insists that "where conviction begins, the field of rhetoric ends" (82).

Dialogic Writing in Advanced Composition

The theorists I have discussed posit advanced thinking and writing as the opposites of ready conviction, and they challenge those of us who teach advanced composition to reconsider what our subject is and how it might be taught. Notably, each identifies close-mindedness in students and teachers with closed rhetorical forms, and each would replace the mechanical recitation of divisions and subdivisions with prose that moves through variegated substance. Further, the writing of each suggests that dialogue—understood as an interplay of voices and perspectives taking place in the mind of a single narrator (as with Aristotle, Montaigne, Vico, De Quincey) or among several characters (as with Plato and Cicero)—creates the dynamic rhetoric of open discourse; dialogic writing necessarily evades the consistency, coherence, and blindness of an insistent "thesis."

Teaching advanced composition may mean introducing "new" genres that require and enfranchise dialogic writing; the most obvious of these genres is the dialogue itself. Perhaps we need to encourage our advanced students to engage in their own dialogic writing. For example, the following is a dialogue assignment that encourages students to keep an issue alive; the definition of advanced composition that I have followed through the history of rhetoric is implicit in the topic and constraints for this assignment. Writing is identified with the "unexplored, unsettled, ambiguous, or confusing," so that our student writers—following Plato—practice writing as *engaged ignorance*. However, maintaining that ignorance means *research*; only by "piling up" (Montaigne's term) substantial and inconsistent propositions can students continue to think and defer its opposite—thoughtlessness. The students' research must be comprehensive rather than "focused"—their minds filled with a drama of voices.

In line with the letter and the spirit of the historical texts I have surveyed, this assignment insists upon *substance* while discouraging a particular *stance*. Further, with its emphasis on planned discourse, it encourages license without vagueness; thus, students are warned against words which "tumble out under the blindest accidents of the moment" (De Quincey 142). Following Aristotle and Cicero, they must know all sides of an issue. Following Vico, they must create a *sensus communis*, or common sense, by enlarging the lexicon of viewpoints that comprise human history and decisions. Following De Quincey, they must set aside conviction to practice rhetoric.

Appendix: Sample Assignment

The Dialogue

Topic: An unexplored, unsettled, ambiguous, or confusing element of a subject that matters.

Characters

(1) Three experts on your topic, each with a different viewpoint. These are *real* experts, with significant reputations and published work (which you have reviewed).

(2) Two curious, critical, undecided students with a substantial interest in the topic.

Constraints

(1) No one makes stupid or uncharacteristic statements.

(2) No one wins; that is, no one view finally seems more intelligent, persuasive, or inclusive than the others.

(3) Each character speaks at least three times, for at least half a page at each turn.

(4) The experts occasionally quote or paraphrase themselves or each other; each character is familiar with the others' published work.

(5) No one delivers "throwaway" lines or transitions, such as "How true, tell me more."

(6) Each character's words are planned and crafted. This is thoughtful deliberate writing, neither spontaneous nor casual, as if the characters had revised and edited their spoken words for publication (see, for instance, the occasional dialogues that have appeared in the "Forum" section of recent issues of *Harper's*).

Works Cited

Aristotle. *The Rhetoric of Aristotle*. Trans. Lane Cooper. Englewood Cliffs, NJ: Prentice, 1932.

Bacon, Francis. *The Advancement of Learning*. Ed. G.W. Kitchin. Totowa, NJ: Rowman, 1973.

Blair, Hugh. *Lectures on Rhetoric and Belles-Lettres*. Ed. Harold F. Harding. Carbondale: Southern Illinois UP, 1965. 2 vols.

Cicero. *De Oratore (On Oratory and Orators)*. Trans. J.S. Watson. Carbondale: Southern Illinois UP, 1970.

Covino, William A. *The Art of Wondering: A Revisionist Return to the History of Rhetoric*. Portsmouth, NH: Boynton, 1988.

De Quincey, Thomas. *Selected Essays on Rhetoric*. Ed. Frederick Burwick. Carbondale: Southern Illinois UP, 1967.

Descartes, René. *Discourse on Method*. Trans. Paul J. Olscamp. Indianapolis: Bobbs, 1965.

Knoblauch, C.H., and Lil Brannon. *Rhetorical Traditions and the Teaching of Writing*. Upper Montclair, NJ: Boynton, 1984.

Montaigne, Michel de. *The Complete Essays of Montaigne*. Trans. Donald M. Frame. Stanford: Stanford UP, 1958.

Plato. *Phaedrus*. Trans. W.C. Helmbold and W.G. Rabinowitz. Indianapolis: Bobbs, 1956.

Ramus, Peter. *Arguments in Rhetoric against Quintilian*. Trans. Carole Newlands. DeKalb: Northern Illinois UP, 1986.

Sprat, Thomas. *History of the Royal Society*. Ed. Jackson Cope and Harold Jones. St. Louis: Washington UP, 1958.

Vico, Giambattista. *On the Study Methods of Our Time*. Trans. Elio Gianturco. Indianapolis: Bobbs, 1965.

What Is *Advanced* About Advanced Composition?: A Theory of Expertise in Writing

by Michael Carter

It was impossible for Bernice Dicks to hide her discouragement as she described the state of advanced composition in 1982. Based on an exhaustive review of the literature—telling in its brevity—and a detailed survey, Dicks somberly announced that except for the fact that it is a nonfiction writing course with freshman composition as a prerequisite, advanced composition has distressingly eluded definition (173-78). It is neither fish nor fowl. Or, as a relative of mine used to say in explanation of why he disliked casseroles, it contains no histologically identifiable matter. Dicks summed up her findings this way:

> Unfortunately, the wealth of models [offered by this survey] suggests again that advanced composition may well prove impossible to define once and for all: if, as Peter Dowell at Emory wrote to me, "the content is at the discretion (or whim) of the individual instructor," then we really are no farther along toward a statement about the course than we were when CCCC started out in 1954 to pin the creature to the wall. (186)

And we have not come much farther since 1982. The difficulty in pinning the creature to the wall is that we can't identify it, we can't say what is advanced about advanced composition. In an earlier survey, Michael Hogan found that most teachers of advanced composition consider their courses extensions of freshman composition, as indicated by the fact that most of the textbooks used in advanced composition classes were freshman texts (22-23). Dicks also found that the lack of definition for advanced composition encouraged teachers simply to incorporate the same format they use in their freshman classes, "requiring a 'harder' textbook, more writing, and increased one-on-one attention" (181). Indeed, two of the most popular textbooks for advanced composition, one by Maxine Hairston and the other by Richard M. Coe, are nearly indistinguishable from most freshman rhetorics, differing in degree rather than in kind.

I believe, however, that advanced composition should be more than just a "harder" freshman course. If advanced composition is to have any viability at all, it

---

Reprinted from *Teaching Advanced Composition: Why and How*, Ed. Katherine H. Adams and John Adams, Portsmouth, NH: Boynton/Cook, 1991. Reprinted with permission.

must be founded on a theory that (1) shows how advanced composition is different in kind from freshman composition and (2) shows how advanced composition is developmentally related to freshman composition. The "harder" approach achieves only the latter.

In this paper I propose such a theory, which I call a theory of expertise in writing. The premise is that an advanced composition could lead a student toward expertise in writing. The question, of course, is what is expertise in writing? Is it the ability to write without grammatical errors or to write with complex syntax? Is it the possession of a large repertory of structural models or of powerful composing strategies? Indeed, I suggest that one of the problems with teaching writing in general and certainly with teaching advanced composition in particular is that we do not know what it is that comprises expertise in writing. The theory that I offer here may help to solve this problem.

This theory of expertise in writing is founded on psychologists' research in expertise. At its most basic, I define the development of expertise as the movement from behavior that is governed by general process strategies to behavior that is governed by specialized knowledge. The development of expertise *in writing* is the movement from global writing strategies to sophisticated knowledge of special rhetorical situations. Expertise, then, is the result of specialized knowledge that comes from experience in a specific writing situation. As this knowledge grows, the writer is able to write within that situation (and others that are similar) much more quickly and efficiently. This concept of expertise in writing is particularly appropriate to this discussion of advanced composition because the concept offers a way to identify what advanced writing is. In addition, it points to a broader structure on which a full writing curriculum may be built.

The Relationship Between General and Specific Knowledge

The issue of expertise is crucial to education because our concept of *what* proficiency is and *how* we become proficient—that is, how we achieve expertise—rules our educational philosophy. In our century, the notion of expertise has been characterized by a pendulum swinging back and forth between general and specific knowledge.

At the beginning of this century, education was imbued with the generalist philosophy that had dominated teaching for many centuries. Generalists conceived of education as a mental discipline and the mind as a sort of muscle that must be strengthened by rigorous exercise. The best known of these Nautilus machines for the mind was Latin, the standard of mental regimen for centuries. The idea was that the mental discipline that one would gain by studying Latin could be transferred to performance in specific domains outside of Latin. This generalist theory of transferability, intuitive at best, was undermined early in the century by the psychologist E.L. Thorndike whose research in the transfer of learning demonstrated that learning one skill, however general, has little effect on performance in another skill. Thorndike's studies laid to rest, for a while, the muscle metaphor of education and encouraged educators to develop curricula that stressed specific instruction for specific skills—the rise of practical education (Glaser 93).

The swing back toward generalism was initiated by the information-processing boom of the sixties and seventies, the main advocates of which were cognitive psychologists whose goal was to understand human cognition through the use of computers. Early computers, of course, were simply very rapid calculators, programmed to work according to certain specific algorithms. The breakthrough for information-processing theorists came when they discovered that they could program computers to "think" the way people think, not by the specific formulas of algorithms but by heuristics (Dreyfus and Dreyfus 5-6). The epitome of the early "thinking" computers was Newell and Simon's *General Problem Solver*, a computer program that could solve a variety of problems using as its primary heuristic strategy a means-ends analysis (Newell and Simon 414-38). A study by Ernst and Newell showed that by focusing on this heuristic, *General Problem Solver* had achieved broad generality without any loss of specific problem-solving power. The implications of this research were all too clear: performance is based largely on an underlying strategic process that could be isolated, studied, and taught; thus, successful performance was a result of the application of powerful heuristic strategies. This research launched the general process movement of the seventies, characterized by courses in problem-solving techniques that, like Latin of old, promised general, transferable powers that would improve performance in many areas (Glaser 95-96). Expertise was once again considered mainly a function of generality—this time, general processes.

The general process movement seems to have suffered the same fate as Latin. Mayer reports that there is little evidence of the transferability of general process skills to specific areas of performance (344-45). The problem is that the work of the information-processing theorists was based primarily on puzzles and games—context-free, "knowledge-lean" problems that demand human subjects to perform without the use of specialized knowledge or skills. In other words, the research results have been misleading: they highlighted the use of general procedures because that is all that was necessary for solving the kinds of problems the researchers used (Glaser 96).

Recent research on the differences between experts and novices demonstrates that expertise is a function of specialization.[1] Studies of experts in many fields—from chess players to physicists—have demonstrated that experts are successful in their fields because they bring to their performance "domain-specific knowledge" attained through much experience within that domain. Indeed, it is no accident that *expert* and *experience* share the same Latin root. Novices, on the other hand, are novices specifically because they lack this knowledge and are forced to rely on general process skills and surface-level features of a problem.[2]

Psychologist Robert Glaser offers schema theory as a way of explaining the significant role of domain-specific knowledge in expert performance. He describes schemata as modifiable structures that act much like theories: schemata are internal

---

[1] Two excellent reviews of this research may be found in Bransford et al. and in Glaser. These reviews are particularly helpful because they discuss the research in terms of its educational implications.

[2] See, for instance, Bransford et al. 1079; Chi, Glaser, and Rees; Chi, Feltovich, and Glaser; Larkin, "Teaching Problem Solving" and "The Role of"; and Schoenfeld and Herrmann.

models that form the bases for testable hypotheses and may be modified if the hypotheses prove inadequate to experience. And also like theories, schemata enable us to make predictions and act on these predictions. Experts evidently have very highly organized schematic structures *related to the specific field of their expertise*. Expert schemata are developed and refined over a long time. The process begins with naive schemata or temporary models that, "when they are interrogated, instantiated, or falsified, help organize new knowledge and offer a basis for problem solving that leads to the formation of more complete and expert schemata." Thus, Glaser describes the process of knowledge acquisition as "the successive development of structures which are tested and modified or replaced in ways that facilitate learning and thinking" (101). Schema theory, then, explains how expert knowledge differs from the knowledge of novices and how that expert knowledge is developed.

Just as Thorndike did many years ago, expert-novice researchers have forced us to reevaluate our ideas of expertise. Can one become an expert by learning general skills that can be transferred to tasks in specific domains? Expert-novice researchers suggest not. Rather, expertise is very much a product of knowledge within the specific field, which allows the expert to act much more effectively and efficiently than those who do not possess that knowledge.

Educational psychology has returned to a domain-specific concept of expertise. But the search for a theory of expertise in writing demands an accounting of the relationship between general skills and specific knowledge, especially how specific knowledge is developed—that is, how expertise is achieved. Understanding this relationship will be crucial to understanding what is advanced about advanced composition.

One of the best explanations of the relationship between general skills and specific knowledge in the development of expertise may be found in *Mind Over Machine* by Hubert and Stuart Dreyfus, the former a philosopher and the latter a computer scientist. In this book, the Dreyfuses trace five stages in the acquisition of expertise. Though the primary purpose of their book is to demonstrate why artificial intelligence cannot achieve full human intelligence, the book also helps us understand what makes an expert.

In stage one, the novice learns "context-free rules," which means that he or she performs on the basis of a set of rules that are applied regardless of the situation. For example, a third-year medical student learns the procedures for taking a patient's history and physical and uses these procedures no matter who the patient is or what the problem is. The novice becomes an advanced beginner, stage two, with some experience in applying the rules and with the acquisition of more sophisticated context-free rules. Applying the rules in specific situations allows the learner to begin to see that the rules are meaningful, not a result of arbitrary decree. Rules begin to become situational as distinguished from context-free. Continuing the example, as a first-year resident the doctor applies the procedures of taking a history and physical in more specific situations but still has trouble pulling out the relevant data for diagnosis and treatment.

Stage three, or competence, comes with more experience in real situations and is marked by less of a reliance on rules and more of an adoption of hierarchical decision-making procedures. At this level, the performer has achieved a much greater awareness of the variables in a situation and must choose a plan to organize the variables in order to improve performance. Later in her residency, the doctor still has to rely on the rules of diagnosis and treatment but manages these rules more effectively and even knows when to break them.

The next stage is proficiency. Up to this point the learner's performance has been essentially rule governed; even when the rules were broken, performance was based on a conscious decision stemming from a perceived goal. Going beyond competence is to go beyond reliance on rules. At this stage, performance relies more on "holistic similarity recognition" than on the conscious decomposition of the features of a situation, more on know-how and intuition than on rationality. In other words, performance is based on the recognition of familiar situational patterns that are formed after much experience. As a chief resident, the doctor has seen so many patients that she hardly thinks about the rules anymore, depending instead on her experience to guide her response.

Expertise, the final stage, is marked by an even more fluid performance that is seldom based on analytic, conscious deliberation. The skill is so much a part of the performer that he or she is not really aware of it: experts do what works. There is little need to analyze a situation into decision and action because the expert has built up a large repertory of situations, each of which encompasses decision and action. Experts react intuitively to most situations without having to rely on rules or plans; instead, they rely on the familiarity that comes from experience (Dreyfus and Dreyfus 16-36). After working for a while in private practice, the doctor has developed a "feel" for patients and can elicit and process information she needs for diagnosis and treatment very quickly and efficiently.

According to the Dreyfuses' scenario, the development of expertise is the movement from a dependence on rules to guide behavior to a dependence on the *intuition* founded on experience within a particular domain. Expertise itself may be characterized by domain-specific knowledge, but the route to expertise begins in the realm of general rules that guide behavior. Looked at one way, the development of expertise may be defined as sloughing off the rules and strategies. Looked at another, it is an increasing reliance on knowledge developed in a specific domain. It is important to note, however, that the interaction of rules and domain-specific knowledge is not merely coincidental but causative. It is *because* of the increase in domain-specific knowledge that the performer needs to rely less and less on operational rules. And it is *because* operational rules demand a diminishing amount of cognitive energy that the performer can develop and use more and more sophisticated knowledge schemata. Thus, the two work together to help in the development of expertise.

This model suggests two key features for a theory of expertise. The first is that expertise is a function of specialization. No one can be an expert in general. The second feature is that the development of expertise is a process of moving from general skills to domain knowledge. General skills and context-free rules are a necessary step toward expertise. There are a few cases in which the intuition of expertise is generated without beginning at the early rule-guided stages, but such cases almost by definition fall into the category of *idiot savant*. But this developmental continuum can move in the reverse direction, too. It is necessary to fall back on a solid basis of rule-guided behavior at times when one is out of the domain of one's expertise (Glaser 102; Bransford et al. 1083). Returning to the example of the doctor, even though she is an expert in her own field, when she encounters a problem that is outside her specialization, she is once again a relative novice and must fall back on the rules and/or seek advice from experts.

The relationship between general skills and domain-specific knowledge also offers a model for learning, a concept of progress. The theory of expertise presents a concept of learning as moving toward expertise. Learners begin as novices, relying on the rules that guide performance. The act of learning may be understood as the development of more sophisticated schemata accompanied by the diminishing need for rules. Learning, however, need not always end in expertise; indeed, I would speculate that learning rarely leads to expertise, given the amount of experience that expertise demands. Any movement along the continuum toward expertise may be called learning.

Expertise: The Idea of an Advanced Composition

The purpose of this paper is to offer a way to describe expertise in writing. This concept is important to composition because our notions of expertise, whether recognized or not, must guide our research and pedagogy. It is particularly important to advanced composition, because the way we define expertise must indicate what we think is advanced about writing.

The theory of expertise has two major implications for the teaching of writing. First, expertise in writing is a function of specialization. There is no such thing as an expert writer in general. Writers become experts only within rhetorical contexts in which they gain much experience and facility. Instead of being an expert in all kinds of journalism, for instance, a writer may be an expert at writing market analyses for the *Wall Street Journal* or at writing movie reviews in the *New Yorker*. Instead of being an expert in all children's literature, a writer develops expertise in producing illustrated books for three- and four-year-olds or in writing young adult fiction. Thus, the domains within which writers develop the domain-specific knowledge that leads to expertise are rhetorical contexts.

Let me hasten to add that expertise in writing does not necessarily imply that writing becomes easy. Rather, expertise within a particular rhetorical context allows the writer to perform more efficiently within that context. This streamlining of performance is made possible by the diminishing necessity, as writers gain expertise, for calling on explicit rules to guide the writing act. And because writers spend less energy on process strategies, they can spend more energy on higher-level aspects of discourse. Writers who must write outside their areas of expertise must call again on general process strategies to guide their performance.

The second implication is that the development of expertise in writing is a movement from the application of general process skills to the application of specialized knowledge based on experience within a specific domain. Learning to write, then, means starting with generalizable skills and strategies practiced in generalized writing situations. By *generalized writing situations* I do not mean the *general* topics written to *general* audiences, which invite vacuous, *general* prose. Rather, I mean a wide variety of writing contexts or (a little farther along the continuum toward expertise) writing that focuses on the broad academic community. At this point, the emphasis of writing is more on the application of the generalizable skills and strategies than on the special characteristics of the kind of discourse. These may include such strategies as exploratory heuristics (looping, cubing, tagmemics, etc.), methods for identifying and analyzing audiences, tactics for organizing ideas, and so on.

At the middle point of this developmental continuum, general skills and specific knowledge bear an approximately equal influence on writing and writing pedagogy. To get to this level, writers have gained more control over the general strategies by using them in more specific contexts. Pedagogical concerns shift from teaching generalizable strategies to helping students apply those strategies in specific contexts; thus, the strategies become more specialized. A key part of this movement toward the specific is the concentration on a particular rhetorical context and a greater concern for the specialized features of that context. In short, writers learn to apply more specialized strategies to specific writing contexts. As writers go beyond this point toward expertise, they depend less and less on explicit strategies and rely more and more on the *intuition* developed through the experience of writing within a particular rhetorical context. Such expertise, of course, takes a long time to develop and is certainly beyond the expectations of a single year of freshman composition and probably even advanced college writing. The idea is to guide students *toward* expertise.

This application of the theory of expertise to writing has specific implications for advanced composition. I began this paper with Bernice Dick's lament for advanced composition. The problem was that most advanced composition courses were nothing more than "hard" freshman composition courses. I suggested that for advanced composition to be a viable course in the college curriculum it must be founded on a theory that (1) shows how advanced composition differs *in kind* from freshman composition and (2) shows how advanced composition is developmentally related to freshman composition. I think that the theory of expertise in writing meets both of these criteria.

First, the theory of expertise in writing provides an answer to the question, what is *advanced* about advanced composition? Whereas freshman composition is mainly concerned with more generalized discourse contexts and has as its goal the development of generalizable skills, advanced composition is mainly concerned with more specialized discourse contexts and has as its goal the specialization of general skills and the development of knowledge related to writing in specific fields. Thus, expertise is *not* defined simply as achieving greater facility with general skills, whether they be grammar, style, or process strategies. Rather, the purpose of the advanced composition course is to lead students toward the expertise of specialization.

The idea of specialization in advanced composition is not new. W. Ross Winterowd, for instance, distinguished between transferable skills and local skills and pointed to local skills as the focus for advanced composition. Richard Fulkerson divided discourse into the elements of writer, reader, text, and universe and recommended that advanced courses could allow the student to specialize in one of these, for example, courses in advanced self-expression or advanced rhetoric. J.C. Mathes set up the specialized writing categories of public discourse, social systems, and organizational communication, suggesting that each one offers certain advanced skills that advanced students must master. And Faigley and Hansen describe a writing-across-the-curriculum program in which students write in specialized contexts according to their majors: fine arts and humanities, social sciences, natural sciences and technologies, and business. Though the idea of specialization in advanced composition is not new, the theory of expertise provides a theoretical foundation for advanced composition that clearly distinguishes it from freshman composition.

It is the *discipline-specific* program that provides the clearest approach to specialization in writing. According to the theory I have presented, the goal of such advanced courses should be to lead students toward expertise in their disciplines by: (1) teaching them the role that writing plays in the construction of knowledge in their disciplines; (2) helping them analyze the discourse of the discipline so they can learn the specialized features of that discourse and the role that those features play in the discourse community; and (3) providing them opportunities for writing within the discipline, to apply the general strategies they have previously learned to specialized situations.

This idea of advanced composition as a discipline-specific course may raise fears in the hearts of composition teachers. We tend to see ourselves as generalists, yet the theory of expertise suggests that the focus of advanced composition is specialization, a suggestion that may generate doubts about our role in these courses. What sort of contribution could we make? I think that no matter what the teaching arrangement for such courses—composition teacher only, team teaching with a specialist, or specialist only—the composition specialist possesses skills and knowledge that are crucial to the course. According to the theory of expertise, experts writing within their own specialization are usually not aware of what makes their performance effective. *Our* expertise as writing specialists provides a corrective for the blindness that comes with expertise in other disciplines, the blindness that may not allow experts to see the specialized features of their discourse, the role of discourse in creating knowledge within their discourse communities, or the procedures they use when they write. So we experts in writing are crucial because we can bring to discipline-specific discourse our knowledge of discourse analysis, of knowledge structures in discourse communities, and of writing process. Whether we construct a course with the help of experts and teach it ourselves (e.g., Faigley and Hansen; Moore and Peterson) or guide those experts in teaching writing themselves (e.g., Fulwiler), writing teachers must be the keystone in building advanced writing courses, a role that could have the additional benefit of letting our colleagues in other fields discover that we are more than just the drill sergeants of grammar.

In addition to showing how advanced composition differs from freshman composition, the theory of expertise also shows how the two are related. The continuum from novice to expert suggests that expertise builds on general skills; thus, both general skills and specialization are important in the development of expertise. It is the role of earlier composition courses, particularly high school and college freshman courses, to teach students explicit strategies for the writing process, general strategies that students may apply in a variety of domains. Earlier courses should also lay the groundwork for discourse analysis, perhaps focusing on the relatively broad domain of writing in college. Advanced composition courses should build on this knowledge of strategies and metadiscourse to help students both understand and write more effectively in specific rhetorical contexts.

Another way of understanding this relationship is to go back to the Dreyfuses' five steps toward expertise. I would describe high school and freshman composition as leading students through the steps of beginner and advanced beginner in the context of academic and professional discourse, learning relatively context-free rules and applying them in such a way that the rules start to become situational. Advanced composition picks up at that point and leads students through competence and proficiency. Competence represents a mastery over the rules and a much greater awareness of how they apply to specific situations. Proficiency is characterized by a dependency less on rules and more on the intuition that comes from experience in writing within a particular context. Expertise itself is perhaps beyond the abilities of college students, requiring extensive experience within a field.

I have offered this theory of expertise in writing as one way of clearing up the identity crisis that advanced composition has suffered for so long. But I think that the theory also demonstrates the importance of advanced writing courses in colleges. It encourages us to take a wider perspective of growth in writing ability, to see the teaching of writing as part of a broader development of expertise. Indeed, the concept of expertise in writing provides both the justification and the theoretical structure for a full college writing curriculum, whether it is advanced writing courses offered in the English department or writing-across-the-curriculum courses taught by specialists in the field or a combination of both. If we limit writing instruction to the generalizable skills and relatively general writing contexts of the freshman course—or even the "harder" courses offered by some as advanced composition—then we are only partially doing our jobs as writing teachers. Our job is to lead students toward expertise in writing, a journey that freshman composition only begins.

Works Cited

Bransford, John, et al. "Teaching Thinking and Problem Solving: Research Foundations." *American Psychologist* 41 (1986): 1078-89.

Chi, Michelene T.H., Robert Glaser, and Ernest Rees. "Expertise in Problem Solving." *Advances in the Psychology of Human Intelligence*. Vol. 1. Ed. Robert J. Sternberg. Hillsdale, NJ: Erlbaum, 1982. 7-75.

Chi, Michelene T.H., Paul J.Feltovich, and Robert Glaser. "Categorization and Representation of Physics Problems by Experts and Novices." *Cognitive Science* 5 (1981): 121-52.

Coe, Richard M. *Form and Substance: An Advanced Rhetoric*. New York: Wiley, 1981.

Dicks, Bernice W. "State of the Art in Advanced Expository Writing: One Genus, Many Species." *Journal of Advanced Composition* 3 (1983): 172-91.

Dreyfus, Hubert L., and Stuart E. Dreyfus. *Mind Over Machine: The Power of Human Intuition and Expertise in the Era of the Computer*. New York: Free, 1986.

Ernst, George W., and Allen Newell. *GPS: A Case Study in Generality and Problem Solving*. New York: Academic, 1969.

Faigley, Lester, and Kristine Hansen. "Learning to Write in the Social Sciences." *College Composition and Communication* 36 (1985): 140-49.

Fulkerson, Richard. "Some Theoretical Speculations on the Advanced Composition Curriculum." *Journal of Advanced Composition* 1 (1980): 9-12.

Fulwiler, Toby. "How Well Does Writing Across the Curriculum Work?" *College English* 46 (1984): 113-25.

Glaser, Robert. "Education and Thinking: The Role of Knowledge." *American Psychologist* 39 (1984): 93-104.

Hairston, Maxine. *Successful Writing*. 2nd ed. New York: Norton, 1986.

Hogan, Michael P. "Advanced Composition: A Survey." *Journal of Advanced Composition* 1 (1980): 21-29.

Larkin, Jill H. "The Role of Problem Representation in Physics." *Mental Models*. Ed. Diedre Gentner and Albert L. Stevens. Hillsdale, NJ: Erlbaum, 1983. 75-98.

____. "Teaching Problem Solving in Physics: The Psychological Lab." *Problem Solving and Education: Issues in Teaching and Research*. Ed. David T. Tuma and Frederic Reif. Hillsdale, NJ: Erlbaum, 1980. 111-25.

Mathes, J.C. "A Taxonomy of Communication Acts for the Design of Advanced Writing Courses." *Journal of Advanced Composition* 1 (1980): 53-57.

Mayer, Richard E. *Thinking, Problem Solving, Cognition*. New York: Freeman, 1983.

Moore, Leslie E., and Linda H. Peterson. "Convention as Connection: Linking the Composition Course to the English and College Curriculum." *College Composition and Communication* 37 (1986): 466-77.

Newell, Allen, and Herbert A. Simon. *Human Problem Solving*. Englewood Cliffs, NJ: Prentice, 1972.

Schoenfeld, Alan H., and Douglas J. Herrmann. "Problem Perception and Knowledge Structure in Expert and Novice Mathematical Problem Solvers." *Journal of Experimental Psychology* 8 (1982): 484-94.

Wintered, W. Ross. "Transferable and Local Writing Skills." *Journal of Advanced Composition* I (1980): 1-3.

What We Could Tell Advanced Student Writers about Audience

by Helen Rothschild Ewald

I think it's fair to say that a sense of audience is generally assumed of advanced composition students. In first-year composition, students have learned that audience is a crucial component of a rhetorical situation, they have encountered the relationship between audience analysis and textual decisions, and they have used peer groups as an audience during the writing process. It thus seems reasonable to assume that advanced student writers can effectively "consider their audience" during composing. And while advanced students may occasionally need to be reminded of the principles and significance of audience analysis, they will generally know enough about audience to generate rhetorically adequate discourse. Advanced students' competence in audience-based concerns leaves them free to make writing a genuine "exploration of ideas, a quest for purpose, and a projection of oneself" (Kroll 183). Their competence allows their instructor to concentrate on other aspects of discourse, such as developing a persona. Right? Perhaps. In this paper I explore what we *could* tell advanced student writers about audience based on current principles of reading theory. Whether or not we choose to introduce students to a reading-based concept of audience depends on issues I address at the end of this article.

Audience and Meaning

We could tell advanced student writers that in any given rhetorical situation the reader may do as much to make meaning as the writer. Reading theorists agree that "reading should be thought of as a constructive rather than as a receptive process" (Haas and Flower 167). In the constructivist view,

> The emphasis shifts from the structure of the text as an independent, immutable entity to structure and meaning as imposed on the text by the reader. It is assumed that although the text constrains the possible meanings readers with different knowledge, interests, and perspectives, or the same reader in different contexts, may construct quite different interpretations. (Goetz and Armbruster 214)

In short, the reader is as much an author of meaning as the writer.

Reprinted from the *Journal of Advanced Composition* 11 (1991): 147-58. Reprinted with permission.

Recent changes in communication models reflect this developing recognition of the reader as creator. Over time, communication theorists have all but abandoned the notion of the audience as a receiver or "decoder." Wilbur Schramm's series of communication models effectively dramatizes the movement away from seeing the audience as decoder. His first model, which bears a striking similarity to Claude Shannon's well-known schematic diagram of communication, pictures the audience as a decoder. His second model, however, introduces the notion that the audience, while still a decoder, shares fields of experience with the "encoder" or sender, and that these common fields of experience enable communication. Thus, in his second model Schramm acknowledges in a small but significant way the audience's role in creating meaning. Schramm's third model pictures communication as an interaction "with both parties encoding, interpreting, decoding, transmitting and receiving signals" (Severin and Tankard 35). Schramm's icon representing the audience has become virtually identical to that representing the sender. The audience has ceased to be a mere "receiver" of discourse.

The reader's power to generate meaning is not as apparent, however, in versions of the communication triangle used in some composition classes, explicitly or implicitly, to represent the rhetorical situation. As James Kinneavy points out, the communication triangle itself traditionally features four components: "a person who encodes a message, the signal (language) which carries the message, the reality to which the message refers, and the decoder (receiver of the message)" (19). Although Kinneavy acknowledges that the components are "actually much more complex" than the traditional communication triangle suggests (19), he nevertheless continues to designate the audience as the decoding component.[1] Unfortunately, such labeling of the audience as "decoder" can foster the misimpression that the audience's role is merely to receive and decipher the writer's message (see Hunter 282).

To acknowledge the reader's power to generate meaning, the communication triangle would better be characterized as a communication circle in which both writer and reader are sending and receiving messages. At the very least, the triangle would have to resemble Newcomb's Symmetry Model, in which the reader's orientation toward the writer and subject is as important as the writer's orientation toward the reader and subject. A revised communication triangle based on Newcomb's model would feature arrows pointing both toward and away from the reader and writer, thus supporting the proposition that the writer and reader are equal participants in the creation of discourse meaning.

Although audience has more or less continued to be identified as the decoding element in the communication triangle, the composition student has not necessarily remained ignorant of the reader's encoding powers. The reader as a constructive rather than a merely receptive figure has crept into some composition texts. The

---

[1] Although Kinneavy continues to identify the audience as a "decoder" in his later composition text, *Writing in the Liberal Arts Tradition* (1985), one suspects he might be simplifying his own case. As his *Theory* suggests, Kinneavy has a complex vision of audience as an element embodied in discourse itself. The implication of this embodiment to the decoding or encoding function of the reader, however, remains undeveloped.

constructive reader, for example, lurks behind Young, Becker, and Pike's extensive discussion of audience in *Rhetoric: Discovery and Change*. Their emphasis on discourse as a cooperative venture between writer and reader equalizes the reader's place in the making of discourse. Similarly, their caution that writers as well as readers experience change as a result of discourse encounters implicitly enhances the reader's status. The constructive reader also appears in Linda Flower's *Problem Solving Strategies for Writing*. Flower establishes that readers "form their own concepts," that they are "creative rather than passive, and that they *make meaning* using various strategies" (131-38). Readers are, potentially at least, a liberated lot in Jim Corder's *Contemporary Writing: Process and Practice*. They have their own histories and ways of perceiving, which at times can make them a recalcitrant, rebellious, or even renegade audience (42). The constructive reader is the keynote in Paul Anderson's *Technical Writing: A Reader-Centered Approach* as well. Anderson cites reading research when discussing audience and emphasizes that "instead of *receiving* meaning when we read, we interact with the text to *create* meaning." Anderson acknowledges further that "reading depends at least as much on what we bring to the page as it does on what is printed on the page" (25).

Given the creative reader's appearance in a number of textbook discussions of audience, the idea that readers are constructive rather than receptive might not be totally foreign to advanced student writers. We thus might be able to discuss the encoding powers of readers without causing surprise. However, when we begin discussing how writers should cope with this constructive reader, we may have some difficulty. When textbook authors give advice to writers on handling the creative reader, they tend to offer recommendations on using linguistic and textual properties to best advantage, an approach that is still writer-centered. For example, Flower reasons that if readers make meaning by using frameworks, drawing on expectations, and chunking material, then writers should "consider their audience" by using hierarchical structures, setting up and fulfilling expectations, and chunking information in their texts. Anderson gives similar guidance to technical writers, recommending adequate detail, a persuasive sequence for that detail, topic sentences, headings, lists, indexes, and tables of contents as reader aids. Corder recommends illustrative detail as well as specific and concrete language. And Young, Becker and Pike offer classical and Rogerian patterns of argument as effective rhetorical strategies. In giving such advice, textbook authors tacitly imply that the reader, given a carefully devised text, will be taking cues from the writer. The reader, through bottom-up processing, will be guided through the text by the text itself. However, this implication runs counter to what reading researchers have found concerning reader-text relationships.

Audience and Text

We might be obliged to tell advanced student writers, therefore, that the concept of a "reader-based" text, insofar as it assumes that readers derive meaning from linguistic and semantic textual properties, is at best "severely limited" (Goetz and Armbruster 202). The putative role of reader input in interpreting texts has led most reading theorists to agree that approaches to discourse that see comprehension as a function of the reader's ability to decipher textual language are likely to fail. In "Discourse and Linguistic Theory," for example, Jerry Morgan and Manfred Sellner systematically explode various meaning-in-the-text approaches. Specifically, they attack M.A.K. Halliday and Ruqaiya Hasan's treatment of cohesion, Gerald Prince's and David Rumelhart's separate examinations of story structure or "story grammar," and Teun van Dijk's linguistic theory of discourse. In each case, Morgan and Sellner show that certain content assumptions *made by the reader* and brought to the text account for the phenomena the researchers are examining. In other words, they find that meaning is not exclusively, or even primarily, a function of linguistic or textual properties.

Morgan and Sellner would attack previously cited recommendations for "reader-based" writing on much the same grounds; that is, these recommendations assume meaning is primarily in the text. This criticism is ironic in that such recommendations have originated in the textbook writers' research into the activity of reading. Nevertheless, missing from or deftly subordinated in these recommendations is the sense that reader expectations brought to the text (in the form of schemata or data structures) will influence and even determine how the text will be interpreted (see de Beaugrande 163).

Writers, then, must learn to appreciate the role of reader input in interpretation. Instead of depending on purely text-based strategies to produce reader-based writing, writers must learn to project accurately the various schemata that readers will bring to the text. In so doing, the writer's aim would *not* be, for example, to discover how much a reader knows about the topic in order to decide which details to include or exclude in the eventual text. Such a concern with textual detail again wrongly assumes that readers derive meaning primarily from text specifics. Rather, the writer should be concerned with such issues as these:

- What schemata (including organizational frameworks) might the reader associate with the subject?

- What schemata are necessarily embedded in or appropriate to the subject?

- Does the reader possess the "appropriate" schemata?

Asking these questions is not the same as asking, "What details are in my subject and important to include for my reader?" Rather, asking these questions is acknowledging that each reader or community of readers characteristically understands the subject in terms of something else—namely, a network of schemata brought to the text. Paradoxically, writers achieve reader-based prose by distancing themselves from the prose-as-text and by focusing on readers as they create meaning.

Audience and Peer Readers

Peer readers are often used in composition classrooms to enable such a focus on the reader's process of making meaning during text negotiation. Unfortunately, the peer group experience is not uniformly successful or always grounded on sound reading theory principles. We might have to tell advanced writers, then, that a peer audience in a composition class is sometimes but a pale representation of discourse communities at large. Student writers may often feel, for example, that peer readers can be readily accommodated by a change in phrasing or stylistic gambit and that they can with impunity shun any critical advice peer readers offer. Thomas Newkirk has found that peer readers are characteristically easy to please, especially if they can identify with the writer's subject or ideas (310). Moreover, Diana George asserts that student writers, for their part, are typically suspicious of their peers' advice and freely ignore peer group injunctions when revising (322). The result in such cases is that peer readers in composition classes tend to look for ways they can identify with what writers have to say and tend to make comments that do not require the writer to make substantive changes in their discourse. This, in turn, reinforces student writers' tendency to see themselves as in charge of not only what they have to say, but also of how they are to say it.

Discourse communities are far more powerful than this image suggests. First, the community and not the individual writer controls the discourse. Discourse communities remove the individual autonomous writer from center stage and replace him or her with a socially constituted system defined by "the characteristics of all other writers and writings in systems" (Cooper 367-68).

Second, it is unwise, if not perilous, for the writer to ignore community injunctions. Discourse communities are there for the writer to write *within*, not *to or for*. The writer demonstrates membership in a community through the use of its conventions. Discourse communities define themselves through conventions or paradigms, which can take various forms, including documentation practices, "in-house style format guides, and group or disciplinary injunctions such as 'do not use the first person'" (Freed and Broadhead 157). These paradigms are part of the network of schemata that readers bring to the text and that validate the writer's community membership. It is possible, of course, for writer and reader alike to belong to more than one discourse community (see Coles and Wall 313).

Third, discourse communities are not necessarily easy to please. These communities not only define themselves through paradigms that constrain the writer's use of linguistic and textual properties, but also through paradigms that determine semantic content. In this regard, Walzer suggests that writers can discover the significance of their data by communicating with members of various discourse communities (155). More dramatically, Bruffee asserts that what writers have to say actually originates within the discourse community to which they belong (784).

Reading theory provides insight into how discourse communities control what a writer has to say. The power of discourse communities to generate a writer's content is analogous to the power of an audience to construct a writer's text according to its interests, attitudes and purposes. The influence of reader interest and attitude on the interpretation and structure of discourse has been repeatedly demonstrated by reading researchers. Using ambiguous passages, researchers have found, for example, that with a passage that could describe either a card game or a musical quartet rehearsal, music students were far more likely to construct the quartet interpretation than were other students (Goetz and Armbruster 215). Reader attitudes have also been found to have a profound effect on comprehension. Researchers have convincingly shown that

> Individuals with a strong stand on issues that they are ego-involved with will interpret statements about that issue differently than individuals without a stand on the issue. For example, the former typically see statements the latter judged to be neutral as being favorable to the stand opposite theirs. Statements that are moderately acceptable are assimilated to their position and judged more favorable to it than is actually the case. (Spiro 255)

In light of these findings, Spiro concludes, "Once again, the cognitive impact of prose comprehension incorporates an aspect contributed by the comprehender and not from the text itself" (255).

A reader's purposes also influence how he or she constructs meaning. Louise Rosenblatt has identified two broad purposes that might inform a reader's reading: *efferent* (when the aim is to bring something away from the text) and *aesthetic* (when the aim is to be involved in the text). One purpose is information seeking; the other, experience seeking. The key term here is "seeking." Readers actively seek information (or experience) relevant to their current needs or goals. According to David Rumelhart, this seeking process goes hand-in-hand with the interpretation process, mentioned above in terms of schemata brought to the text (51). If a reader's expectations determine what the reader sees in the text, the reader's purpose tells the reader where to look for it. Interestingly, if a reader does not find what he or she is looking for, the reader will commonly import additional meaning or detail to the text (Rumelhart 35-37). Moreover, text-presented entries are commonly altered "to produce a better match" with the reader's world-knowledge and, indeed, these entries become "indistinguishable in the reader's mind" from his or her inferences and "spreading activations" (de Beaugrande 232-33). In short, the reader *makes* the text.

Writers would do well, therefore, to ask such questions as these:

- What are my reader's interests and attitudes?

- How are these interests and attitudes likely to alter what the text presents?

- What are my reader's purposes in reading my text?

- How will these purposes influence the reader's use of the text?

Such questions would complement other questions designed to identify the reader's discourse community and its attendant constraints. They would remind the writer that it is the reader who "consummates" the discourse act (see Augustine and Winterowd 135).

Audience and Writing Instruction

We could tell advanced student writers that the audience is by nature an *en-*

coder, that what the audience brings to the text is as important as (if not more important than) what the text itself presents. We could tell them that audiences characteristically alter what the text presents to produce a better match between what the text says and what they know. We could tell advanced student writers that the audience as a discourse community functions much like the audience as an individual reader: encoding, anticipating, altering what the text has to say. We *could* tell student writers all these things. But should we? Should we encourage our writers to see their audiences as the constructive readers that reading research suggests they are?

There are reasons for caution. One reason entails the apparent difficulty, perhaps impossibility, of establishing a reader-centered approach to the writer's composing process. As we have seen, textbook authors may indeed view audience in the same way that reading researchers do; however, when turning to discuss how writers could or should think about audience during composing, they tend to offer advice that counters reading theory tenets. That is, they tend to privilege either the encoding writer or the encoded text. This tendency receives overt expression when composition theorists such as Peter Elbow recommend "ignoring" audience, especially during the initial stages of composing. Indeed, the writer's right to his or her own text is a powerful idea in writing instruction. Having to develop a reader-centered approach to a writer's composing, therefore, might be analogous to having to remediate Common Error where the teacher must "keep in mind the cost to himself and the student of mastering certain forms [in our case, the constructive view of audience] and be ready to cut his losses when the investment seems no longer commensurate with the return" (Shaughnessy 122).

A second reason for caution, as several distinguished researchers have argued, is that it is impossible in any case to teach the rhetorical competence necessary to understand a concept such as that of the constructing reader. According to Augustine and Winterowd, rhetorical competence, like linguistic competence, is intuitive, acquired through years of exposure to models, mostly "imperfect" ones (143). To teach a writer to compose discourse that effects a "felicitous exchange" between writer and reader, therefore, involves more complexity and time than a composition course affords. Advanced composition teachers who adopt the position that audiences are constructive thus may find themselves in a position akin to that of E.D. Hirsch when he adopted a constructivist attitude toward "readability." Initially, Hirsch's definition of readability assumed a decoding reader. In *The Philosophy of Composition*, he examined the need for semantic closure and discourse pointers during text processing. However, as he eventually discovered, his understanding of the reader's operations was based on several questionable assumptions about reading (Dillon 1) and failed to consider reading as an "act of personal interpretation, evaluation, and affective response" (Kroll 178). Hirsch placed too much emphasis on what the writer had constructed and ignored what the reader would be constructing. Hirsch recanted this text-oriented position in "Reading, Writing, and Cultural Literacy," where he finds that the cultural information possessed by readers is more important than the stylistic quality of the text itself (142-43). In this essay, Hirsch equates writing conventions with "changing elements of cultural knowledge" (147), and he maintains that such knowledge cannot really be taught. To teach writers the cultural knowledge that would enable them to "know what other writers and readers know within literate culture" takes time, if not a lifetime (145-47). Thus, Hirsch finds himself dressed up in a new theory of reader "with no place to go." The theory precludes its own teaching.

Reading research which informs the vision of the constructing reader is admittedly in its infancy. Reading researchers Goetz and Armbruster call the existing literature investigating the psychological correlates of text structure "almost embarrassingly meager and rudimentary, given the import and complexity of the area" (201). Notwithstanding this admission, Spiro asserts that the constructivist view of reading is "unassailable" (250). For this reason, we would do well to introduce advanced student writers to a concept of audience that features the reader as creator. To do so, however, we might first have to abandon the notion of the writer as romantic hero involved in an independent quest for self-realization and truth. We might, instead, have to emphasize that all discourse, even so-called expressive discourse, is collaborative.

To assume such a stance would bring us close to the philosophy of Mikhail Bakhtin, who offers a model of reality where "there is no room for—and perhaps no conceptual possibility of—an independent unconscious" (Emerson 26). Bakhtin's work, in fact, holds considerable promise for composition researchers.[2] His concept of dialogism, for example, suggests a useful perspective on writers, readers, and the composing process. Dialogism, in part, attempts to dissolve the traditional oppositions of the individual to society, of self to other, of "the specific utterance to the totality of language," and of "particular actions to the world of norms and conventions" (Morrison xi). Because dialogism finds traditional oppositions such as self-versus-other untenable, it suggests that the image of the writer as an encoder separate from the reader might be equally untenable. In this regard, Bakhtin emphasizes that all discourse is a *response*, rather than, say, an individual "quest for purpose" or "a projection of oneself." At the same time, Bakhtin finds authorship an important, even a moral act. To be sure, the implications of Bakhtin's thought for composition theory and pedagogy defy easy synthesis. Synthesis, in fact, is not a Bakhtinian impulse. Dialogism, after all, is not dialectic. But Bakhtin, in speaking to issues of language, may offer the composition teacher a theoretical touchstone for discussing audience and its encoding role in discourse.

If we emphasize the creativity of the reader to our advanced student writers, we will also have to abandon the notion that the text is the sole, even primary, repository of meaning in written discourse. We will have to add to their understanding of how discourse itself works. In so doing, we might discuss, at least in a preliminary way, the work of Augustine and Winterowd, who have studied the writer-reader transaction from a speech-act perspective. Their work posits the types of "models" of written discourse that embody the encoding power of the reader. These models not only identify the propositional intention of a textual statement, but

---

[2] Schuster addresses this very point. Interestingly, he also notes that Bakhtin's version of the "rhetorical triangle" was a circle with "speaker, hero, and listener whirling around the circumference" (596).

also suggest the various possible rhetorical and "super" intentions which might be brought to that statement by writer and reader alike (132). Experience with such models enables both writer and reader to share a recognition of the deep-structure performative values which "govern writers' purposes and readers' expectations in discourse" (135).[3]

Finally, we will have to design our pedagogy so that it enables advanced writers to acknowledge the creative reader during the composing process. Such a design would entail an emphasis on the reading process both when discussing composing choices and when using peer groups for input and feedback. For example, instead of discussing classical and Rogerian argument as potential rhetorical strategies to be used as aids in "developing discourse designed to change the reader's image" (Young, Becker, and Pike 229), we would introduce these and other conventional patterns of arrangement as schemata extant in the discourse community and brought to the text by the member reader. Arrangement options can be classified according to the type of processing they implicitly demand of such a reader. Those that favor top-down processing are based, like classical argument, on established forms or schemata brought to the text. Schema-based options require that the reader be acquainted with various organizational structures existing "outside the text." These options represent socially shared strategies of response, ways of "sorting factors, sizing up situations" that have become part of the rhetorical competence of those belonging to a particular discourse community, a community that the advanced student writer is being asked to join (Coe 19).

The reader, through top-down processing, uses these frameworks brought to the text as a primary source for interpretation and evaluation (de Beaugrande 163). Arrangement options favoring bottom-up processing, on the other hand, are rooted in text-specific strategies. These text-based options tend to find their initial identity in linguistic and textual properties. For example, the sentence, "He was a compelling presence from the start, this Iowa-born farm boy who wore all black and no hat, and swept his full blond hair back away from his ruddy face," becomes a transition primarily because of its place in the text and not because it takes a form that has been traditionally recognized as transitional by the discourse community. The reader, in theory at least, must look to such text-specific entries to negotiate the text successfully. In so doing, the reader relies to a certain extent on bottom-up processing to complete the discourse act.

This is not to say that reading is ever exclusively a top-down or a bottom-up procedure. Reading almost always involves the integration of these two processes, with top-down dominating (Spiro 255; Morgan and Sellner 181-95). What is important here is that the advanced student writer, in looking at arrangement options as involving certain types of reader processing, learn to perceive various organizational choices in terms of the reader. These organizational choices are "aids to effect meaning," not because the writer is using them, but because the *reader* is.

---

[3] In recommending Augustine and Winterowd's ideas for student review, I recognize that the authors themselves think that the best use of their theory is as "an aid to the teacher's formal understanding of the discipline more than as an immediate editing tool for the student" (143). What I am arguing for, however, is an increased awareness on the student's part as well.

Works Cited

Anderson, Paul V. *Technical Writing: A Reader-Centered Approach.* San Diego: Harcourt, 1987.

Augustine, Dorothy, and W. Ross Winterowd. "Speech Acts and the Reader-Writer Connection." *Convergences: Transactions in Reading and Writing.* Ed. Bruce T. Petersen. Urbana: NCTE, 1986. 127-48.

Bruffee, Kenneth A. "Social Construction, Language, and the Authority of Knowledge: A Bibliographical Essay." *College English* 48 (1986): 773-90.

Coe, Richard M. "An Apology for Form, or, Who Took the Form Out of the Process?" *College English* 49 (1987): 13-28.

Coles, Nicholas, and Susan M. Wall. "Conflict and Power in the Reader-Responses of Adult Basic Writers." *College English* 49 (1987): 298-314.

Cooper, Marilyn M. "The Ecology of Writing." *College English* 48 (1986): 364-75.

Corder, Jim W. *Contemporary Writing: Process and Practice.* 1979. Glenview, IL: Scott, 1983.

de Beaugrande Robert. *Text, Discourse, and Process: Toward a Multidisciplinary Science of Texts.* Norwood, NJ: Ablex, 1980.

Dillon, George L. *Constructing Texts: Elements of a Theory of Composition and Style.* Bloomington: Indiana UP, 1981.

Elbow, Peter. "Closing My Eyes as I Speak: An Argument for Ignoring Audience." *College English* 49 (1987): 50-69.

Emerson, Caryl. "The Outer World and Inner Speech: Bakhtin, Vygotsky, and the Internalization of Language." *Bakhtin: Essays and Dialogues on His Work.* Ed. Gary Saul Morrison. Chicago: U of Chicago P, 1986. 21-40.

Flower, Linda. *Problem-Solving Strategies for Writing.* New York: Harcourt, 1981.

Freed, Richard C., and Glenn J. Broadhead. "Discourse Communities, Sacred Texts, and Institutional Norms." *College Composition and Communication* 38 (1987): 154-65.

George, Diana. "Working with Peer Groups in the Composition Class." *College Composition and Communication* 35 (1984): 320-26.

Goetz, Ernest T., and Bonnie B. Armbruster. "Psychological Correlates of Text Structure." Spiro, et al. 201-20.

Haas, Christina, and Linda Flower. "Rhetorical Reading Strategies and the Construction of Meaning." *College Composition and Communication* 39 (1988): 167-83.

Hirsch, E.D., Jr. *The Philosophy of Composition.* Chicago: U of Chicago P, 1977.

_____. "Reading, Writing, and Cultural Literacy." *Composition and Literature: Bridging the Gap.* Ed. Winifred Bryan Horner. Chicago: U of Chicago P, 1983. 141-47.

Hunter, Paul. "'that we have divided/In three our kingdom': The Communication Triangle and *A Theory of Discourse*. *College English* 48 (1986): 279-87.

Kinneavy, James L. *A Theory of Discourse.* New York: Norton, 1971.

Kroll, Barry M. "Writing for Readers: Three Perspectives on Audience." *College Composition and Communication* 35 (1984): 172-85.

Morgan, Jerry L., and Manfred F. Sellner. "Discourse and Linguistic Theory." Spiro, et al. 165-200.

Morson, Gary Saul, ed. *Bakhtin: Essays and Dialogues on His Work.* Chicago: U of Chicago P, 1986.

Newcomb, Theodore. "An Approach to the Study of Communicative Acts." *Psychological Review* 60 (1953): 393-404.

Newkirk, Thomas. "Direction and Misdirection in Peer Response." *College Composition and Communication* 35 (1984): 301-11.

Rosenblatt, Louise. *The Reader, The Text, The Poem: The Transactional Theory of Literary Work.* Carbondale: Southern Illinois UP, 1978.

Rumelhart, David E. "Schemata: The Building Blocks of Cognition." Spiro, et al. 33-58.

Schramm, Wilbur, ed. *The Process and Effects of Mass Communication.* Urbana: U of Illinois P, 1954.

Schuster, Charles I. "Mikhail Bakhtin as Rhetorical Theorist." *College English* 47 (1985): 594-607.

Severin, Werner J., and James W. Tankard, Jr. *Communication Theories: Origins, Methods, Uses.* New York: Hastings, 1979.

Shaughnessy, Mina P. *Errors and Expectations.* New York: Oxford UP, 1977.

Spiro, Rand J. "Constructive Processes in Prose Comprehension and Recall." Spiro, et al. 249-78.

Spiro, Rand J., Bertram C. Bruce, and William F. Brewer, eds. *Theoretical Issues in Reading Comprehension.* Hillsdale, NJ: Erlbaum, 1980.

Walzer, Arthur E. "Articles from the 'California Divorce Project': A Case Study of the Concept of Audience." *College Composition and Communication* 36 (1985): 150-59.

Young, Richard E., Alton L. Becker, and Kenneth L. Pike. *Rhetoric: Discovery and Change.* New York: Harcourt, 1970.

Balancing Individual Projects and Collaborative Learning in an Advanced Writing Class

by Felicia Mitchell

When we design a course in writing, we join that debate "over whether we should see individual cognition or social and cultural context as the motive force in literate acts" (Flower 282). To remind us of this debate, Linda Flower recently asked, "Can we . . . reconcile a commitment to nurturing a personal voice, individual purpose, or an inner, self-directed process of making meaning, with rhetoric's traditional assumption that both inquiry and purpose are responses to rhetorical situations, or with the more recent assertions that inquiry in writing must start with social, cultural, or political awareness?" (282). Those three commitments are not really incongruous. All three can be found "reconciled" in the advanced composition course described below. As a course built by students around individualized projects, it encourages students to apply general principles to specialized tasks. "Good writers," according to Richard M. Coe, "know how to apply general principles of composition to particular writing tasks and contexts" (412).

With so many different projects resulting from this approach, students' divergent interests must be shared in an atmosphere of collaboration. John Trimbur has stated that "one of the goals of collaborative learning is to replace the traditional hierarchical relations of teaching and learning with the practices of participatory democracy" (611). Yet even collaborative models need to leave the instructor with a certain authority. For example, James A. Reither and Douglas Vipond, whose teaching model is based on collaboration, suggest that "the most powerful way to arrange this kind of situation is to organize a course so students collaboratively investigate a more or less original scholarly question or field. The teacher sets a long-range research project or question for the class, casting the students as members of a research group" (863).

The final exam in my course acts as that "long-range research project." This assignment, which is submitted to students on the first day of class, summarizes related tasks from the course and illustrates how collaboration can be encouraged through a common assignment:

> For your final examination, you will prepare a style handbook based on
> the type of writing you have studied closely. In it, you will identify the

From *College Composition and Communication* 43 (1992): 393-400. © by NCTE. Reprinted with permission.

of writing; define your audience; compare/contrast this type of writing to other models we have studied; classify stylistic elements; synthesize what you have learned about writing from peers and relate it to your specialization; analyze examples of text from your writing and from the annotated bibliography of sources; and evaluate the usefulness or relevance of this type of writing. You will be evaluated on the handbook's comprehensiveness, accuracy, readability, and organization, as I assess how much you have learned from the annotated bibliography project, reading assignments, writing projects, oral reports, lectures, workshops, and so on.

While individuals specialize in a particular type of writing in this final project, all students are called upon to see interrelationships throughout the course. In what follows, I will sketch an outline of the class, describe how selected students have responded to different elements of it, and comment on what I have learned using this approach. For the sake of organization, I have simplified and adapted Flower's framework.

The Pressure and the Potential of the Social Context

The student's first task is to choose a context for expression. Past projects have situated students in many environments, from the battered women's shelter to the architect's drawing board to the dentist's office. After (and during) choice of context comes the search for models. What type of writing is produced in a particular environment or context? Why? An annotated bibliography project answers these questions as the student rhetorically and stylistically analyzes models. The bibliography assignment I make early in the course states,

> You will analyze the texts of at least 20 models of expository writing from your area of academic and/or professional interest; three of these models must be considered "classics" in the field. Each entry may focus on a particular stylistic element, or it may look at a number of elements such as diction, tone, format, organizational strategy, and sentence types. Your job is to provide a consistently-rigorous, comprehensive analysis of text. Many of our discussions of reading assignments will help you to learn how to analyze text. Also, we will spend one class session to discuss your proposed project, and each of you will meet with me individually to firm up your project. We will spend a class session workshopping analyses before you turn in the final project. This bibliography will establish your personal framework for your participation in the course.

As students search for and read models, I teach them how to analyze text to see what makes a piece of writing work on the page and to understand how the text was constructed. Several communication models including Kinneavy's are introduced. Examples of levels of diction and syntax are used for analysis so students can see how language is adapted to different audiences.

Searching for models can lead to some initial contact outside the college. Interested in battered women's shelters, Paula Webber wanted to find out how public service announcements, brochures, pamphlets, and posters can appeal to people least likely to want to change self-defeating behavior; she combined a study of persuasive techniques with her analysis of models largely provided by a human services agency. Amanda Gilmer collected and studied the models of rhetoric used by the pro-life movement. Greg MacMillan visited numerous automobile dealers to explore those posters, brochures, and pamphlets available to prospective buyers.

Even when students do not interact with outside agencies, they can develop a sense of professionalism and gain credibility in the class to stand as experts in their different areas. Christy Rector, for example, practiced writing a *belles lettres* type of essay after analyzing essays in mainstream literary journals. Other students find models in trade journals, magazines, books, and the like. Anne P. Thomas read among essays by female, feminist writers utilizing the personal voice. Taught in good English style to do what she called "suppress the self and become enculturated," Thomas was delighted to find "invaluable lessons in writing, expression, and ultimately, feminism." She wrote in the introduction to her bibliography: "I have been given authority from them to write from the very soul of me, to write without trying to give equal time to 'the other side' in every instance, and to write from my personal experience. I think I expected to learn that. At least, I needed to hear it. But what I did not expect to learn was the value of the familiar writing style—the value of humor, of kindness, of everyday speech."

Creating Goals

The pressure and potential of a social context, then, lead individual students to contemplate their relation to a discourse community and, correspondingly, to propose a semester's emphasis. Formal development of writing assignments grows out of the bibliography project and helps students to articulate goals. These assignments also help me to gauge students' intentions. The following heuristic for helping students construct assignments involves a series of prompts based on rhetorical dimensions, instructional dimensions, and cognitive objectives:

My topic is. . . .
The occasion for which this paper is suited is. . . .
My audience is. . . .
In order to prepare to write this paper, I must. . . .
The primary purpose of this piece of writing is. . . .
A secondary purpose might include. . . .
The style appropriate to this type of writing is. . . .
My paper will be organized according to this strategy. . . .
A primary mode of exposition will be. . . .
Secondary modes of expression may include. . . .
I anticipate the following length. . . .
The time frame for working from preparation through drafts to final copy is. . . .
The following format is suitable for preparing my manuscript. . . .
The following criteria should be included in my writing's evaluation. . . .

Assignments submitted with papers usually are not as detailed as this heuristic would suggest they could be. Topic, purpose, audience, and style get the most attention. Eddie James's observation that "entertainment writers usually try to appeal to the masses, which means writing on about a seventh-grade level" introduced his description of the style he utilized in an article on the evolution of the singer Tiffany. Sometimes assignments change during the process of sharing work with the class. Jonathan Jonas decided to direct one of his sermons to a youth ministry as the class led him to realize that his examples and tone in one sermon were more appropriate for teenagers.

It is at this planning stage that things will go wrong, if I am not careful to work closely with students as they design their writing projects. Poor choice of models can lead to poor writing assignments and thus to poor experiences. One semester, for example, a future English teacher interested in reviews of adolescent literature chose all models from one source—paragraph-long reviews (more advertisement than criticism) given to librarians to enable them to make their decisions about book purchasing. My early suggestion—which *remained* a suggestion because in the first days of teaching this course I allowed students too much freedom—that she also look at the more popular journals in language education did not make an impression. She set no real goals and learned little from writing her capsule reviews. Not seeing the connection between models and assignments can also hurt writing projects. Once a student with an interest in public relations writing ignored the models reviewed for her bibliography and instead largely repeated writing tasks she had done in other courses and did not learn anything new. She did not use the bibliography project to grow but saw it as a discrete activity unrelated to the rest of the semester.

Working with students who do not push themselves enough, I have learned to intervene more during the planning stage. Consequently, when Peter Gretz wanted to write provocative, fundamentalist prose, I was able to steer him away from his initial desire to write personal essays about his views to find public avenues for expressing his opinions. The heuristic helped him to think his goals through and develop assignments. And his opinions gained more authority as he found he could channel them into articles suitable for the type of Christian magazines he studied. Other students have benefited from this type of intervention as well.

Negotiating the Context: Skills and Process

To negotiate context and accomplish goals, students end up exploring the individual writing skills of the authors they read and the basic writing needs in their respective areas of interest, and they learn to relate these to the projects they develop. To encourage a process approach to writing and build community, I assign homework exercises, oral reports during which students introduce a concept or technique from their project to the class and encourage the class to relate it to other types of writing, peer-review workshops, oral readings, multiple drafts, and so on.

Homework exercises which help students to look more closely at how language works are based on models of writing in a special class reader composed of writing by faculty, staff, alumni, and students of Emory & Henry College. Students learn to analyze and discuss stylistic elements such as tone, or to replicate organizational strategies found in, for example, a research report. While exercises in style related to the annotated bibliography help students to emulate other writers, exercises drawn from models in a common reader lead them to experiment with their emerging textual authority to transform text and to create it. For instance, in response to a series of homework exercises which were related to a geographer's field report on tobacco barns and which prompted students to rewrite a section of it in their own particular styles, Leigh Ann Skeens said: "At first glance, I did not see how movie reviews and tobacco barns could possibly relate. What I realized, though, was that my technique of using positive and negative adjectives to convey my opinion in a subtle way made rewriting this article much easier. I was able to create a positive or subjective tone in the article that had been missing before, so that more people would find the piece interesting to read rather than boring because of all its information and jargon."

In addition to offering models for analysis, the reader provides a common reading experience and shows students that the college houses a varied community of writers. Students like the reader because they know or know of the authors. Professors and other authority figures seem a little more real. And when a homework assignment guides students to analyze the changes made in a series of drafts for an essay published in the alumni magazine, they find more respect for the work of the hidden but industrious support staff. John Allman, who had previously perceived the president only as administrator, was pleasantly surprised by an assignment comparing a speech he made to a group of civic leaders at a Jewish community center to its revision as an editorial in *The Chronicle of Higher Education*. In analyzing the transformation of language from spoken to written, in discussing the constraints different audiences place on a writer, this student found the president's humanity in a piece he had written on why he has dedicated his life to teaching the holocaust.

Workshops and peer review are successful despite the students' seemingly divergent interests, as well as because of them. As students gain familiarity with different projects, they are able to respond to writing as hypothetical audiences and as objective critics. Process and context interrelate. Robert Allen, already editor of and a writer for the school newspaper, reported this in a course evaluation: "Reading my papers aloud not only gave me some needed experience in speaking within a group, but helped me gain confidence in my own writing." It is interesting to note that Allen used "within a group" instead of "to a group"; despite his singular writing project, he found solidarity within the group. As community spirit grows, trust allows students to criticize well. Regina Ellis noted that she "liked having immediate feedback, whether positive or negative, so that I could learn how audiences perceived my written intentions." Feedback is an integral component of the course. Students offer critiques of each other's initial drafts, and I respond to a final draft which is in turn revised for the portfolio, which is submitted at the end of the course for a grade.

Creating Meaning

The selection of a social context, creation of writing goals, and subsequent negotiations all lead to the primary purpose of the course, which is to encourage students to create meaning and develop a sense of themselves as authors. Discussions of the role of prior knowledge in the construction of meaning by both writers and audiences help students see how writing is learning, not just telling. Amanda Gilmer began her project by reading widely in the rhetoric of the anti-abortion or pro-life movement. She collected brochures from religious organizations and articles from religious magazines. Initial reading of her models led Amanda also to read "objective" pieces on the two sides to the abortion debate in order to understand what she would be fighting against. Then after her first anti-abortion pieces, she decided to compose some pro-choice "rhetoric" to get inside the heads of pro-choicers. Strong in her own convictions, Amanda broadened her perspective not to change beliefs but to enhance her general knowledge and make her rhetoric more logical.

Students also like to create meaning from their own experiences. If they choose to specialize in the "personal essay," they must select a publication source that will guide their process and keep their writing from being solely expressive. They must find a context for their expression. Charlene Joye, a returning student and mother, wrote a series of newspaper columns on effective parenting. Ben Robertson wrote this of Charlene's project in his course evaluation: "The theoretical and the political are not difficult to talk about for most people, but to merge them with one's own experience is another matter. Charly comes to my mind, perhaps because she got so very personal; she put her own experience of being a mother, including what she considers some of her failures, into papers that looked into the problems involved in effective parenting." Stylistic considerations which grow out of a sense of a real audience help students to slant and package personal meaning.

Affecting Others through Writing

Unless students put their writing to work outside the course, effects on others are primarily course-related. The most immediate effect is on simple writing growth. As students listen to oral reports and read the myriad styles of writing, their definitions of writing grow; in turn, they find that they have more control over the process than they might have thought previously. Michael Miller, who had worked on perfecting a "new journalism" style, noted in a course evaluation that "Connie [whose project was based on magazine-style scientific writing, such as that found in *Discovery*] really helped me with my problems with concreteness and abstract images. She showed me how to be more solid so people can understand what I have to say. She also taught me how to integrate facts into my images." The divergent interests and projects also have an effect on students as they learn about, for example, car advertisements, edible wild plants, or feminism. Some of the subjects they are introduced to are more palatable, it seems, because instruction in them comes from peers as information, not as gospel. Elizabeth McWhorter, who during the first week of class asked me if she would be required to use the inclusive language required by the college's Inclusive Language Policy (to which I said, "No, as long as you avoid the issue."), responded to an oral report and the discussion that ensued in her course evaluation: "I would say Anne Thomas's project was farthest from my interests because of the feminist overtones. I don't consider myself a feminist but found that I agree with a lot of her ideas in the paper about how she tried to relate her newfound feminist ideas to her high school friends. They seemed to consider the subject completely irrelevant so they misunderstood her. I saw myself at first like one of those friends but thought more deeply about feminism and found that I agree now with most of what it suggests."

Collaboration and the Teacher

Writing instruction at its best empowers; there's no place for indoctrination. Phyllis Spiegel, discussing the difference between passive and active learning, criticized indoctrination in her 1988 commencement speech at Emory & Henry College: "Unless students stand up and demand their education, they will be powerless to learn what they feel is important to them." In her advanced writing course, she had observed to me earlier, she was allowed to demand and learn what was important to her. So many people writing about composition instruction today also agree that students should learn what is important to them. Yet we are timid to experiment with or continue some of the very methods designed to empower students (or else we do not trust students to know what is best). Reither and Vipond acknowledge that timidity or mistrust and report that "traditional classroom concerns have not been superseded by such prior questions as how and why these features of writing might originate, how, why and where they might be learned, and what kinds of circumstances, needs, and motives lead people to want to learn and use them" (855).

Perhaps some of us are afraid to grant students authority because we fear that our roles will be undermined, that our education will go unheard. It is true that between the first day of class and the last, my students are responsible for learning what is important to them. But the instructor does not become obsolete. My job is to orchestrate: I probe students to find out what they really want to focus on; help them find models of writing; discuss the elements of style and teach students to analyze style as a basis for designing their projects; ask questions that encourage deeper reading of models; comment on drafts; present evaluative workshops based on common patterns of error in each set of papers that I read; push students to work beyond what they perceive as their capacities. I also keep roll, grade portfolios and final examinations, talk about my own writing process, and share projects. My identity as a teacher then grows in proportion to my students' growth as writers.

Works Cited

Coe, Richard M. *Process, Form, and Substance: A Rhetoric for Advanced Writers.* Englewood Cliffs: Prentice, 1990.

Flower, Linda. "Cognition, Context, and Theory Building." *College Composition and Communication* 40 (1989): 282-311.

Kinneavy, James. *A Theory of Discourse.* Englewood Cliffs: Prentice, 1971.

Reither, James A., and Douglas Vipond. "Writing as Collaboration." *College English* 51 (1989): 855-67.

Trimbur, John. "Critiquing Collaborative Learning." *College English* 51 (Oct. 1989): 602-16.

Denial, Conflagration, Pride: Three Stages in the Development of an Advanced Writing Requirement

by Ann Kimble Loux and Rebecca M. Stoddart

The following narrative describes the long road to a successful advanced writing requirement taught entirely by the full-time faculty of a small liberal arts college. We hope that our story will suggest short cuts for other writing teachers and administrators, and that the illustration of how all can end well will encourage others on the journey.

Background and Context

The Saint Mary's College writing-across-the-disciplines program is entering its twenty-first year; thus it has managed to survive for a generation. Thanks in part to circumstances such as size and a faculty dedicated to teaching—1,700 students, small classes and a 11/1 student faculty ratio—over two-thirds of the faculty have become involved through the years with teaching writing to students at every level. During a curricular review in 1983, faculty at the college, with a few dissenting opinions, decided to integrate an ambitious advanced writing requirement (advanced W), taught entirely by full-time faculty, into all twenty-one majors at the college. General satisfaction with the achievements of the introductory level W in content courses led faculty to believe that students were capable of sustaining comparable progress in their majors. Thus faculty instituted a curricular revision, having agreed only on the idealistic goal of involving every teacher at the college in teaching writing.

With the aid of a three-year development grant from the Lilly Foundation, faculty in each department set out to articulate specific writing goals for graduating seniors: They asked what writing chemists and sociologists are asked to do; what writing tasks are handed to a new employee at IBM; what expectations graduate schools have in terms of writing skills. After considerable discussion and compromise, faculty specified the kinds of assignments their majors were to collect in a portfolio and detailed logistics for submitting and evaluating these papers.

In introductory-level writing courses across the curriculum, faculty had been working for ten years with college-wide evaluation of portfolios and were generally pleased with the results. Evaluation had become more consistent over the years; even more important, portfolio review served as a brief and comprehensive

From *College Composition and Communication* 45 (1994): 521-34. © 1994 by NCTE. Reprinted with permission.

in-service training session for both new and experienced writing teachers. Over the last few years, the review had become an opportunity for faculty to display students' progress with pride and to receive compliments from their colleagues on the general success of a set of portfolios. Because portfolios had proved so successful in introductory W courses, teachers of majors' courses decided to use a similar collection and review process for the advanced W. The hope was that the prospect of a portfolio would enlarge the students' sense of audience beyond their individual teachers and simultaneously engage teachers in deliberation about writing pedagogy, encouraging a developmental progression of assignments and courses through the major. At the outset most faculty members conceded the theoretical need to compromise and reach consensus on standards if they expected to evaluate portfolios fairly.

Although some members of the writing program steering committee argued for college-wide standards, in the end department faculty developed criteria for the advanced W on their own, with only general models and advice from writing program directors. A long tradition of autonomous departments at the college made any other process unrealistic. In addition, writing program history suggested that because it had been allowed to develop organically and idiosyncratically within departments, the introductory W was imaginative in ways no outside organizer could have anticipated. The directors of the writing program (one each from the disciplines of biology, English, humanistic studies, philosophy, and psychology) also believed that faculty who articulated their own goals and developed their own methods were more likely to improve and promote the program in the future.

Because any new requirement for graduation can apply only to incoming freshman, departments had between three and four years to work out procedures on paper and to experiment with the most challenging components of the new requirement. Faculty spent the first year formulating advanced W proposals, and the next four semesters developing assignments, responding to drafts, working through revisions, and evaluating sample portfolios. National writing consultants and successful teachers from the college offered as much advice as teachers were able to absorb. Nothing seemed too difficult during those exploratory years; at times enthusiasm even ran high. After all, most discussions were hypothetical and the samples rarely involved messy papers and threatened students.

The First Stage: Denial

In August of 1989, the summer before beginning the gradual implementation of departmental advanced W proposals, the co-directors of the program sent out a questionnaire asking faculty how they expected the new requirement to change their major. Surprisingly, every respondent but one anticipated little or no effect. In some respects this optimism was a good sign. Confident that they were already doing all they could to teach writing, departments expected little change. In other respects this expectation that the advanced W would not affect the major signaled that a number of faculty were either unwilling to take the new requirement seriously or unable to conceptualize additional possibilities for integrating writing assignments and content. Two departments simply changed labels, making their senior comprehensives equivalent to the advanced W requirement. Numerous faculty declared writing irrelevant or impossible to include in their syllabuses. In one large department where few instructors were writers, faculty no doubt realized full well that taking writing seriously would have a huge impact on their major. Rather than make a commitment in that direction, however, they agreed to see how other departments dealt with the new requirement before taking portfolio collection and review seriously. In a side-step that avoided the whole evaluation procedure, their majors were simply required to file three "B" papers with the department secretary.

The best indication that faculty did not yet see writing and learning as integrally related was the fact that *no* department deleted or recombined content and writing assignments in order to compensate for the added work required to complete a portfolio. Cutting content, regardless of the reason, was regarded as a savage and unnecessary operation by the vast majority of faculty members. Instead, virtually every department moved in the opposite direction, using the advanced W as an "add-on" to their major curriculum. One department, for example, specified that the third required paper in the portfolio had to be the research paper which some faculty members had always yearned to include somewhere in the major. But nowhere did the department add instruction in research methods or step-by-step assistance with completing such a complex intellectual task. Another department detailed five challenging assignments for the portfolio; however, only two of those five assignments were built into major courses. The advanced W in these instances was manipulated into a "wish list" or a directed reading, without credit for either students or faculty members.

Not only did many departments increase previous writing requirements, but in virtually every major an additional substantial burden was added to students' loads by the expectation that they complete revisions on their portfolio submissions outside of class—often as long as a year after completing the course in which the paper was submitted. Thus students were simultaneously writing new papers and revising old ones, to an exacting standard in many cases. The writing program coordinators, worried about the directions things were taking, attempted to respond to escalating student and faculty complaints and emphasized the integration of drafts into faculty syllabuses. But discontent among both students and faculty was growing.

The Second Stage: Conflagration

During the second year of the advanced W both faculty and student frustration with the new requirement reached its height. Faculty who were comfortable and confident teachers of content suddenly found themselves to be halting and questioning teachers of writing. "I made so many mistakes," the humble groaned, "How can my students write about art or Aristophanes when they can't connect a subject with a verb?" the frustrated complained. As majors faced the challenge of writing about increasingly difficult subject matter, their writing often seemed to deteriorate rather than improve.

The general approach of simply adding on writing topics to an already unwieldy curriculum insured that early experiences with the advanced W would be quick and clear disasters. The number of new assignments probably also hastened the bitter news the advanced W was destined to place squarely in front of faculty noses: Stu-

dents were not being taught to write nearly as well in their major classes as had
been assumed. Prior to the advanced W the picture had not looked nearly so bleak
to faculty who never or rarely assigned writing or who dealt with only a paper or
two in each class—in batches of twenty to thirty, always with the major focus on content. Forced by advanced W submissions to take a comprehensive and focused
view of the writing weaknesses among each department's majors, faculty were overwhelmed, despairing, and angry. Especially threatening to individual faculty members was the fact that papers originally submitted in their own classes were often
found unsatisfactory when reevaluated within a portfolio to meet the advanced W
requirement.

The implications of this new accumulation of information were disturbing. Students had been graduating regularly with poor to mediocre writing skills, which faculty had successfully ignored. More devastating still, students had been preparing
papers their teachers would not objectively evaluate as satisfactory, but these same
teachers had not stopped covering material long enough to help students develop
the writing skills necessary to complete their papers satisfactorily. With such a clear
profile of the lack of writing skills in virtually all disciplines, faculty were forced into
a difficult choice: Would they deny or ignore that the students were not learning, or
would they organize to help them? Not surprisingly, many teachers at the college
developed a line of defensive and blame-laying behaviors, too personal and distract-
ing to chronicle here. More challenging to explore is why, in department after department, perceptions of what students in general were accomplishing were so out
of sync with what individual students had actually been producing all along. Why
were so many faculty overwhelmed by a sense of inadequacy and despair the first
year of the advanced W requirement?

There were good reasons why teachers—particularly those in business, the sciences, and social sciences—felt frustrated and overwhelmed in their first attempts to
teach and evaluate writing along with content material in major courses. Their own
educational backgrounds had rarely prepared them to be writing teachers; even
among humanists few had the experience of handling a class full of flawed first
drafts. Unaccustomed to seeing beyond mistakes of every variety to a paper's potential, new writing teachers often felt powerless to meet the enormously varied
needs in a class of twenty-five individuals. Few colleagues in any discipline could
recall writing drafts or revising papers during their own undergraduate years. Most
college teachers learned to revise for a master's thesis or dissertation, when they
knew quite a lot about the material and were highly motivated to perform well.
There was a world of difference, therefore, between what many teachers expected
from a draft and what undergraduates were capable of generating. There was a
world of difference, too, between faculty members' current writing context and that
of their students. Most teachers worked so long on a few pages of prose that they
scarcely remembered the mess of their first attempts. They also typically produced
far fewer words over several years than some students were asked to produce in
one semester. As a result, novice writing teachers tended to expect entirely too
much of their students initially and then to become discouraged and even bitter
early in the writing process.

While most teachers outside the humanities recalled any number of excellent content teachers, many remembered only poor writing teaching in their disciplines. Faculty in the social and natural sciences did not learn good methods for helping students become autonomous writers in graduate school. In order to do research in someone else's laboratory, like many other graduate students, they typically had to agree to work on a mentor's project or on an individual project that dove-tailed nicely with ongoing work. When the time came to write up results, they had little input or recognition. Unfortunately, this model did not work well in their own teaching of undergraduates; it led them to be too directive of their students' compositions.

Another reason some non-humanities faculty had difficulty adjusting to teaching writing was that for years they had relied on tests to validate students' learning. Ordinarily class performances on objective tests approximated a bell-shaped curve: a high percentage of Bs, some As and Cs and only a small number of Ds. Faculty even saw students' occasional failures as expected and let them drop one quiz grade. If a test failed to produce a satisfactory bell shape, the teacher redesigned the test and/or teaching methods until things came out as they should. In this context faculty rested easy that the occasional failure fit into a pattern of how humans learn. When faculty accustomed to such predictable results began to make formal writing assignments in their major classes, their ease with themselves as teachers was suddenly challenged. On a first advanced W assignment, for example, the novice writing teacher typically faced a whole class of "rewrites," a whole set of results at the lower end of the curve. As yet unable to anticipate students' slow progress through revision, these novices were likely to become discouraged and interpret their students' "failures" as their own. Faculty who made the mistake of giving grades on these early drafts were besieged by distraught students who also, precipitously, perceived themselves as having failed.

The whole matter of grading further exacerbated the discomfort of novice writing teachers. Those who were accustomed to more objective and clear-cut measures were often uncomfortable with the inevitably subjective and emotionally sensitive components of grading writing, regardless of how hard they tried to objectify the product with explicit directions and numerical evaluation. Nor was the matter as simple for the inexperienced writing teacher as recording the grades, handing back the papers, and moving on to new material. Teaching writing well requires teachers to help students make something out of those messy beginnings both might much rather forget. Grades on papers are thus necessarily delayed longer than on tests, and both teachers and students often found this new delay in closure anxiety-provoking.

If individual faculty members were this dissatisfied with themselves as writing teachers, it is not difficult to imagine the level of frustration when whole departments of unhappy individuals met behind closed doors to thrash out their standards of evaluation. Before the new advanced W requirement, faculty were fully aware of the differences in standards within departments, but as often as possible, they tried to ignore rather than resolve these differences, no doubt having concluded long ago that it was good for students to negotiate a variety of well-informed if idiosyncratic preferences. Such individualism went unquestioned when there was no audience for writing beyond the classroom teacher, but it wreaked havoc on portfolio readings. In the end students suffered.

During the first and second year of advanced portfolio review, conflicting faculty criteria got in the way of a more appropriate focus on learning to teach writing. Faculty often found themselves split between those who believed that undergraduates should be writing for a general audience and those who wanted students rigorously trained in professional writing. If a student's personal narrative was submitted to a faculty member who assigned only research papers, the ensuing suggestions for revision often left the student confused and angry. On occasion when students' literature reviews or technical research reports were submitted to faculty members fresh out of graduate school, the demands for stylistic correctness left students wondering what the criteria for publication in a professional journal had to do with them. Faculty within the same department also disagreed frequently and vehemently about when work on a portfolio submission was complete. Many evaluators took to heart— with a vengeance—the dictum that writing is revision. In the first year of portfolio submission, paper after paper was returned to student after student with extensive suggestions for revision. It did not matter how many semesters earlier the paper had been written, if the faculty advisor was no longer on the continent, if papers written later in the major did not show any of the same weaknesses. Indeed, students were often so distracted by extensive revisions on faintly-remembered past efforts that their focus was splintered from the class work at hand.

Although disputes over standards within departments were fully expected, other departmental decisions came as more of a surprise—the choice, for example, by several departments during the first and second year of the advanced W to read the entire portfolios of graduating seniors in March or April. It was, of course, impossible at that point to have a serious evaluation because it was not humane either to make substantial demands for revision or to deny graduation to a senior at the end of second semester. More problematic still, students were given virtually no chance to learn from their mistakes, much less bask in success. If they received a poor portfolio review just prior to graduation students felt insulted; those who received praise felt unfulfilled, given the hastiness of those ninth-hour assessments.

Put in the most pragmatic terms, the aim of portfolio review was to use social pressure to bring about better teaching of writing. In the early months of the process, however, many teachers had anything but such collegial feelings. In fact, both novice and experienced teachers of writing described feeling exposed and threatened when their students' papers fell into the hands of their colleagues. Before the advanced W, both well and poorly designed assignments had remained private. Portfolio review, however, brought all writing teachers into the marketplace and exposed their wares for inspection by critical eyes. The possibilities for developing open pedagogical exchanges remained attractive; however, the discomfort caused by such a public teaching forum, especially for those long accustomed to privacy, presented a major hurdle.

Finally, the most common objection of all—among even a dedicated and enlightened facult—was the complaint that teaching writing took too much time and that the results were not worth the agony. Dutiful faculty were almost swept away by waves of revisions, from courses present and past. Anguished reports from students made it sound as if teachers had incorporated dozens of writing topics, scores of drafts and revisions into the curriculum, far too many for anyone on either side of the desk to handle. On bad days such objections appeared to be irrefutable. By the spring of 1991, the second year of the graduation requirement, the advanced W seemed not such a good idea at all. In the midst of so much doubt over whether the new addition to the curriculum was helping students learn better or eroding morale across the campus, a few outspoken opponents of the requirement called a meeting of departmental chairs and proposed the elimination of the advanced W as a graduation requirement, effective immediately. Attending the meeting, however, were also defenders of the requirement who blocked its precipitous elimination from the curriculum. After two years faculty seemed to be polarized on the subject of the advanced writing requirement. Caught in the thick of the dispute, writing program directors wondered whether continuing such a controversial requirement would do more harm than good.

The Third Stage: Taking Pride In Major Accomplishments

Fortunately, by graduation in the spring of 1992 there was a pervasive sense among faculty that student writing had improved substantially during the previous three years and that this improvement was the direct result of the advanced W requirement. Portfolio reviews had become more pleasurable than painful, in many cases occasions of pride for both teacher and student. It took the majority of a dedicated and intelligent faculty somewhat less than three years to retrain themselves as effective writing teachers and to set up procedures and guidelines to help students develop good portfolios. This remarkable turnabout occurred at least in part because the demolition proved more difficult than anticipated: The annoying writing program refused to take its cue and gracefully exit. The real cause of such a major shift in attitude, however, came from more positive sources—from thorough groundwork and from trust and responsibility.

Part of its support system during this period of stress was the writing program's diverse leadership. During the early years of the introductory W, the program was directed by members of the English Department. With the movement toward the advanced W, faculty from psychology, philosophy, biology and humanistic studies moved gradually into positions as co-chairs. Currently four faculty direct the program each year for the compensation of a one-course reduction each. This organization has, the directors of the program suspect, been a fortunate choice. There is no *one* writing person, no one-dimensional fanatic from the English Department, no outside agitator bringing in newfangled ideas that mean a lot of extra work for everyone. Leadership that wears many hats, that permeates many departments and committees does not provide an easy target for anger and abuse.

From the outset of the advanced writing requirement each department had been responsible for establishing criteria for portfolio collection and review. Thus it was common knowledge, regardless of all projection and blame slinging, who was responsible when difficulties arose. Just as departments had been trusted to formulate their original criteria, they were also trusted to work out the glitches in their early drafts. In addition to offering encouragement and trying to build confidence among novice writing teachers, writing program directors scrambled to find help for a faculty in search of good teaching techniques. The best sources of successful methods proved to be from colleagues who were further along in the struggle than others. Many faculty gained credibility among their colleagues when they published papers on methods for teaching writing in major courses. The writing program sponsored numerous workshops where successful and published writing teachers addressed faculty complaints and questions, both directly and indirectly. Prior to each workshop writing program directors worked with speakers through several drafts of their presentations to insure the pertinence and quality of their remarks. Carefully chosen from across all disciplines, workshop presenters made the most persuasive case possible for the feasibility and desirability of the advanced W. Several faculty described how they struck a balance between their students' need to learn to write and their need to master content. They were most successful with assignments, these teachers reported, when they placed themselves and the discipline in the background and the student's interest and ability to communicate in the foreground. The authors of articles on teaching writing in education (Bryant, Traxler and Watson), math (Joanne Snow), and nursing (Cynthia Danford) described assignments that were developmentally and professionally appropriate for undergraduates. As a result, faculty began to gauge the quality of their assignments by whether the majority of their classes produced drafts with potential and revisions that showed progress.

A positive surprise was the eagerness with which many teachers in the professional disciplines accepted the challenge of integrating instruction in writing with content material. For example, Jerome McElroy, an economics professor, offered a workshop based on an article he had published in which he described how he had experimented with writing a paper himself along with his students over the course of a senior seminar. Instead of beginning with a draft of the entire paper, both professor and students wrote the first part of their papers, the introduction, and completed that section before they moved on to the second component, the research review, and so on, until all more or less simultaneously reached the data analyses and conclusions of their papers. Similarly, the two of us described methods of sequencing assignments that asked students to begin with a narrative and gradually add research findings to support their arguments or, alternately, to begin with one angle of a comparison (such as an analysis of a typical product of the educational system in B.F. Skinner's *Walden Two*) and extend the paper to include the second aspect of the comparison (such as an analysis of a typical product of the educational system in Carolyn Chute's *The Beans of Egypt, Maine*). Dividing writing topics into segments and completing each portion sequentially has been, according to teachers in both the professional disciplines and the humanities, one of the most successful pedagogical methods presented in writing workshops.

Professional dialogues within their disciplines about teaching writing as a vehicle to content mastery helped bring faculty to a more supportive stance toward the advanced W. As they had several years of experience, teachers at the college were quick to share their expertise with colleagues from other institutions struggling to integrate the teaching of writing and content. By the end of the third year of the new requirement, faculty in biology, economics, education, math, and nursing had made conference presentations, served as consultants, and written articles describing how incorporating writing into the curriculum was having synergistic effects upon their majors' high-level thinking skills: the ability to understand and critique hypotheses, question assumptions, develop theories, draw inferences, speculate about results. During the third year of the requirement most departments that had been frustrated by the advanced W made changes that were both sensible for faculty and helpful for students. Two years of workshops challenged faculty to enjoy the benefits of teaching—rather than simply assigning—writing in major classes. Several departments also began to study the sequence of courses, including writing topics, in their majors. Structural and procedural reorganizations usually involved managing the length, number and flow of papers. The process of reviewing a complete portfolio at the end of the major was also often reexamined and modified.

The single most significant change in writing pedagogy across the disciplines was the introduction of drafts into many syllabi. As faculty built drafts into the development of papers, conversations at writing workshops improved remarkably. Faculty began to discuss such sophisticated questions as whether or not to grade drafts, how many drafts and revisions were enough, how to get students—not teachers—to do the real work of revising, how to insure that faculty were aided and not abused by the word processor's capacity to generate clean copies. Faculty spread the word that student progress was gratifying even after the addition of one draft; stacks of revised papers proved to be so much less frustrating that building drafts into syllabi became almost popular. Faculty who would not incorporate drafts into their courses got little sympathy when they complained about dismal results. The growing emphasis on drafting and revising *within* courses gradually paved the way for smoother evaluation procedures. No longer were students expected to revise submissions for their portfolios outside of class; in most departments papers needed to have a teacher's approval by the end of the semester before they could be submitted for the advanced W. The need to receive this endorsement encouraged students to take their written work, and deadlines for assignments, more seriously.

Faculty who became convinced of the success of working through developmental stages within single assignments soon extended this insight to bear on entire courses and departmental requirements. During writing program workshops, teachers illustrated how they planned writing experiences in a developmental sequence, beginning, for example, with a summary or report or description and working through to a personal argument and then to speculation about possible explanations of the data collected. In several departments that later served as models, faculty sat down together, often for days, and honed a sequence of courses and assignments for the entire major (see Traxler and Watson for a sequence in education). Sophomore and junior psychology majors wrote two or more reflection papers and critiques of journal articles, assigned in several courses. Reflection papers and reviews of single articles were well within the range of beginning majors and good preparation for the research-based position paper or literature review assigned later in the junior and senior years. Such planning distributed the load of teaching writing across a department and insured a manageable schedule of writing assignments for students as they moved through the major.

The sequencing of portfolio evaluation followed naturally from the sequencing of writing topics within a major. This sensible move toward evaluating submission-by-submission helped both students and faculty focus on progress rather than on the failings of the less mature papers. Evaluating papers submitted early in a major's writing career also alerted faculty to which students had serious writing weaknesses and allowed time for intervention. Students were much happier with this more gradual approach to portfolio evaluation; juniors in psychology, like typical younger siblings, pointed out that the faculty were spending too much time with seniors and their portfolios, neglecting the sophomores and juniors, just when these new majors were ready to focus on writing. These students acknowledged as well that they wanted specific help with their weaknesses and recognition of their progress long before a portfolio was finally approved. As the number of papers, with their component revisions, seemed to multiply, many faculty began to question when enough was enough. "Too Much Writing as Bad as Too Little," was the topic of a workshop late in the third year of the advanced W. In essence, the faculty had come full circle and were ready to address the mistake made earlier when departments added on the advanced W requirement but failed to subtract anything from already overloaded major curricula. Faculty were finally asking what should be cut out of the curriculum to make room for writing, what kinds of writing assignments were more valuable than others, and what were appropriate lengths for undergraduate assignments.

A reality principle emerged the third year of the advanced W to replace the perfectionistic tendencies that had characterized faculty's evaluation standards during the first two years of the requirement. Working with drafts in their courses taught faculty how much improvement in students' writing they could realistically expect within a semester, how much progress could be made across the four semesters in most majors. As faculty within departments implemented and revised their requirements, they also revised their sense of the advanced W's goal: to help undergraduates write skillfully within their major disciplines, not to produce publication-quality prose.

Students' solid backing often in that most persuasive form—letters from graduates—of those teachers who offered them instruction in writing, provided invaluable support for the new requirement. The more energetic and capable students endorsed the advanced W from the beginning (certainly for classes who graduated after theirs); by 1992 even weaker students began to take enormous pride in overcoming what many of them later described almost as a disability, their initial terror of writing. It took students two years to organize and articulate their responses to the advanced W, but when they spoke at a workshop in late spring of 1991, they were astute and practical. In so many words, members of the student academic council told the faculty that the student body was ready and willing to learn to write; these student leaders asked directly, was the faculty willing to teach them? Students were ardent in their support of completing assignments step by step; they described the opportunity to draft and revise as a necessary component of any fair writing assignment. Seniors as well as beginning students across campus began to enquire of department chairs and the directors of the writing program why particular teachers did not assign drafts and thus permit them to profit from their mistakes.

In the past three years, then, there has been a major shift in the pedagogy of many faculty at Saint Mary's College as a result of an upper-level writing requirement. For some faculty the new writing requirement was initially radical, disturbing, difficult to manage. More recently, however, many teachers describe teaching writing as one of the more rewarding aspects of their work. The college's new graduation requirement has led to a faculty development program of unforeseen magnitude. The challenge of helping students learn to write has revitalized older faculty and inspired their younger colleagues. Monthly writing workshops are widely acknowledged to be the one place on campus where teachers from all disciplines gather and talk seriously about pedagogy. One month recently-tenured faculty from the French department explained how the writing process works with undergraduates learning a new language; the next month a newly appointed cognitive psychologist described why an upper-level writing requirement is essential for developing higher-level thinking skills. Recently appointed and graying faculty leave their research and computers, attend these workshops, and focus their attention on how good writing teaching serves the best interests of students. It is an enormous boost to look back on how much faculty across the college have accomplished in developing a whole new area of expertise, as well as to realize how much better the students are writing.

Works Cited

Brown, Ann. "Writing to Learn and Communicate in Mathematics: An Assignment in Abstract Algebra." *MAA Notes* 16 (1989): 1131-33.

Bryant, Susan, Mary Ann Traxler, and Karilee Watson. "Empowerment of Practitioners through Professional Writing: Creating a Writing Program for an Undergraduate Teacher Education Program." *Teacher Education: Preparing Teachers for School Reform.* Eds. Pamela J. Farris and Jerry A. Summers. Midwest Association of Teacher Educators. DeKalb, IL: April, 1993.

Chute, Carolyn. *The Beans of Egypt, Maine.* New York: Warner, 1985.

Danford, Cynthia M. "Writing in Nursing Education: Peer Review of Drafts." *Nurse Educator* 15.4 (1990): 5-6.

McElroy, Jerome. "The Mentor Model in the Senior Writing Seminar." *The Teaching Professor* 4.8 (1990): 2.

Nekvasil, Nancy P. "Adding Writing Proficiency to Undergraduate Biology Research—A Formula for Success at Saint Mary's." *Journal of College Science Teaching.* 20 (1991): 292-93.

Skinner, B.F. *Walden Two.* Toronto: Macmillan, 1948.

Snow, Joanne Erdman. "The Advanced Writing Requirement at Saint Mary's College." *Writing to Learn Mathematics and Science.* Ed. Paul Connolly and Teresa Vilardi. New York: Teachers College P, 1989, 193-97.

_____. "Writing Assignments and Course Content: Using Writing to Teach Mathematics." *MAA Notes* 16 (1990): 113-14.

Stoddart, Rebecca M. and Ann K. Loux. "And, not but: Moving from Monologue to Dialogue in Introductory Psychology/English Courses." *Teaching of Psychology* 19 (1992): 145-49.

Traxler, Mary Ann and Karilee Watson. "Writing Across the Curriculum: Creating a Professional Writing Sequence for a Teacher Education Program." The Fifth National Forum, The Association of Independent Liberal Arts Colleges for Teacher Education. Ed. Tom Warren. Beloit, WI, August, 1993.

Part 3:
Curricular Content and Emphases

A Special Course
in Advanced Composition
for Prospective Teachers

by Richard L. Larson

Most of the major recent pronouncements about the training of elementary and secondary teachers leave no doubt that those whose duties will eventually include the teaching of writing ought themselves to take courses in writing. Many of these declarations specify the skills such courses should develop. For example, when listing the requirements that should be established for those who will graduate from college with teaching certificates in secondary English, the Commission on English, College Entrance Examination Board, recommends work in "rhetoric and composition above the freshman level."[1] Alvina Burrows commends to elementary teachers the "experience of trying to write in order to analyze some of their own reactions in the composing process and to regain some measure of satisfaction in writing."[2] The Commission on the English Curriculum, National Council of Teachers of English, asserts that "in his college years the prospective [secondary] teacher of English should attain a considerable amount of understanding of how language works in connected discourse, a high degree of skill in writing of various types, and an ability to analyze the writings of others to discover their strengths and weaknesses and to make suggestions for improvement."[3] The Commission goes on to recommend that teachers study logic, the utility of different organizational patterns, the values of different kinds of sentence structure, and ways of choosing appropriate words and idioms. Needless to say, the Commission recommends work in expository writing and in the evaluation of writing for all prospective teachers of English.

On the training of elementary teachers, the Commission observes:

> The elementary school teacher needs help in two areas of writing. The first is well-ordered, logical presentation of facts or ideas, involving critical thinking and organization. The second is personal and imaginative writing.[4]

Reprinted from *Journal of Teacher Education* 20 (1969): 168-74. Copyright by the American Association of Colleges for Teacher Education. Reprinted with permission.

[1] College Entrance Examination Board, Commission on English. *Freedom and Discipline in English.* New York: the Board, 1965. p.10.

[2] Burrows, Alvina. "Academic and Professional Training in Composition." *A Source Book on English Institutes for Elementary Teachers.* Champaign, Illinois: National Council of Teachers of English, 1965. p. 52.

[3] National Council of Teachers of English, Commission on the English Curriculum. *The Education of Teachers of English for American Schools and Colleges.* Champaign, Ill.: the Council, 1963. p. 259.

[4] Ibid., p. 65.

The Commission then advocates a course in advanced composition for all elementary teachers. Professor Thomas Parkinson goes further:

> [The elementary teacher] should know something of the composition of artifacts, . . . how books, poems, sentences are put together, what principles of order and effect are at stake in *King Lear, The Brothers Karamazov,* Yeats's "Crazy Jane" poems. . . . The elementary teacher who is equipped with a genuine understanding of composition at its most complex and dense is better able to understand the questions of composition that affect her own writing, her own presentation of material, her selection of works that should be treated in full by her pupils. . . . She should be able to read and construe, clarify, summarize, and present. She should also have some idea of what the creative process is about, what goes into the composition of verse especially so that verse will not seem to her and to her pupils the inexplicable confusion of a lunatic who abjures prose for reasons that are probably suspect.[5]

Even if he does not become and has no hope of becoming proficient in expository or narrative writing, these authorities agree that the teacher should know how difficult—and how exciting—it can be to design an argument, arrange a paragraph, shape a sentence, invent a metaphor, and choose from many possibilities the precise word to fit a given context. These experiences will help teachers to understand the problems—the agonies, if you will—that students experience as they write. With understanding will come patience and sympathy, not to mention a heightened ability to offer appropriate guidance at moments when the students are most perplexed. Moreover, the effort of trying to write well helps the teacher to recognize and value good writing so that he can, in turn, encourage his students to try to produce good writing.

The frequency of these urgings suggests that many planners of curricula for preparing English teachers do not yet share these experienced teachers' conviction that new teachers should have studied advanced composition. To find out how widely the recommendations of the NCTE's Curriculum Commission and those of the Commission on English are now being followed, an inquiry was made of a sampling of universities across the nation to ascertain what sorts of writing courses they require of teachers. On the assumption that the training of persons to engage in a public service such as teaching is most likely to be felt as a responsibility by state-supported universities, questionnaires were sent to the principal public universities in each state, but a few private institutions that prepare large numbers of teachers were also included. In all, seventy-eight institutions are reported on.

The results confirm that many institutions that prepare teachers of English have not yet heeded the proposals of the professional groups. To be sure, most teachers preparing for work in secondary schools, where English is usually a separate subject, are required to take advanced courses in writing. Fifty-eight (74 percent) of the

---

[5] *A Source Book on English Institutes for Elementary Teachers, op. cit.,* pp. 24-25.

78 universities polled require at least one course in advanced exposition; at two-thirds of these, the requirement is a three-hour course. Only four of the 78 (5 percent) require these prospective teachers to take work in writing narrative or fiction, though a few other respondents said that their advanced courses in writing included work in narrative writing. At fourteen universities, the course in advanced exposition was only recommended, not required; and at six more, no course in advanced exposition was either recommended or required. At 25 percent of the institutions polled, then, advanced exposition is still not required of prospective secondary teachers.[6]

Teachers preparing to teach in elementary school are even less likely to take courses in advanced writing before going out to teach. Only 18 of the 78 universities polled (23 percent) require courses in advanced expository writing of prospective elementary teachers (usually one three-hour course); and only two (about 2.5 percent), a course in the writing of narrative or fiction. Twenty-seven universities (35 percent) recommend a course in advanced writing for prospective elementary teachers;[7] but 33 (42 percent) neither require nor recommend such a course, and of the 58 percent that do require or recommend it, only seven give special attention to the needs of elementary teachers, who will probably be asking students for a much greater variety of personal (often imaginative) and practical writing than will secondary teachers.[8] Comments by several of the respondents imply that their departments of English have little or no knowledge, let alone control, of what prospective elementary teachers must take to prepare themselves to teach English. Apparently the argument that elementary teachers need advanced training in writing themselves is not widely heeded among planners of curricula for such teachers; there is clearly a need for continued efforts by professional groups to assure that all teachers of English, in all grades, get the necessary advanced training in writing.

As professional groups continue these efforts, however, they are increasingly confronted with a practical issue: whether prospective teachers of English need special courses in composition different from those open to regular majors in English and to students preparing to enter professions other than teaching. The literature quoted from at the beginning is far from explicit on whether prospective teachers should have a course uniquely tailored for their needs. The want of explicitness is understandable, since the profession's first task is to see that prospective teachers get at least some training in writing. As a matter of tactics, arguments over the details of the course and demands that departments create special courses to be taken by teachers alone may well be deferred until after the initial objective is reached and secured. If necessary, professional groups can refer preservice teachers to

---

[6] This figure, perhaps significantly, contrasts with the 40 percent obtained in a survey taken three years ago of about two-thirds as many institutions.

[7] These figures contrast with the 16 percent of schools polled (in the smaller survey three years ago) that required a course in advanced exposition of elementary teachers and the 29 percent that recommended such a course.

[8] For a discussion of the kinds of writing that might figure in elementary school programs, see Saunders, Dorothy. "Composition in the Elementary School." *Report of School and College Conference on English*. New York: Barnard College, 1965. pp. 17-28.

courses now offered in various departments of many universities, courses in logic and semantics, for example, for important theoretical training that will at least partially supplement a general course in advanced composition.

Even so, the issue of what kind of writing course teachers should take sharply divides the planners of curricula for teachers. Of the universities in which a course in advanced exposition and/or narration is required or recommended for secondary teachers, 38 (roughly two-thirds) ask only that the teacher take the same course as any other interested student, but 20 (about one-third) have a special course in writing for prospective teachers. Of the 45 universities that require or recommend a writing course for elementary teachers, 28 (again almost two-thirds) said they would accept the same writing course that any interested student may take, but eleven said they provide a special course for prospective teachers, though not necessarily for prospective elementary teachers. (The other six universities that require an advanced course in writing did not respond directly to this question.) In addition, a few universities reported that they were in the process of developing courses designed specifically for future teachers.

We can approach the question of whether or not such courses are desirable by taking note of the interests of a prospective teacher and determining whether these interests are likely to be satisfied by the same course that serves future engineers, lawyers, businessmen, and public administrators, whose last contact with a classroom will come when they receive their degrees. Some comments by Martin Steinmann, Jr., are pertinent:

> There are two senses of "knowing": knowing *how* and knowing *that*. In the first sense, a person is said to know something (a language, say) if he possesses a certain ability, if he can perform in certain ways (speak the language). He has knowledge because he knows *how* to do something. In the second sense, he is said to know something (a language, say) if he possesses either a theory (of grammar and semantics) explaining exercise of a certain ability (speaking the language) or information about some historically given events (certain utterances). He has knowledge because he knows *that* something is the case. Neither sort of knowledge entails the other.[9]

Professor Steinmann is talking about "knowing" rhetoric (he is discussing different kinds of research on rhetoric), but his words apply equally to all activities that relate to writing. The engineer and businessman need only to know *how*; the teacher needs both to know *how* and to know *that*, or, perhaps better for our purposes, to know *why*. Indeed, the teacher needs more to know that or why than to know how, for the teacher of sub-collegiate grades lives not so much by performing as by explaining, by helping others to perform. He must be able to reveal to his students the choices that confront them as they write and the possible consequences of those choices, and enough about how words work and thoughts connect so that he can set tasks before his students in the order and against the background that will help them perform at their best. By so doing, he will help students enjoy and want

---

[9] Steinmann, Martin, Jr. "Rhetorical Research." *College English* 27: 278-85; January 1966.

to continue writing. In order to do so, he needs theories and information; he needs to know *that*. Because the focus in such courses is almost entirely on performing, there is reason to doubt that the ordinary course in advanced exposition, whose main purpose is to help the student learn *how*, will also help the teacher sufficiently to know *that* or *why*.

Also helpful in determining the kind of advanced writing course a teacher needs are comments of the NCTE's Commission on the Curriculum quoted earlier. The teacher needs "an ability to analyze the writing of others to discover their strengths and weaknesses and to make suggestions for their improvement"; in short, he needs to be a good reader. Some will contend, without doubt, that the experience of reading imaginative literature, coupled with practice in writing, will be quite sufficient to train future teachers as readers. Few will deny that studying imaginative literature helps teachers to read better; but the purposes, the principles of order, and the tasks that language must perform in exposition, are not the same as in imaginative literature. Even if all three were the same in both kinds of writing, the purposes for which a good teacher reads exposition still differs from the purpose for which he reads literature. He reads a literary work in order to interpret it and enlarge his experience, not to improve the work; but he reads his students' expository papers so that he can advise them and help them to improve their writing.

Those of us who supervise freshman composition know that the staff members who are most perceptive in reading novels and poems are not always lucid commentators on professional essays or constructive annotators of their students' themes. The prospective teacher of English needs a writing course that will train him in the analysis and constructive criticism of expository prose. He needs a special kind of course in advanced writing, in most cases different from the one open to all students in a university. The design of this special course for teachers should incorporate the following features not likely to be included in a general course:

1. *Exploration of the problems of finding and organizing data that are encountered in each assignment.* As in any good course in composition, the student in this course should be assisted in the finding of materials to include in his paper, that is, in invention, as well as in perceiving possible arrangements of those data and choose among those patterns of order. But the prospective teacher, even more than the general student, needs to be made conscious of the habits of observation and inquiry that help in the discovery and generating of ideas so that he can, in turn, help his students to develop these habits. Similarly, the prospective teacher needs even more skill than the general student in evaluating strategies for the arranging of material. He will need not only to organize material well himself but also to be able to explain the value of different strategies to his students. The student of business or law, for example, may need to know only enough about writing extended definitions to be sure that he and his reader are talking about the same subject. But the teacher, if he is to teach defining effectively, needs a more comprehensive understanding of the occasions when definition is needed, the purpose of defining, various techniques for defining, and ways of evaluating and improving definition.

2. *Consideration of some fundamentals of modern rhetoric.* There is no need for extended study of rhetorical theory, but future teachers should recognize that

writing is a series of choices among alternatives and that a good writer must shape his discourse carefully to make it reach its intended audience effectively and accomplish its intended purpose. This view of rhetoric does not imply that the writer is a cunning deceiver but rather that even the writing of exposition can be artful. And it encourages teachers to approach their writing and that of their students with such questions as these: Whom am I addressing? On what occasion am I addressing him? What is my purpose in speaking? What is my relationship to him? What tone of voice ought I to assume in this discourse? What kinds of language will best enable me to achieve my purpose in addressing this audience?

3. *Study of how language establishes a voice, an identity, for the writer whether or not he consciously intends to establish one.* If it is important for the writer to decide how he wants to appear to his reader, it is essential that he know how his language establishes the distinctive identity he assumes each time he writes. The prospective teacher, who will need not only to be heard in a suitable voice when he writes but also to explain to students exactly what choices of language are most directly audible to the reader's ear, should consider questions such as these: How do a writer's favorite sentence patterns affect the way he is heard? How do the figures of speech he uses establish his attitude toward his subject? How do his adverbs and adjectives help to create impressions of him? What elements of his language does a writer need most carefully to control if he is concerned with his reader's estimate of his intelligence, character, and personality? The prospective teacher should develop more than usual sensitivity to the workings of words in expository prose.

4. *Practice in reading exposition and describing strong and weak points of substance, structure, and expression in any essay.*[10] The pieces examined might be professional essays as well as themes written by members of the class. In studying these essays, the class would strive, not just to identify models for imitation or to locate major ideas, but to judge their overall effectiveness. Especially in themes by their classmates, students might be asked to suggest revisions in such a way that the authors could understand and follow their suggestions. Such practice would train future teachers to recognize infirm structure, vagueness, ambiguity, redundancy, inconsistency, and inappropriateness of voice and help them learn to express their evaluations, not in language of subjective reaction (e.g., by epithets such as "confused," "boring," "nonsense"), but in words that would guide a reader of their comments to a better performance in his next essay.

5. *Attention to the reasons for making each writing assignment.* Besides asking the student to complete the assignment, the instructor can discuss with the class his reasons for believing the assignment worth the attention of a student of writing. Such discussion would alert the prospective teacher to the need for care in planning his composition curriculum and in designing individual assignments. It would also help him to see the reasoning used in planning assignments and to appraise the value of the assignment itself. The last purpose is particularly important because, if the proponents of the spiral theory of learning are correct, the prospective teacher

---

[10] For suggestions about reading and evaluation of essays, see Larson, Richard L. "Teaching the Analysis of Expository Prose." *English Journal* 57: 1156-62; November 1968.

may later want to give a more elementary version of the same assignment to his own students. No task of the teacher of composition is more important than the designing of good assignments and their successful administration; yet, few tasks are more neglected in books about the teaching of English.

6. *Some practice in nonexpository forms of writing.* Not all the writing of subcollegiate students is, or should be, expository; they often benefit from trying to communicate their experiences in fiction or poetry. A prospective teacher should have the experience and confront some of the theoretical problems of writing narrative and poetry, so that he can guide his students to an understanding of the special qualities of language and structure that distinguish a good poem or story.

7. *Explicit attention to ways of writing analyses and evaluations of literary works.* Since most teachers of English in secondary schools will handle courses in which the study of literature is combined with the study of composition, these teachers should confront the problems of making and defending inferences about characterization, structure, and meaning in literary works. They should also practice reaching and explaining a value judgment on the texts discussed by references to the language and structure found in these texts.

Many teachers today seem to avoid the actual teaching of composition. They assign themes hastily, annotate them with correction symbols, and give grades, but they do not ensure that their students practice a wide range of writing, do not aid them to identify and solve their writing problems, and do not help them to improve their writing from one assignment to the next.[11] Teachers might teach composition much more willingly and effectively if they had come during their training to a better understanding of the art of composition and of the why and how of teaching it. Such an understanding they could well obtain in a special course of writing tailored to the distinctive needs of prospective teachers.

---

[11] For recent comments on the amount of actual teaching that takes place when students are working on composition, see Applebee, Roger K. "National Study of High School English Programs: A Record of English Teaching Today." *English Journal* 55: 273-81; March 1966. Squire, James. "National Study of High School English Programs: A School for All Seasons." *Ibid.*, pp. 282-90. Squire, James R., and Applebee, Roger K. *High School English Instruction Today: The National Study of High School English Programs.* New York: Appleton-Century-Crofts, 1968.

Incorporating Sentence Combining into the Advanced Composition Class

by Gary A. Olson

Perhaps at no other time has theoretical linguistics—specifically, the transformational generative model—been applied on such a universally practical level as in the case of sentence combining. Researchers over the past decade and a half have established convincingly the pedagogical efficacy of sentence combining (Miller and Ney in 1968; Mellon in 1969; Hunt and O'Donnell in 1970; Obenchain in 1971; Vitale, et al. in 1971; O'Hare in 1973; Fischer in 1973; Perron in 1974; Combs in 1975, 1976; Pedersen in 1977; Morenberg, et al. in 1978). It is clear that practice in combining sentences can lead to sustained qualitative increases in syntactic fluency. Unfortunately, however, sentence combining has acquired the reputation of being principally a lower-level phenomenon: rarely do we ever hear of sentence combining in connection with courses more advanced than freshman English; and Ney's study (in 1976) concluding that there is not even any convincing evidence that sentence combining helps college freshman is well known, despite the cogent refutation by Morenberg, Daiker, and Kerek (in 1978). Although sentence combining was developed originally for the high school grades and now is used widely on the freshman level, it is not logical to presume that it cannot be an effective tool in the advanced composition class as well.

Actually, sentence combining is pedagogically viable regardless of the students' level of syntactic proficiency. Perhaps the greatest virtue of sentence combining is that it alerts writers to the variety of linguistic options available to them, and makes the pursuit of options and variant transformations a conscious endeavor. In "Applications of Transformational Grammar," Diane Bornstein writes, "A transformational grammar . . . provides knowledge about how language functions and can raise intuitive knowledge of a language to a conscious level. Moreover, it can make people more aware of the stylistic options that are available in their language" (*An Introduction to Transformational Grammar* [Cambridge: Winthrop, 1977], p. 209). This consciousness-raising is important to all writers, even the most sophisticated. Obviously, advanced writers will possess more of a variety of possible sentence patterns to choose from than beginning writers will. But I believe it is probably natural for even advanced writers to rely for long periods of time on the particular patterns they have learned, before they begin to incorporate new patterns into their reper-

Reprinted from the *Journal of Advanced Composition* 2 (1981): 119-26. Reprinted with permission.

toires. Practice in sentence combining, even at the more advanced levels, exposes writers to variant structures and reaffirms the value of continually examining options while writing.

In addition, sentence combining helps students attain *semantic* as well as syntactic sophistication. In combining sentences, students in my advanced class seem to seek words that are more contextually accurate, which compress the meaning of several words into one. For example, instead of saying "a medicine that kills bacteria," the student is likely to seek out the word *antibiotic*. Similarly, the simple and common transformation of a deep structure sentence into a single adjective is another example of this process. In other words, practice in effecting transformations is linked with lexical selection. Semantic accuracy is a fundamental element of good writing, and it is especially important that the advanced student learn to be alert for the most precise words. I am convinced that practice in sentence combining helps students acquire this habit. Another benefit of sentence combining in the advanced class is that students learn to manipulate punctuation creatively. Since its inception, sentence combining has been credited with helping beginning students learn the basics of punctuation. However, it also helps advanced students already knowledgeable in the rudiments of mechanics to perceive punctuation as a malleable rather than rigid phenomenon—something which *they* can manipulate to increase the accuracy and originality of self-expression. When working with sentence combining in class, we consciously sought transformations involving various methods of punctuation. In fact, on a purely quantitative basis, the students exhibited an increase in the use of internal punctuation from papers 1 to 14. I counted the number of internal punctuation marks (commas, semicolons, colons, dashes) in both sets of papers and discovered that the average amount of punctuation per paragraph increased 55%. Obviously, this item of information is not necessarily significant, but it does illustrate that each student used more punctuation at the end of the semester, perhaps an indication that some syntactic growth did occur.

In addition, I have observed that sentence combining helps transform *linguistic competence* into *linguistic performance*. That is, writers begin to take intuitive linguistic "knowledge" and apply it on a practical level in their prose; passively held knowledge of the language becomes actively employed rhetoric. For example, in the beginning of this last semester, most of my advanced students *knew* of left-branching structures and were able to produce them upon request, but rarely used them in their own writing; however, after a semester of sentence combining, almost *all* of these pupils (one exception) produce left-branch structures spontaneously in their prose. These results are significant. Students were able to take structures that they as native speakers (and readers) of English were familiar with but did not normally use, and, through sentence combining, were able to internalize them so well that they now employ them regularly and successfully. Of course, I am not saying anything new; sentence combining is supposed to cause intuitive knowledge to surface, but usually we speak about this in relation to beginning writers. Nevertheless, I am convinced that sentence combining is just as effective in the advanced composition class.

Before examining some writing samples, I wish to describe briefly how I incorporated sentence combining into the syllabus of my advanced composition class here at the University of Alabama. During the semester, we spent ten full hours engaged in combining activities; this was 23% of our total semester time. This may seem excessive for an advanced class, but I wanted to emphasize syntactic growth, and I did not wish to duplicate Ross and Ney's (reported in 1971 and 1976 respectively) poor results by investing insufficient class time in the combining exercises. Usually, we spent entire fifty-minute class periods on sentence combining, rather than, say, ten minutes during every class.

My methodology was simple. We used only "open" exercises, with no cues or predetermined structures that students were asked to imitate. Since the students were all seniors, most of whom were already writing at relatively high levels, I felt that it was important to allow them maximum opportunity for creativity and originality. In fact, not only did we use open exercises, but the pupils were entirely free to replace words in the exercises with ones they deemed more appropriate, or to alter the structures in any manner.

We alternated between two simple formats: class discussion of exercises on overhead transparencies, and group competition over mimeographed exercises. I did not construct my own exercises; the transparencies and worksheets were derived directly from several of the available textbooks, usually Strong's *Sentence Combining: A Composing Book* or Daiker, Kerek, and Morenberg's *The Writer's Options*. Although these texts are directed at lower level students, they are nonetheless useful in the advanced class. It seems to me that it is practice *in* the process of combining sentences that is important; the level of combining exercise is not as essential as one might assume. When we utilize sentence combining we are helping students learn a *process*—the process of embedding information into sentences while attaining effectiveness, clarity, and stylistic variety—and I believe we can help students accomplish this using the available texts. This is not to suggest that a text directed specifically at the advanced level would not be useful, only that it is not essential.

Before introducing sentence combining to the class, I provided students with a relatively detailed synopsis of the "theory" of linguistic transformations and how sentence combining derived from it. This theoretical base stimulated the students' intellects, causing them, I believe, to respond more readily and enthusiastically than they might have otherwise; they began to perceive the method as something more sophisticated than a simple game. Usually, we engaged in sentence combining on days in which papers were due, creating some relaxation of tension after the anxiety of writing each paper. When discussing transformations on overhead transparencies, we tried to exhaust every possible variation, using the full range of punctuation and syntactic structures. Everyone was asked to participate in the discussion. When using mimeographed exercises, groups of three students decided which combinations were the "most effective" given a particular purpose and audience. The groups then voted which group's renditions were most effective. This procedure introduced an element of competition and challenge which in turn made the tasks intellectually stimulating to the students—a factor of special importance when dealing with graduating seniors who inevitably have things other than composition on their minds.

Whenever we engaged in combining activities, we discussed stylistic options: use of absolutes, appositives, participles, semicolons, dashes, and so on. Unless we were voting on structures that were "most effective" given a particular purpose and audience, we always kept in mind that there is no "best" structure. I heavily emphasized "revision" in this course and encouraged students repeatedly to experiment with various options in the revision stage. Similarly, I encouraged students who kept an optional journal to experiment with the combining process in their daily writing. In fact, experimentation with sentence combining in journals seemed to be an effective way for students to achieve syntactic growth. Evidently, writers especially learn to *internalize* the embedding process when they experiment with optional structures in their daily personal writing.

By the semester's end, I had a strongly intuitive sense that our emphasis on sentence combining had a positive effect on the students' writing abilities, but I had no actual "evidence." In order to obtain a more dependable estimation of whether the students' prose did exhibit syntactic growth, and if so how much, I examined papers 1, 8, and 14 of each of the 10 students in the class. I applied to these papers two of the criteria—T-units and words per clause—established by Hunt (in 1965) and others as dependable indicators of possible syntactic development. In no way do I present this information as empirical or conclusive evidence that sentence combining worked in the advanced class; rather, I am presenting it as data which seem to support my intuitive impression that the advanced students all made *some* gains in syntactic proficiency and that sentence combining, since we had emphasized it so strongly throughout the semester, may have been a contributing factor. It is important to note that the students had no knowledge that their writing would be the subject of a study; in fact, neither did I until the semester's end.

Reprinted below are the second paragraphs of a student's papers 1, 8, and 14. I chose this student's papers randomly, without any previous considerations.

Paper 1

If you talk to one of the true horse lovers, you'll find he is very dedicated to the animals. He has a great pride in what his horse can do. He works long hours caring for his big pet. And you can see this fierce dedication and pride in the owner of a seven foot Puissance Wall jumper, and in the owner of a Texas cowpony, to the owner of a backyard pleasure horse. Why do these people have such a strong love for these animals? Where do they get this interest in the sport?

Paper 8

A Feminist Movement existed for several centuries in the form of isolated groups of women rebelling against the subservient role of housewife which men and society forced upon women. Some of these groups of women banded together and acquired the right to vote for all American women, accomplishing a major victory for the Feminist Movement at that time. As technology improved over the years in areas of mass media and communication, knowledge of the Feminist Movement grew, enabling women to organize into large, powerful groups. By the 1960s and 1970s, the Feminist Movement exploded with action and support leading to the drafting of the Equal Rights Amendment, which states, "Equality of rights under the law shall not be denied or abridged by the United States or by any State on account of sex." With continued support, the ERA or similar legislation may yet obtain legal equality for women.

Paper 14

The Indians at first reacted in fear of the mounted Conquistadors; perhaps the Indians thought they were seeing one animal in the mounted conquistador and his horse. The Indians soon overcame their fear, however, After a momentary panic, the Indians' fear changed to hatred of the horses. Because of this hatred, the Indians slew vast numbers of the Spanish horses. Later, the Indians discovered the use of horses for food, barter, and labor. Roe refers to the extreme terror the Indians of Spanish America experienced when they first encountered horses, and then the phenomenal speed in which they overcame their fears to control the horses with equestrian mastery rivaling the best in the world.

The increase in syntactic sophistication is reflected in these three writing samples. Number 1 is composed of short subject-verb complement sentences. One sentence is a left-branching structure. The author does not use punctuation imaginatively. A comma is used in the first sentence to separate the prepositional phrase from the main clause, and commas are used to separate the series in the fourth sentence; but the writer uses no other internal punctuation. In addition, the paragraph shows incidents of wordiness and awkwardness. For example, the fourth sentence can be made clearer if we eliminate the third *and*, and replace *to* with *or even in*.

In contrast, there is more of a variety of structures in paper 8. The author employs left- and right-branching structures; in fact, the third sentence contains both. The paragraph, sentences, and clauses all are longer than those of paper 1. The sentences contain a greater density of information than those in paper 1, and the level of specificity is also greater.

Similarly, paper 14 exhibits continued syntactic growth. The level of complexity of the sentences is greater than that of 8 or 1, and the sentences also contain a density of information at least equal to that of 8, if not more. The author employs a variety of structures, in one instance using a semicolon to join independent clauses. Even the semantic component of paper 14 illustrates a sense of growth.

These samples are meant to illustrate the *type* of growth I have observed in student writing throughout the semester. When applied to the papers, Hunt's well-known criteria give further insight into the class' general syntactic development. In every case, the words per clause increased from the first to the fourteenth paper. (It is important to note that since I am dealing with a limited number of students, I was actually able to count the words per clause; Hunt derived the "average" words per clause of his samples by dividing the total number of words by the total number of clauses.) The mean average of growth in words per clause for the class as a whole was 5.5 words, with individual students achieving increases of as high as 8.6 and as low as 1.2 words. Eighty percent of the class showed increases of higher than 3.3 words (see Table). These data are certainly encouraging; they indicate that *some* growth has occurred, measured by a usually dependable indicator. Since we have no control group, we cannot assert necessarily that sentence combining is responsible for the increases; but we can presume the sentence combining had *some* influence on the growth, especially since the very objective of sentence combining is to promote syntactic development and since we had spent a full 23% of our semester on combining activities.

In addition, syntactic development is reflected in the ratio of T-units per sentence, though not as impressively as in the words per clause category. The data indicate that 70% of the writers registered some improvement (a lower ratio of T-units per sentence on paper 14 than paper 1). The class as a whole improved .03 T-units per sentence over the semester; however, if we exclude the two students who registered negative improvement, the result is a bit higher: .09 less T-units per sentence (see Table). This latter number is closer to the development ratio we should expect to find judging from Hunt's study: around .10 to .15. Nevertheless, the fact that 70% of the class made such improvement is encouraging. Another factor to consider is that each of the students is writing at about the level, judging from T-units per sentence, that Hunt established as "superior adult": around 1.24. It is possible, and even likely, that writers do not usually progress much beyond Hunt's "superior adult" (now "skilled adult") range, that the T-units per sentence category does not measure growth beyond this particular level.

Table

Students	Net Increase of Words Per Clause (Papers 1 to 14)	Variation of T-Units Per Sentence
A	7.2	-.02
B	3.9	+.02
C	5.5	-.03
D	8.6	+.12
E	8.4	-.22
F	1.9	-.01
G	7.5	-.09
H	3.4	-.22
I	1.2	-.15
J	7.5	-.04
Class	5.5	-.03

This study does not set out to *prove* that sentence combining was successful in the advanced composition class; it does attempt to establish that sentence combining should not be "written off" as a method restricted to developmental composition or freshman English. My professional judgment as well as some usually reliable indicators show that *some* syntactic growth occurred in each student's writing throughout the semester. Since we strongly emphasized sentence combining throughout the semester, it is reasonable to assume that it played *some* role in the writers' development. The next step is to conduct a controlled experiment, involving several advanced composition classes, to determine more clearly exactly what effect sentence combining does have on the senior level. But before we can take this step, we must reexamine our preconceptions; we must be willing to accept that sentence combining *might* be a viable pedagogical method on the senior level.

Writing for Publication in an Advanced Course for Undergraduates

by Wilma Clark

When I first thought of involving a "real-world" editor in my writing seminar, I envisioned a professional consultation on editing. Bold strokes of the blue pencil would slice across the pages of my students' manuscripts, leaving handwritten drops of brilliance to bleed forth in tight phrases and fresh metaphors. Having submitted the best prose we were capable collectively of producing, we would watch breathlessly as a real editor applied the finishing touches.

But when our editor arrived at the end of the semester with the sheaf of manuscripts we had sent him, he had not made a mark on any student's paper! He spoke to the class and then to individuals in conference about the importance of two things: (1) a topic that fits the publication and the audience, and (2) an enticing lead. He had seen no reason to mark on the papers because "the writing itself [was] of high quality."

Dan Chabot was on the editorial staff of *Insight* magazine, a Sunday supplement to the *Milwaukee Journal*. I was teaching English 303, Seminar in Expository Writing, a core course in a new writing minor. Serving students in both the technical/professional and the creative tracks of the minor, English 303 draws skilled, motivated writers who have completed prerequisites in freshman composition and sophomore expository writing. Our department had decided that the primary objective distinguishing a course for students of this caliber should be writing for publication.

Funded by a small curriculum development grant, I sought an editor who would read a manuscript from each student in the course and then visit the class to discuss the papers with us. It was important, of course, to find a publication that would provide a realistic market for my students and one that would consider pieces written in the *expository* mode. *Insight* magazine was our most likely target. It features essays about Wisconsin by Wisconsin writers, seeks autobiographical sketches with a philosophical twist, uses free-lance as well as staff-written articles in most issues, and includes, in some articles at least, the kind of prose we wanted to practice in the seminar. I contacted *Insight*, Dan Chabot agreed to the plan, and we sent him the manuscripts about one month before his visit to our class.

Knowing that an editor would actually read and discuss the papers with us added an exciting dimension to this class. It changed *writing for publication* from an

Reprinted from the *Journal of Advanced Composition* 3 (1982): 24-36. Reprinted with permission.

abstract, school-time exercise to a concrete real-world challenge. It energized the class, making students and instructor alike stretch and grow to a degree that would not ordinarily occur in a school-contained writing course. However, the first time I taught the course, problems arose that I had not been expecting. I was surprised to discover how limited the possibilities are for undergraduates attempting to publish in the expository mode. Even more surprising to me was the fact that my students' greatest challenge was not to polish style but, rather, to focus and shape the whole piece. I was sure that these students had practiced adapting material to specific audiences in many school assignments over the years. And yet, when substantive revision proved necessary now for real-world discourse, they seemed almost hypnotically disabled. In this article I will discuss the problems I encountered upon first teaching English 303, the changes I plan in future offerings of the course, and the reasons I will continue to involve a professional editor in this writing seminar.

Before focusing on the problems in the course and the impact of Chabot's visit, I would like to explain briefly how we organized the class. The first half of the semester was spent in preparing essays to send to Chabot. We analyzed the *Insight* issue every week for types of article topics developed, varieties in style and tone. Each week students produced approximately four typed pages in response to an assignment meant to help them identify a piece suitable for *Insight* (e.g., autobiographical incident, description of a place, personal opinion essay, biographical sketch). Weekly papers were considered drafts, and the writer was asked to note at the top of the paper what "stage" the draft was in (e.g., "free write," "taking shape," "nearing completion") and to specify to the reader what kind of criticism was wanted (e.g, "ideas for my best angle on this topic," "identify information gaps," "note boring passages"). By about the sixth week of class, each student had chosen one of these pieces to develop and polish. By mid-semester we had a pile of "finished" manuscripts to send off to Chabot. The remainder of the semester was devoted to informative, analytical writing, culminating in a professional article in the major discipline.

A key feature of the course was a system of peer critiquing which we adapted from John Trimble, author of one of our texts, *Writing with Style* (Prentice-Hall, 1975). From hearing Trimble at CCCC meetings and from visiting his classes in Austin, Texas, I gleaned a method of intensive evaluation whereby every student's weekly paper receives a written response from every other student in the class as well as a written critique from the instructor. In addition, each student, at least once during the semester, presents a paper for discussion by the whole class.

An immediate problem in such a course is to find an expository form in which undergraduates are marketable. In one of our course texts (*The New Strategy of Style*, 2nd ed., McGraw-Hill, 1978), Winston Weathers and Otis Winchester discuss discriminating features of five types of publishable exposition: the popular article, the professional article, the personal essay, the formal essay, and the critical review. We soon discovered that the popular informative articles in *Insight* were usually assigned to staff writers (as are critical reviews in most magazines). My students did not have the means to follow a new Wisconsin representative during his first five days in Washington or the time to interview bank and shopping mall executives, horticulturists, owners of a green-plant renting corporation, and secretaries in lush tropical offices to do a story on the business of renting exotic plants in Milwaukee. Besides, these popular articles begin to sound like feature stories—which, at our school at least, are to be assigned not in English courses but in feature writing courses in the Journalism Department.

The formal essay is normally written by an established authority who, according to Weathers and Winchester, is not concerned primarily with information or scientific conclusions but is permitted "judgments and ideas designed to influence or change the reader's intellectual perspective." Coming from an undergraduate, this kind of writing would be rejected as "unsupported generalization." Formal essays are written by people like Joseph Wood Krutch or Harvey Cox of the Harvard Divinity School on lofty topics such as "Life, Liberty, and the Pursuit of Welfare" or "Understanding Islam: No More Holy Wars." My students have not gathered the wisdom needed to soar at these heights, nor have I.

Professional articles are almost as unrealistic for undergraduates. The professional journals publish articles by professors and researchers, and occasionally by graduate students. In our course we spent half the semester on professional writing, as an important type of prose for students to know how so they might produce "sometime in the future," but although I encouraged students to submit their articles to the journals, I don't know of any who did. It is rare for an undergraduate to have the expertise necessary to inform a professional article.

This leaves the personal essay, "a fragment of autobiography . . . inevitably self-revealing," according to our textbook writers. Here my students were authorities, and this was the kind of material that *Insight* sought from the free-lancers. However, the personal essay is only one kind of expository prose. The limitation on the kinds of exposition accessible to students wishing to publish remains a problem as I develop this course.

When Chabot arrived with our manuscripts just before final exams, he spoke repeatedly throughout the day about leads. Introductions which we had thought were interesting as well as literate, Chabot found dull and slow. One paper began with a passage from Wordsworth. "It has become a cliche to start an article with quoted poetry. Try something fresh," Chabot recommended.

I had praised John for the following lead in his article on investment gemstones:

> The 1.45 carat stone attracts light and bounces it back in vibrant bands. It radiates with a fiery green intensity. The emerald-cut, natural garnet gem measures 5.35 x 7.74 x 3.86 millimeters. Moderately flawed, its estimated worth is $5,800.00.

Chabot asked for a more appealing lead. I defended it for specific diction: *bounces, vibrant, radiates, fiery green.* "Yes, but then read on. All those digits. The Sunday morning reader won't take the time to process that numerical information." Well, of course, we suddenly saw what he meant.

In writing for a popular audience, one must remove all obstacles, make the way smooth and inviting. Chabot liked the following lead in Melissa's paper and so did we:

As I wake it is there, it has grown up around me in the night without my knowledge, and I am seduced by it. It makes me want to abandon my day's activities to contemplate the stitching on my quilt, explore the recesses under my bed. (from "Stillness")

Aside from lethargic leads in many of the essays, Chabot liked the style of the writing itself. This matter of style had been my first surprise in the course. I had expected that the greatest need in a class at this advanced level would be to work on style, and that the students would need to be coaxed into careful editing in order to "tighten, sharpen, and brighten" the page, as Trimble put it.

How wrong I was. I simply had not been prepared for the enthusiasm with which these students pursued style. They copied out striking images from prose they admired. They used transparencies on the overhead projector to study sentences they had modeled on the sixty-four stylistic patterns provided by Weathers and Winchester. While editing one another's drafts, they slashed through verbiage without mercy, determined to "tighten" the page into compact prose. They were enamored of the precise word, and several had the gift for fresh imagery. Melissa's still summer afternoon was accentuated by "warm, warm concrete, like bathwater, warm enough to place a cheek against." Tracy's instructor, dedicated to dance but eschewing the flashy clothes and brilliant make-up of many of her peers, was "a pigeon in a nest of peacocks." Indeed, I would agree, on the basis of students in this course at least, that William Stone was right in observing recently that the more advanced the students, the more able they will be to approximate the skill of experienced writers (noted by Nancy Sommers) in "rewriting at the sentence level."[1] And I do believe in the accuracy of Chabot's judgment: with words and sentences, my students had talent, which they enjoyed exercising; with regard to diction and syntax, they could produce publishable prose.

Our problem it turned out was with the more global matters—focusing on the topic to interest the reader, finding a structure to unify the piece, shaping to create momentum. "Remember, these readers are not teachers paid to finish your article," my students would remind each other, and yet they couldn't seem to accomplish what they knew intellectually had to be done.

And this was my biggest surprise in the course. I was expecting students who could reorganize material when necessary to accomplish a purpose with a specific audience. I soon discovered, however, that on this point my class did *not* follow the pattern suggested by Stone in the article noted above: that 300-level writers can handle organizational problems when rewriting more easily than they can solve sentence-level revision problems.[2] Indeed, although my class relished the game-like calisthenics of editing for style, they were often confounded by the fundamental work of *revision*, in the sense of *re*-seeing, *re*-shaping the whole piece as Donald Murray and others have explained it.[3]

---

[1] William B. Stone, "Rewriting in Advanced Composition," *Journal of Advanced Composition* 1 (1980): 74-77.
[2] Stone 76.
[3] Donald M. Murray, "The Maker's Eye: Revising Your Own Manuscripts," *Subject and Strategy: A Rhetorical Reader.* Ed. Paul Eschholz and Alfred Rosa (New York: St. Martin's, 1978), 400-05.

In examining their drafts, students had great difficulty in identifying an angle on the topic that would truly interest the general readers who purchase *Insight*. And nothing had prepared me for these students' rock-ribbed resistance to reshaping a draft into a structural whole once an appealing angle had been identified.

Benjamin's article on earth-sheltered homes was full of dimensions, weights, BTU's, and dollar savings. But the reader would also want to know how it feels to live in an earth-sheltered home. Nancy described "The Joynt," a unique saloon near our campus which features cultural stars of the stature of Ahmal Jamar and John Ciardi, even though only 150 patrons can squeeze into the place at one concert. Nancy described the place and the owner, but readers would want to know how it feels to be at a concert there and *why* Woody Herman or the Herd, Odetta or Donald Hall would decide to perform in this small place.

Susan's piece on her first parachute jump was hilarious. "What sane person would abandon a perfectly good airplane?" But although we laughed, we asked, "So what?" What was the point? Susan labored, found a focus (the growth of the human spirit in meeting and overcoming danger), and embedded new sections into her original essay at various points. But now the contrast between tones of light humor and philosophical wisdom was jarring.

Dana wrote several drafts on abuses in the financial aid system. Her examples of outright abuse alarmed us, but deep within every draft we detected a contradiction. She would write cogently on the unfairness of subsidizing the lives of some young people and not of others. Suddenly it didn't seem right that twenty-year-old factory workers should pay taxes to supply grants and interest-free loans for twenty-year-old college students. But then she would suddenly allude to the legitimate claims for support by a "student who would be unable to attend college without financial aid." Are needy students entitled to financial help, or not? Dana could never decide. Her inability to clarify basic assumptions created a snag for the close reader attempting to follow her analysis of what constitutes "abuse" in financial aid.

My students' problem was not intellectual but rather psychological. Benjamin knew he needed to visit two or three earth sheltered homes, interview the residents, and reveal the experience of living in such homes. Nancy needed to interview Ciardi and Odetta, who both appeared at the Joynt while our course was underway. But neither of these students could muster more than a half-hearted effort at revision. They had worked too hard on polishing their pieces as originally shaped.

Dana wrote with passion on financial aid abuses, and as a stylist she was the most talented in our class. But she could never achieve a clarification of her basic premise—even though we had made her aware of the contradiction in her essay. Susan loved her sky jumping story, and she was pleased with the theme which our critiques had prompted her to discover. But she could not bring herself to reopen the paper, to begin a completely fresh draft so as to weave the two threads of her essay into one whole cloth.

Encompassed daily by the creative energy and upbeat spirit of the students in this class, I was baffled by their unwillingness to undertake substantial revision—even when we were quite confident that we had identified changes necessary for turning a piece into a publishable article. Perhaps since the students had worked so hard to impress an editor with stylistic flair, they hadn't enough energy left to solve basic problems. Or perhaps writing for a *real* audience beyond school created complex demands that they had never had practice in meeting.

At any rate, when Chabot came, he did not, as I have already indicated, edit manuscripts for us with a dazzling professional sweep. Instead, he showed students, as indeed I had been trying to show them all semester, that they must solve basic problems before indulging themselves in the delights of stylistic embellishment. He told Benjamin and Nancy to interview key people to bring life into their essays. He told Dana that she must clarify her thesis. He complimented Susan on her use of humor. "It's the light touch. Not many writers can make that work." He asked her to smooth out the piece and resubmit it to him.

Of all the papers in the course, Melissa's essay on "Stillness" came the closest to being published. It was a collection of exquisite images, organized more like a poem than an essay. In class we had pressed for some conceptual framework, some point. But even Melissa couldn't round out the structure to bring this very fine piece to completion. Chabot liked it enough to take it back to Milwaukee to the articles editor at *Insight*. But within two weeks Melissa had it back, with a note from this second editor: "It needs a rallying point, some event or action around which to develop a solution to a problem or a special insight. The manuscript needs dramatic structure."

Like all instructors who stand back after teaching a course the first time, I now have a clearer view about what to emphasize in the class the second time around. What I must do above all is find ways to help students keep a piece open until fundamental rhetorical problems have been solved. To illustrate the fruitlessness of working hard without solving basic problems, I will, of course, be able to draw many examples from my first English 303 class. From the outset, I will be able to demonstrate for students that, to avoid rejection by an editor, they must become willing to delay closure until the piece is truly working to accomplish their purposes.

To teach students *how* to develop an essay while delaying closure, I must become more efficient in suggesting practical ways by which they can benefit from the relevant insights abounding in current composition theory and research. The research of Linda Flower and John Hayes, for example, will help me emphasize that the primary task of a writer is to analyze the rhetorical situation. Flower and Hayes have shown that *the* most striking difference between good and poor writers is the ability of the former to analyze the topic in terms of the audience and to plan ways to write so as to affect that audience in the desired way.[4]

Then, even as the students are clarifying the purposes of the written piece, I must show them strategies for developing the essay before they feel a sense of closure on the piece. For some writers, jot listing on different days over a long period of time—*before* attempting any drafts—is the most efficient way to discover the shape and central meaning of an essay. According to Howard Gardner, a psychologist researching artistic capacities, this "top-down" approach—selecting a ready-made schema

---

[4] Linda Flower and John R. Hayes, "The Cognition of Discovery: Defining a Rhetorical Problem," *College Composition and Communication* 31 (1980): 21-32.

or planning one before filling in the details—is a common method of composing among musicians as well as writers.[5] Other writers thrive on the "bottom-up" method, experimenting with free-writes whereby they approach the topic in completely different ways at different times, letting the right-brained imagination explore possibilities before the left brain begins to select details and arrange material into an orderly pattern. Freewriting calls to mind the French tradition of the *brouillon* (literally, a scrambled mess) to which Elaine Maimon alludes when exhorting writing instructors to encourage students "to produce these scrambled messes as a part of the composing process."[6] Some writers spend hours, days, on the lead, using the opening of the piece to force their own decisions about thesis, tone, and shape. Addressing area teachers in our writing project recently, Lucy McCormick Calkins elaborated on this method in which a carefully developed lead determines the shape of the whole essay.[7] Thanks to Linda Flower, we now have a whole textbook for teaching strategies whereby writers can proceed to accomplish their goals with regard to their intended audiences.[8]

The trick is to help each student identify methods that are most efficient for him or her—methods of *working* (without procrastination) but yet remaining at the same time *open to changes* until the best reconciliation is achieved between the writer's intentions and their fulfillment. Understanding the revision process as Nancy Sommers describes it may help students develop a greater tolerance for the discomfort they experience until the piece is finished. According to Sommers, revision for experienced writers is "holistic" (they consider needed changes in both the parts and in the whole simultaneously) and "recursive" (they remain open to needed changes of all kinds throughout the writing of the piece even though giving more attention to the shape of the argument in early drafts and more attention to style in later drafts). Sommers emphasizes that experienced writers can recognize *dissonance*, "the incongruities between intention and execution." In contrast with beginning writers who resist deviating from an original plan, experienced writers are willing to exploit this dissonance to discover new possibilities while they are revising. And they have the ability to stick with a piece until harmony between intention and execution is finally achieved.[9]

Utilizing such insights more effectively, I will be better prepared to meet my students' needs the next time I teach English 303. Even so, I doubt that I would be able to accomplish the objectives of the course fully without the help of a professional editor. I have discovered that the contact with a real-world editor effects students profoundly and should be retained as a key element of the course. I say this even though none of my students has as yet sold an essay to *Insight* magazine. In fact, I am beginning to believe that *rejection* by a real editor is what will help

---

[5] Howard Gardner, "Composing Symphonies and Dinner Parties." *Psychology Today*. April, 1980, 18-27.
[6] Elaine Maimon, "Talking to Strangers," *College Composition and Communication* 30 (1979), 367.
[7] Effective leads grace the many articles (in *Language Arts* and other journals) in which Lucy McCormick Calkins has described the composing processes of young children.
[8] Linda Flower, *Problem-Solving Strategies for Writing* (New York: Harcourt, 1981).
[9] Nancy Sommers, "Revision Strategies of Student Writers and Experienced Adult Writers,"*College Composition and Communication* 31 (1980): 378-88.

students at this level the most.

Rejection by Chabot jolted my students into a sudden realization of the great difference between writing for school and writing for publication. In school, they had evidently been permitted to ride along on pockets of excellence, even when deficiencies were apparent. Benjamin's information on earth-sheltered homes was so detailed and technically accurate that a pleased instructor in a typical writing course would have marked it "A+," obviating Benjamin's need to act upon the suggestion, perhaps added by the instructor as an afterthought, to consider ways of increasing in the article's appeal to the average reader. Dana's writing was consistently imaginative and dynamic.

> *Need*—a word that forever changes color. When I was a freshman I needed a stereo; a sophomore, I needed to go to Daytona during spring break. My father needs a snow-blower. My mother has always needed a vacation. I am receiving $7500 in interest-free loans because I am a student and "need" the money. Others are paying for my use of these funds because they are not students. Something doesn't seem right.

Persuaded by the energy of her style, students and instructor would have awarded her highest honors in most writing classes, as we did. She would never have felt the need to act upon the suggestion to resolve the contradiction hidden within her essay.

In school, writers are rewarded for pieces of excellence. But to publish in the world beyond school, they must achieve both excellence of the parts and harmony of the whole. This is what Chabot really taught my class. John had worked hard and enthusiastically for eight weeks on an article on gemstone investing and was rejected in one breath, "Not appropriate for *Insight*. Our readers are not the wealthy elite." Melissa had revised the diction and chiseled the imagery with painstaking effort. "You need a rallying point, some dramatic structure to hold the piece together." The teacher praises the strengths to encourage learning and growth. The editor notes the flaw which makes the piece unusable. Perhaps writers need this kind of abrupt rejection from the professionals before they will believe how essential it is to stay with an article until it is truly finished, and what an utter waste of time it is to attempt anything less.

The encounter with Chabot recharged the students in my class. By semester's end, Nancy was planning to interview the next celebrity booked at the Joynt, and Benjamin, with renewed zeal, had made appointments to interview families in two earth-sheltered homes. Other students began completely new pieces. A few weeks after the course ended, Dana asked me to critique a new essay aimed at *Insight*. "People must learn to lie more." Chabot would like the lead. "People must recover from the current obsession with honesty and openness; some discretion is needed to protect our relationship with those we love the most." Perhaps the idea had that "ring of truth" that would effect Dana's break into print.

I recognize that not all the students in English 303 will have the talent and drive to publish. I am confident, however, that the course as we are developing it will provide all students in this seminar with a taste of what writing for publication actually involves.

Analyzing Classifications:
Foucault for Advanced Writing

by Carol Snyder

In recently published texts on writing the topic of classification is given scant attention. While some rhetorics and handbooks discuss classification and division as ways of organizing paragraphs, others ignore them altogether. No current text, moreover, offers advanced students the help they need if they are to write well about the classifications they encounter in their fields.[1] Because classifications—of types of literature, behavior, social systems, philosophies, methods, and so on—structure discourse in the disciplines, advanced students are often expected to explain or critically analyze aspects of these arrangements in their papers.

Instead of exploring or challenging the classifications they write about, however, all too frequently students merely rehearse categories and repeat standard distinctions. The absence of argument in these papers suggests that students typically misunderstand the provisional status of classifications and their dependence on disciplinary conventions, tending to regard them as though they were as reliably permanent as the bold-face headings of textbooks make them seem. What such writers need, it seems clear, is a more challenging introduction to division and classification, one that can at once spur the interest that makes for engaged, purposeful writing and promote a better understanding of division and classification as scholarly tools. In response to this need, I have formulated an approach to teaching classification based on the work of Michel Foucault, the French historian of ideas whose "archaeology of knowledge" unearths the workings of classifications in history.[2]

Reprinted from *College Composition and Communication* 35 (1984): 209-16. © 1984 by NCTE. Reprinted with permission.

[1] Maxine Hairston's *Successful Writing: A Rhetoric for Advanced Composition* (New York: Norton, 1981) does not treat classification. Richard M. Coe's *Form and Substance: An Advanced Rhetoric* (New York: John Wiley, 1981) includes the most thorough discussion of classification in any recent text, although the emphasis here is on learning to classify and not on analysis.

[2] Foucault's discussion of classifications is dispersed throughout his concrete historical studies of mental institutions: *Madness and Civilization*, trans. Richard Howard (New York: Pantheon Books, 1965); hospitals: *The Birth of the Clinic*, trans. A.M. Sheridan Smith (New York: Pantheon Books, 1973); penal institutions: *Discipline and Punish* trans. A.M. Sheridan Smith (New York: Vintage Books, 1979); and schools and families: *The History of Sexuality, Vol. 1.*, trans. Robert Hurley (New York: Vintage Books, 1980). Some of his most significant insights, however, are embedded in his more abstruse, theoretical works:*The Order of Things*, trans. A.M. Sheridan Smith (New York: Pantheon Books, 1970); *The Archaeology of Knowledge*, trans. A.M. Sheridan Smith (New York: Pantheon Books, 1972); *Language, Counter-Memory, Practice: Selected Essays and Interviews*, trans. Donald F. Bouchard and Sherry Simon, ed. Donald F. Bouchard (Ithaca, NY: Cornell University Press, 1977); *Power/Knowledge. Selected Interviews and Other Writings 1972-1977*, trans. Colin Gordon, Leo Marshall et. al., ed. Colin Gordon (New York: Pantheon Books, 1980). A useful bibliography appears in *Power/knowledge*.

From Foucault's revolutionary analyses of the rise of discursive categories I have derived a set of principles for understanding classifications—their authority, operations, and effects—and a plan of inquiry students can use both to generate working theses about classifications and to improve the classifications they themselves propose. Following the convention in the natural and social sciences and for ease of reference, I will hereafter use the general term "classification" to designate not only the acts of segregating ranges of entities into classes ("partition" or "division" in rhetoric) and assigning instances to those classes, but also to name the product of these operations, the order or classificatory system so created.[3]

Foucault has a great deal to say about the classifications that structure our discourse and order our institutions. Classifications serve Foucault as keys to the development of the "human sciences," his term for the cluster of modern knowledges of man: a cluster including such fields as medicine, linguistics, ethnology, penology, and psychiatry. To reconstruct these histories, he compares earlier and later classificatory systems in a field for evidence of changes in the way we conceive our subjects. The emergence of a new or revisionary system of classes figures for him as a signal of a conceptual shift. In the decline of eighteenth century "classificatory medicine," for instance, with its tables of essential resemblances between diseases, Foucault sees a turn away from a structural, universalizing reading of organic nature to a reading focussed on the body of the individual patient; nineteenth century typologies of diseases codified knowledge of pathological tissues gained by dissection and clinical observation.[4] As his analyses show, by isolating objects of knowledge, classifications function both to create and limit discourses.

But for Foucault classifications are more than conceptual structures. Because he finds that they often arise in institutional practices or take effect in such practices, he also sees classifications as social instruments, powerful codes whose frequent function is to exclude, confine, or incarcerate "deviant" types. Foucault's histories abound in examples of the power of classifications to shape intellectual and social reality, examples that should prove provocative to students and teachers overly familiar with the biological model of classification on which so many writing texts rely. *Madness and Civilization*, for instance, Foucault's first important history, traces the course of "the great exclusion" that occurred in the mid-seventeenth century as the insane, the poor, and the unemployed were alike classified as "idle" and on that basis thrown together into asylums. This isolation of the mad in asylums, the book proceeds to show, created the conditions in which madness could be both controlled

---

[3] Logically, dividing and grouping are nearly simultaneous acts. By noting symmetries and disparities among items, we create divisions which thereafter serve as classes. Dictionaries and thesauruses recognize the closeness of the two acts when they list "classification" under "division" and vice versa. Rhetoric texts, while often acknowledging that classification is the broader term, preserve a distinction: "division" is used for the initial sorting operation, "classification" for the arranging of given items into groups and the assigning of items to predetermined categories. In the natural and social sciences and symbolic logic, however, "classification" does duty for both operations and for the orderly array of sets produced by a full analysis. Foucault's vocabulary for division and classification is too rich to be emulated here, but his general term of reference is "classification." For my students, drawn as they are from several disciplines, "classification" is the more familiar and thus the clearer term.

[4] This argument is advanced in the first chapter of *The Birth of the Clinic*, "Spaces and Classes."

and studied; eventually, the invention of new techniques for dealing with the insane led to the production of a new order of knowledge, the discipline of psychology, and its refinement of the taxonomy of mental disorders.

Tracing the intellectual history of the last four centuries, Foucault constantly raises questions about the authority of the discourses of experts and the power of institutions to determine the production and application of knowledge. His inquiries into "the author function" in discourses—questions about who is authorized to articulate, modify, circulate, or employ the statements and schemes they contain—can be particularly revealing when applied to classifications, those most anonymous arrangements of ideas.[5] The insights in his concrete historical surveys of modern social institutions also bear on classifications. In these works, for instance, he offers a number of examples of how particular classifications led to the architectural partitioning of hospitals, schools, and prisons while acknowledging that the "art" of distributing individuals in space can also create new objects of knowledge, new ways of categorizing knowledge. In *Discipline and Punish*, he notes that the careful distribution of workers in the late-eighteenth-century factory, while it was meant to allow the efficient supervision of workers and the production process, also occasioned the recording and distilling of information about both laborers and processes. Foucault expresses this insight in the principle that "discipline organizes an analytical space," a space open to observation, calculation, and control.[6] In general, then, Foucault's work should alert us to ask of any specification system when, in what historical circumstances, it emerges, and where, in which institutional contexts, it operates. By making classifications objects of inquiry, Foucault's principles and questions can help students see these deep, often nearly invisible structures and the power they have to inform discursive and social transactions.

To streamline the task of teaching the analysis of classifications in an advanced writing class, I have schematized Foucault's ideas. I open discussion by defining classification, note that classificatory schema surround us in both our discourse and our institutions, and then point out that like all other products of civilization, the products of our acts of classifying and dividing have only an historical reality. From century to century and even decade to decade, these schemes are in the process of being formulated, modified, or discarded. Put as a general principle, we can say that within a specific historical frame, *"classifications both reflect and direct our thinking. The way we order represents the way we think."*[7]

The best way to bring this principle home to students, I have found, is to present them with two subsidiary propositions and some examples. The first proposition is that *we classify only what we consider important: the rise of a taxonomy identifies a new topic of conceptual importance.* A good example is the rise of a taxonomy of sexual deviance in the late nineteenth century. In "The History of Sexuality" Foucault argues provocatively that this development is a signal of that period's

---

[5] "What is an Author?" in *Language, Counter-Memory, Practice*, p. 138.

[6] *Discipline and Punish*, p. 143.

[7] This formulation appears in an essay by Stephen Jay Gould, "The Titular Bishop of Titiopolis," *Natural History* 90 (May, 1981), 22. Gould refers to Foucault's *Madness and Civilization* as a source for the idea.

increasing preoccupation with sexuality and specifically of the "medicalisation of sexuality" which, at least in part, gives rise to the discipline of psychoanalysis.[8] Students can contribute other examples drawn from their own fields.

For the second proposition, I use a statement of paleontologist Stephen Jay Gould from an article of his reviewing Foucault's work: *"Historical changes in classification are the fossilized indicators of conceptual revolution."* Gould's article recounts the breakthrough made by Nicolaus Steno, the founder of modern geology, when he reclassified the appearance of solids within solids as a phenomenon caused by physical forces; before Steno, solids in solids had been explained metaphysically as part of the evidence of the aesthetic hand of God in an original creation.[9] Written for a general audience, Gould's essay is short and clear enough to start students thinking about classification.

The next principle is much harder to state succinctly, for it speaks to a range of power relations between classifications and their objects. In its most global form, the principle holds that *classifications have the power to dispose their objects*. What we classify, I explain, we tend to isolate: discursive classification isolates objects of knowledge; institutions, when they classify their human objects, regulate them as well, assigning them to partitioned locales like hospital wards, classrooms, and prison cells. At this point, Foucault's examples of the institutionalization of the insane and of health services in general are valuable, but my students have been able to provide further examples. Several education students, for instance, have noted that the classification of some children as learning disabled has meant their separation from their classmates and their isolation in specially-controlled environments where they are both taught and studied.

Students are also quick to see another sense in which classifications can be said to have exclusionary power: in discriminating some objects as worthy of attention, classifications necessarily exclude others. The categorization of some branches of the visual arts as "fine" arts is exclusionary in this way. The work of women artists has traditionally been classified as "craft" and on this basis excluded from museums, critical consideration, and textbooks. The situation began to change, in fact, only when feminist art historians analyzed the connections between the classification, the experts authorized to articulate it, and the institutions empowered to sanction it. Brainstorming along these lines, students have discovered many less malign examples of circumscription by classification.

With this preparation, students can usually identify a classification they want to analyze. I encourage them to choose one of some importance in their fields. To help them with their analyses, I have devised a plan of inquiry based on Foucault's principles and the questions he poses about discourse. Using this scheme, students identify the object, the criteria for inclusion and exclusion, the originator and user, the historical locus, and the institutional seting of a classification.

1. *Identify the object of the classification.* What is being classified? Does the classification affect human beings? How? A classification of psy-

---

[8] "The History of Sexuality," in *Power/Knowledge*, p. 191.
[9] Gould, p. 20.

choses, for instance, may purport to classify illnesses and may derive from other classifications of mental disorders, but may take effect on people suffering some mental disorder. If this is the case with your classification, you should identify both the overt object and the human object of the grouping.

These questions remind students to consider the social implications of some ordering schemes. Responding to them, a student who proposed to categorize radiology techniques by describing their mechanical operations and diagnostic functions revised her plan to focus on a risk-benefit analysis of the effects of different radiography procedures on patients. The analysis she eventually wrote gained both descriptive power and an evaluative perspective.

2. *Identify what the classification excludes.* Who or what is being excluded by this classification? Does it privilege or disadvantage any particular group of persons, things, or ideas by assigning them to this class? Examine the difference/s between what falls within and what falls outside the classification. What are the criteria for inclusion in the classification? On what basis are some objects excluded?

The questions about exclusion help students see that the criteria used to establish privileged categories are sometimes slanted. Thus education students have discovered that some of the I.Q. and achievement tests used to divide "the gifted and talented" from their classmates may measure only the cognitive benefits of affluence and ethnic advantage. These questions also encourage students to try to apply classifications and their criteria to new or excluded instances. In one case, for example, a student examining her professor's categorization of the sub-genres of science fiction noted that no examples of recent feminist science fiction figured in his classification. She asserted, finally, that these works could not be made to fit the framework without distorting either the works or the scheme.

3. *Identify the human subjects who devise or use the classification.* What person or group of persons constructed this classification? Who accepts or uses it? To clarify your answers to these questions, you should consider some further questions: a) How did the originators or modifiers of the classification arrive at their conclusions? What did they observe and how? b) Who is authorized now to employ or modify this classification? c) What is the source of authority of the person/s who made the classification or of those who now use it? d) Does any person or group challenge the validity or criticize the effects of this classification? Why?

Probing the authority of classifiers can help students uncover the not always obvious perspectives that classifiers bring to their tasks. Answering these questions, a student working with the American Psychiatric Association's classification of mental disorders, the *Diagnostic and Statistical Manual* (DSM), learned an interesting fact about the formulation of the second edition. She found that it had been developed with the World Health Organization along lines set by the medical model for classifying diseases. The medical orientation carried over unchallenged, she noted, into the most recent (1979) version of the DSM, while other features of the classification were revised in response to various protests by behaviorists, family therapists, and others. Following this lead, she began to think about some of the ways medical classification methods would necessarily falsify psychological diagnosis and to look for telling examples. As this student discovered, classifications connect experts in different fields to create a web of discourse and practice: composition researchers and writing teachers, for instance, now use classifications developed by linguists and cognitive psychologists. Exploring such connections can be fruitful.

4. *Locate the classification in time.* When did it arise? Is there a reason why it could not have been formulated earlier? How was its object regarded before it was classified this way? How did this classification change the way its object was understood or managed?

Once students have identified the makers and users of classifications, they should be prepared to ask some broader questions about the history of the classification. To illustrate, a student writing about the division of nations into first, second, and third worlds had already recorded the information that the classification arose when the leaders of some African and Asian nations at the 1955 Bandung Conference began to refer to themselves as the "third world." Answering these questions, she observed that this discursive reordering of the geopolitical map registered a sense that the postwar division of the world into superpower spheres of influence ignored the possibility of an independent Afro-Asian bloc. From this point she proceeded to judge the political and intellectual consequences of the reordering: while it had not completely succeeded in establishing a new balance of power, she found, it had fostered a genuinely global understanding of the power relations between nations.

5. *Locate the classification in space.* Where was it formulated or modified? Remember that some classifications originate in social or institutional practices and only later take form in discourse. Where is it now used, in what institutional or social sites? How is it understood or administered in those sites?

Institutional regimens produce many de facto classifications. Our schools, for instance, as they divide students by age into grades, assign special spaces to those grades—a partitioning now so familiar we hardly think to write about it. On the other hand, some classificatory grids are both circulated discursively and cast in institutional concrete. These questions open such transformations to analysis. In one case, for instance, a student preparing a paper on some aspect of the Texas Criminal Code succeeded in finding a thesis when he considered the sites in which the Code is realized. Recognizing that the Texas county jails housing misdemeanor offenders are more crowded, violent, and poorly equipped, and provide fewer work outlets and education programs, than the maximum security prisons housing felony offenders, he noted that in this respect misdemeanor offenders actually receive harsher punishments than convicted felons. His discovery led him to assert that in this case the classifying intent of the Code is subverted in practice.

By preparing students to seek meanings, the plan of inquiry provides an essential stimulus to good writing. As they engage with these five groups of questions, students come to see that the classifications that order their disciplines are meaningful human inventions with significant effects, that they are, in fact, *open* to question and explanation, and thus that writing about them might lead to useful discoveries. The questions themselves prompt students to perceive new relationships; those perceptions become the basis for a working thesis about a classification.

Students begin by answering these questions in writing, assembling information they already have or can find by doing some research. They generally stop to construct a tentative thesis when they have located an overlooked connection or a fascinating inconsistency. I advise them, however, to work through all the questions, for the responses to later questions, if applicable, may broaden or complicate the assertions they have formed. Once they have shaped their theses from their discoveries, students are ready to plan an argument. The energy released by these discoveries usually carries over to the composing process, and students find that they can use some of the information generated during their work on invention both to introduce the classification and support the principal assertion.

Beyond helping them discover something worthwhile to say about a particular category or scheme, the invention procedure outlined here should also help students narrow the gap between their own and their professors' attitudes toward classification. Analyzing their classifications for both their internal coherence and their relation to other social or intellectual systems, they are exposed to the full range of critical stances that scholars might assume toward these powerful but provisional tools. Moreover, since they have chosen for analysis a classification from their own disciplines, the experience often serves to sensitize students to the classificatory methods and problems peculiar to those fields. The literature student who uses the plan to analyze a category or genre, for instance, should approach other divisions of literature with a clearer sense of how such categories are formulated and what their limitations might be.

Students who have worked with the scheme are also more likely to classify in their other papers, and I encourage them to return to the scheme to check their formulations. Reviewing these questions, they are reminded to identify the specific object of their classification, their criteria for inclusion and exclusion, the perspective from which they have worked, and the context in which the classification arises or in which it will apply. The review aids students not only to evaluate their own logic but also to make explicit statements in their papers to guide readers to a clear conception of the classifications they offer. Thus the plan of inquiry can function as a revision heuristic.

Whether they write to analyze a classification or to devise one, this approach to teaching classification should help students find their way around the classified spaces of their disciplines and demystify for them one of the basic forms of academic discourse. At the same time, asking and answering the questions Foucault raises can lead students to understand that the construction of classifications, like the production of academic knowledge in general, is strongly affected by and strongly affects social conditions. It may even lead them to a truth about the "truth" our discourses transmit—that, as Foucault puts it, " . . . truth isn't outside power, or lacking in power. . . . Truth is a thing of this world."[10]

---

[10] "Truth and Power," in *Power/Knowledge*, p. 131.

Research Writing in Advanced Composition: An Essay in Definition

by Russell Rutter

For years I have both taught and done technical writing. Since 1975 I have been a technical writing program coordinator. Of necessity—but pleasant necessity—I have worked closely with faculty members and other professionals from many disciplines besides English. I wish to offer here some thoughts about the place of research writing in advanced composition. This article is in essence tentative, intended to isolate one variable—research writing—that will help define more fully just what is meant by the term "advanced composition program."

Advanced Composition and the Continuum of Writing Courses

Composition courses come in a nearly infinite variety of shapes and sizes. For purposes of classification, though, one can envision a continuum of courses. At one end is the course conducted entirely within the classroom. Students write papers on subjects assigned by the instructor, and no resource materials are used except those available on the spot—course texts, class discussion and the memory of personal experience. At the opposite end of the continuum is the course conducted on an interdisciplinary basis. Students write not just in their English classes but in all of their classes. Teachers from all disciplines work together to devise assignments and to improve the quality of writing instruction, and English professors serve as resource persons and facilitators for what is really a campus-wide program. It will be clear that this second type of course is in the traditional sense not a course at all. It is a writing-across-the-curriculum program.

It may be doubted whether so hermetically sealed a composition course as our first example offers actually exists. It is beyond doubt, though, that writing-across-the-curriculum programs, because they involve so many people from so many departments and cost so much money to implement, are (unhappily) very rare. Thousands of advanced students who have passed introductory composition and have no access to a writing-across-the-curriculum program seek to further improve their writing skills. It is for them that advanced composition programs are designed. Because these students come from a variety of disciplines, the advanced composition courses they take must adopt an interdisciplinary perspective. Because these students are engaged in more specialized research and not simply in general education, their

---

Reprinted from the *Journal of Advanced Composition* 6 (1985-86): 131-38. Reprinted with permission.

advanced composition courses must be oriented to research writing. If they are both of these things—interdisciplinary and research-oriented—they move on our hypothetical continuum away from introductory composition and toward the ideal embodied in writing across the curriculum. The essential issue in defining the term "advanced composition program" is this: How does the program approach research writing?

Research Writing in Introductory Composition

It might be objected first, though, that research writing—however it is defined—is part of introductory or "freshman" composition and thus *not* an essential characteristic of advanced composition alone. I have come for several reasons to believe that such is not the case. For one thing, guided readings play too important a part in introductory composition to be dropped. They acquaint students with ideas and issues fundamental to understanding what it means to be a person in these times, understanding that I believe it is the mission of liberal arts, general education courses to provide. Moreover, it has been urged that "some of the cognitive activities that enable one to understand a subject are the same activities that enable one to formulate and support the assertions one makes in one's writing,"[1] in other words, that improving reading skills can improve writing skills. Yet the only way I know to make room for the research-writing unit is to jettison these valuable readings. I am not convinced that the less focused reading done for the research paper is an adequate substitute.

A second answer to the objection mentioned above is that professors in other departments are far less interested in having their freshmen write research papers in introductory composition than in having them write short papers clearly and coherently. The supposed homage they pay to research writing at the freshman level seems limited to a desire that students learn how to make endnotes and bibliographies properly and to know when these are needed. A plain exercise in documentation can teach them this skill.

Finally, there is a third answer to our objection—an answer that is, at least to my mind, decisive. It is highly questionable that true research can be taught by one English instructor to twenty freshmen who possess differing interests *and* little experience with college-level work. Richard Larson has summed the matter up this way:

> We in English have no business claiming to teach "research" when research in different academic disciplines works from distinctive assumptions and follows distinctive patterns of inquiry. . . . Most of us are trained in one discipline only and should be modest enough to admit it.[2]

---

[1] Lee Odell, "Teaching Writing by Teaching the Process of Discovery: An Interdisciplinary Enterprise,"*Cognitive Processes in Writing*, ed. Lee W. Gregg and Erwin R. Steinberg (Hillsdale, New Jersey: Lawrence Erlbaum Associates, 1980), p. 145. See also Joseph Comprone, "Recent Research in Reading and Its Implications for the College Composition Curriculum,"*Rhetoric Review*, 1 (1983), 122-137.

[2] "The 'Research Paper' in the Writing Course: A Non-Form of Writing,"*College English* 4 (1982), 815-16. after I had given this article in its briefer form as an MLA paper, I was asked to serve on the master's thesis committee of a second graduate student in physical education. As of July, 1983, both students had completed their degree programs. The time I spirit working with them and with colleagues in physical edu-

To this eminently reasonable assertion I would add that never once have I met a colleague who expected from English professors the omnicompetence that introductory composition courses featuring "research papers" insist on promising.

Research Writing in Advanced Composition

Research writing, then, to return to the thesis of this article, is the province of the advanced composition course and the advanced composition program. Here students are familiar enough with research methods in their particular areas to be asking questions about organization, audience, style, format, and the like. And they have something to say. This situation, which I encounter frequently in advanced composition, presupposes the existence of outside specialists. Indeed, to a focus on research writing we might add consultation with outside specialists as another key characteristic of the advanced composition program.

Let me illustrate. One of the students who completed my course in Advanced Technical Writing was also completing his master's thesis in the area of physical education. He was an assistant coach of the Illinois State University soccer team, and his thesis developed the idea that training methods, or protocols, should mimic the sport for which the athlete is training. For soccer players, my student contended, a training protocol should consist of short periods of maximum energy output separated by short periods of reduced exertion, because soccer, unlike, say, sprinting, does not require maximum sustained effort but rather spurts of effort.

This was not just theory. There are techniques and mechanisms to monitor the significant functions of the respiratory and motor systems so that the effects of various training protocols can be charted and only desirable types of conditioning retained in the final protocol. One of these mechanisms is called a Digital Read-out Jaeger Ergo-Oxyscreen. As this imposing name implies, the researcher using it must have some acquaintance not only with exercise physiology but also with computer programming and statistical analysis.

The work described here is certainly specialized research, and the writing may justly be called research writing. The paper that my student submitted to me at the end of the course—four chapters of his master's thesis—was surely better than the original version he had shown me fifteen weeks before. Of course, it was more complete because more of the research had been finished, but it was also more coherent, it contained fewer loose ends, and it was stylistically more concise and direct.

If by teaching research writing we mean solely teaching coherence, clarity, the concise style, and so on, we can say that all writing is research writing. The trouble with a definition as general as this is that one suffers from a kind of intellectual want of fresh air. A definition like this is, as someone once said of transcendentalism, a train of fifteen coaches with one passenger on it. If by teaching research writing we mean teaching students to grapple with content and not just with problems of form,

---

cation, statistics, and physiology contributed more toward "teaching research" than any introductory composition "research writing" unit I could have developed on my own. research procedures differ from discipline to discipline, but the composing process is more uniform. See Linda Flower and John R. Hayes, "A Cognitive Process Theory of Writing" CCC 32 (1981), 363-87.

we fool ourselves—certainly not them—if we think we can perform the task alone. As a matter of fact, in the case I just described, the student was receiving guidance from his thesis director. The director and I were engaged in an interdisciplinary research writing cooperative effort, which is just as it should be.[3]

Implementation of Research Writing in Advanced Composition

We in advanced composition have, then, a grand opportunity to broaden the scope of our courses. Let me suggest some preliminary steps for making the most of this opportunity, steps that define not only the nature of advanced composition but also the very way in which an advanced composition program can be conducted and administered.

1. All students enrolled in an advanced composition course should be identified by major, minor or special option, number of completed credit hours, career plans, and special interests. This information should be contained in a card file and, for large-enrollment courses, a tabulation of cards should be maintained. All departments should be singled out for special attention that for two semesters or more provide more than five percent of the students enrolled.

2. Letters should be written that describe succinctly the goals of the course, typical writing assignments, and special features. I have found it best to address such letters to the department chairperson and promise a follow-up telephone call within a week. If all goes well, the chairperson may in the meantime post the letter or send copies of it to advisers and other interested department members.

3. The chairperson should be told in the follow-up call that members of the advanced composition faculty would welcome an opportunity to visit with him/her and other interested faculty to discuss ways of making more useful and directly applicable those writing courses to which students are being sent.

Department chairpersons often delegate responsibility, so advanced composition faculty may meet with a department council or curriculum committee, or be invited to attend a department faculty meeting. These visits enable composition faculty to meet—often for the first time—faculty in other departments who are interested in writing. And that is what this preliminary process is for—to identify "interested persons," like graduate or undergraduate advisors, the chairperson of the curriculum committee, an area coordinator, or simply the departmental writing nut. This last person, by the way, may prove invaluable—may for years have been seeking a good chance to say

---

[3] After I had given this article in its briefer form as an MLA paper, I was asked to serve on the master's thesis committee of a second graduate student in physical education. As of July, 1983, both students had completed their degree programs. The time I spent working with them and with colleagues in physical education, statistics, and physiology contributed more toward "teaching research" than any introductory composition "research writing" unit I could have developed on my own.

to his/her colleagues, "OK, now you have no excuse for not acting. They have even come to us!"

The results of the kind of interdepartmental dialogue just mentioned are as varied as the persons who engage in it. For example, faculty, particularly in departments with large numbers of majors, where detailed tallies are hard to keep, sometimes express surprise that so many of their majors have been electing a given advanced composition course. I mentioned earlier that students are *sent* to advanced composition courses, but they also enroll on their own initiative. If their experiences are favorable, they recommend these courses to their friends. Contacts initiated by advanced composition faculty may permit a relationship to be formalized which students have initiated without formal faculty advisement. Again, knowing more about what other departments expect their majors to learn helps the advanced composition teacher devise assignments that reinforce the teaching done in the major department. Moreover, such interaction makes it possible to develop assignments that can be used exclusively in non-composition courses to aid in the learning process—and to discover assignments that individual professors have developed and found successful in their own courses.[4] English faculty can help strengthen the writing activities in courses taught across the campus by showing that students who write more learn more.[5] In addition they will learn that they possess no monopoly on good writing assignments or on interest in writing as a tool for learning and communication. If the quality of an advanced composition program depends on the extent to which it is an interdisciplinary effort focusing on student research at the advanced level, such a program has much in common, as was suggested earlier, with that more ambitious endeavor called writing across the curriculum.[6] What should in fact distinguish an advanced composition program is its unremitting effort to transcend the narrow boundaries of the English department, to cross the departmental fire breaks that keep higher education so compartmentalized.

Introductory Composition and Advanced Composition Compared

I hear it said occasionally that advanced composition does not differ from introductory composition but rather offers more of the same. This is a dangerous half-truth. It is true insofar as clear writing in English 101 is clear writing in English 301; it is false because no composition program teaches writing in a vacuum—or at least no composition program should. Let me conclude with a distinction. Introduc-

---

[4] Research procedures differ from discipline to discipline, but the composing process is more uniform. See Linda Flower and John R. Hayes, "A Cognitive Process Theory of Writing,"*CCC*, 32 (1981), 365-87.

[5] Janet Emig, "Writing as a Mode of Learning," *CCC*, 28 (1977), 122-28. Reprinted in Gary Tate and Edward P.J. Corbett, eds., *The Writing Teacher's Sourcebook* (New York and Oxford: Oxford UP, 1981), pp. 69-79.

[6] This approach to advanced composition is not limited to technical writing (which is often too narrowly defined anyway). For a discussion of the process approach used in a writing situation that would not be considered technical, see Russell Rutter, "Teaching Writing to Probation Officers: Problems, Methods, and Resources," *CCC*, 33 (1982), 288-95.

tory composition courses should be humanistic, general studies offerings that encourage not only writing but also reading on varied topics and discussions of values, social issues, or ethical questions. Advanced composition courses, by contrast, should zero in not just on good writing but on good specialized writing. You can recognize a good introductory composition program because it compels students to think not only about writing but also about issues that one expects a person with a university education to have considered. And you can recognize a good advanced composition program because it moves its teachers to develop a familiarity with the research areas, often highly specialized, in which the students will exercise the writing skills they acquire, both now and after graduation. A good introductory program forces students to look inward. A good advanced program forces English faculty to look across the campus and beyond. Both programs perform essential educational tasks, and where they function in the manner described here, the problem of research writing will take care of itself.

Preoccupations: Private Writing and Advanced Composition

by Susan Hilligoss

In discussions about cross-disciplinary writing, the college student is typically described as a novice being initiated into a discourse community of academic experts. Most of the documents generated by this entering writer (1) have transactional functions, to use James Britton's term; (2) are public—exams, school essays, term papers, resumés, applications for entrance to programs and employment, reports, memos; and (3) are intended for and validated by experienced members of the community (88). This model of novice and expert is a shorthand that has been fruitful in understanding the social contexts of academic writing, but as a metaphor for classroom practice it has limits. First, because investigation has understandably focused on success in academic writing, the professional or academic discourse community is privileged with a sense of integrity and unity over time, but the novice is not. This discrepancy is not new—typically we have regarded students as newborns at the start of our classes and adults at the end of them—but neither is it helpful. Second, in the novice/expert model, the newcomer writes for only one purpose: to enter the academic community. In effect, the novice writer is seen as having no history, no identity developed over time through other texts, other discourse.

Yet, college students *do* have histories with texts that they have produced. By the time they have spent fourteen or more years in school, they have perhaps written more for school than for any other purpose. They might agree with John Richmond, who concluded from his work with Jamaican teenagers in London, "A great deal of writing is done in school, maybe too much" (quoted in Goswami and Stillman 17). Even so, students have also written other texts with a variety of purposes, some more private than public in function.

Social Theories and Private Writing

Although there is interest in it, private writing as such is still largely unexplored by composition researchers (Britton 23). Elaine Maimon has noted that composition teachers "blur the distinction between private and public writing, to the detriment of both forms" (132). Expressive or speculative journals written in academic settings, valuable as they are, turn a private form to public purposes; according to Susan Florio and Christopher M. Clark, in one elementary classroom the school setting affected the nature of diary writing (126-27).

Reprinted from the *Journal of Advanced Composition* 9 (1989): 124-34. Reprinted with permission.

Private writing is most often voluntary. It includes personal letters and diaries, as well as many brief, usually ephemeral texts such as lists and personal messages. It also includes course notebooks and other self-initiated writing instrumental to transactional purposes. The immediate audience for private writing may be only the writer himself or herself and at most one or two other persons; but even when it is instrumental to a job, schoolwork, or other public or transactional purposes, private writing has its own conventions and traditions. These conventions may be idiosyncratic; Ann E. Berthoff, for example, has pointed out the "highly personal" structure of grocery lists (56). But they may also be shared knowledge about what makes a list, letter, or diary. Indeed one broad collection of disciplines, the humanities, has recognized private documents as central to its traditions of inquiry. That is, a check register or long-term correspondence has interpretive communities—from the immediate readers to investigators at a distance from the writer's community—in the same way that a scientific paper or a poem does. Both private and public writing enter into writers' understanding of themselves as writers and their ability to engage in dialogue with, make sense of, and contribute to not just one but a number of communities. Recognizing both types of writing seems important for all writers but is critical for those who are studying liberal arts, particularly the humanities with their traditional concern for *self* and *identity*.

Convinced that knowledge is socially constructed and that writing in our culture can forge both personal and professional identities within communities, I developed an advanced writing course for liberal arts students based on the connections between private and public writing. Developing this course raised an issue related to the emerging social view of academic discourse: the apparent dissonance between that view and the expressive or personal development view of writing. In the extreme, the social model can be represented by a hypothetical writing-in-the-disciplines program that concerns only formal conventions of academic writing; the expressive or personal development model, by a writing workshop that takes up only the personal writing of its members and has no other reading. In practice, researchers and teachers occupy a knowledgeable and humane middle ground; however, emphasizing the dissonance lets us confront some of our assumptions. I agree with Gerald Graff that English teachers must bring the discipline's conflicts (which frequently have "greater richness and vitality" than the conclusions eventually reached) to their classrooms where they implicitly or explicitly enact their beliefs (14).

Given these conflicting models, teaching advanced expository writing means clarifying values and practices. Theorists like Lester Faigley have distinguished a number of differences between the social and expressive views of writing. For example, Faigley notes the ahistoricity of three main "expressivist" values for writing: "integrity, spontaneity, and originality" (529). Further, citing the Marxist critic Henry Giroux, he suggests that "the expressive view of composing ignores how writing works in the world, hides the social nature of language, and offers a false notion of a 'private' self" (531). That is, in classroom terms, when we teach writing as personal development in an expressive workshop, we tend to hide our assumptions about writing, in particular our Romantic notions of individuality and creativity. Part of the social nature hidden from the students' (and teachers'?) view is the history of inquiry from which expressive courses derive. Yet, as I have said, the social model also tends to ignore history, chiefly the writer's history, but also the history of ideas about personal growth and cognition that inform much inquiry in the humanities. In preparing to teach advanced liberal arts students, I asked two questions. Is there a way to keep the values of expressive workshops and at the same time show workshop members that these practices have historical and social contexts? On the other hand, can the notion of discourse communities be broadened to recognize and indeed privilege the variety of settings in which advanced undergraduate students have written?

Focusing on private writing is one way to address these questions and the opposing views of discourse. Private writing is not writing without a social context, but writing that differs in context from more public writing. In the humanities, the preservation and editing of private documents belongs to the conventions of treating a single life, or a number of lives, as worthy of study, to be revealed as textual artifacts. Private documents have many contexts and purposes, only some of which are expressive.

Also, private writing differs from personal writing. For example, personal narrative, memoir, and autobiography are recognized public genres and embody certain assumptions about context—facts often overlooked in teaching. Conceptions of autobiography differ according to the writer's age and vocation, and probably also by time and place. In a study of autobiographical narratives by three groups differing in age and experience, Richard Beach found that younger adolescents' texts were concerned with action; those of older adolescents and adults with beliefs (62). In their essays, the adults (who were English teachers) were also less likely to retell events and more likely to use description than the younger writers. David Bartholomae and Anthony Petrosky have seen basic writers' autobiographical accounts as characterized by such patterns as "Boy Makes Good" and "Lessons in Life" (33). Lynn Z. Bloom notes that "Autobiographies focusing on childhood (and therefore ending with the subject's leaving home, or beginning college, marriage, parenthood, or a job) are seldom written by politicians, athletes, entertainers, or corporate executives (whose autobiographies emphasize adult performance), but mostly by writers and philosophers" (347). Far from being a genre suited mainly for beginning writers, autobiography, as it is interpreted by members of academic communities, carries sophisticated assumptions about strategies, subjects, purposes, and readership. In sum, the terms "expressive," "personal," "autobiographical," and "private" are not synonymous, viewed within a social model of language.

An Advanced Course about Private Writing

The course that I devised attempted some awareness of the social contexts of private writing and certain types of expressive writing, whether public or private. It was a single and partial answer to some of the issues raised here. The course, Advanced Expository Writing, is intended for third-year students in liberal arts and some science curricula; it fulfills the advanced communication requirement at Clemson University. In the spring of 1987, when I first taught it, class members were majoring in political science, English, psychology, economics, sociology, and chemistry; their work and insights are described here. Most said at the start that they took the course to improve their writing and as an alternative to other less liberal arts oriented advanced communication courses.

I sought to embody these themes in the course. First, we explored many types of connections between public and private writing. Using ordinary texts as evidence, we tried to identify our individual writing traditions, bring them to academic discussion, explore the interpretive communities in which they were produced, and place them in a public tradition of inquiry in the humanities. That sense of public tradition came from reading the private writing of others—writing now published and valued by larger discourse communities. In light of the humanities tradition of privileging the self, we also tried to construct views of ourselves as writers and thinkers, that is, identify our own intellectual preoccupations. We attempted to do the same for published writers.

The goal of class writing was not to write polished autobiography, especially given its problematic status, but to see how writing and texts "constructed" us and gave new opportunities to pursue and extend our preoccupations in several of our discourse communities, including those clustered to form a field or a vocation. Writing was a means to have a voice in an academic community, a voice that knew from whence it came.

As members of an advanced workshop within a liberal arts college, we also tried to enact some of the discursive practices of professionals in the humanities and social sciences. We wrote informal notes to each other, collaborated on one project, respected writers' wishes to keep journals private, encouraged speculative "pieces" composed of fragments, valued our preoccupations as special knowledge already developed, and treated our own texts with the authority accorded other artifacts of scholarly interest. I also sought explicit connections between class members' special interests and academic pursuits, but this was not borne out. The goal of these practices was not to dismiss the social conventions and power relations of the classroom, which as Patricia Bizzell has remarked would be difficult to change even with extraordinary conscious effort (150), but to treat each other more like professionals who typically mix formality and informality in their relations with one another.

Later writing included more public but still expressive forms: a book review, a profile that extended the thinking of an earlier piece, and an exchange of letters with an editor of historical correspondence. Although these genres and subjects are common in advanced expository writing courses, we strove to connect private and public writing, encourage interests formed over time, and understand the social contexts in which specific types of writing arise. For example, reviewing can extend and make public to an implied community an individual's voluntary, fragmented, or instrumental private writing. Editing assumes an interpretive community that not only values learning about the lives of others, but understands the published work as itself an artifact of time and place, a selected and edited version. Members of that community often write informally to each other about their concerns, and that was the focus of our editing work.

Finally, we tried to recognize that not all writing has an academic end and that bringing private writing to academic discussion might change our views of it. As Richard Rodriguez has observed, "While one suffers a diminished sense of private individuality by becoming assimilated into public society, such assimilation makes possible the achievement of public individuality" (26).

Constructing Our Pasts as Writers

In what became the most important personal inquiry, class members reflected on writing from their own histories—a cycle of discussion, writing, and reading repeated through the semester. Over three weeks I introduced several types of private writing or public, expressive writing: journals, diaries, and artistic and scientific notebooks; letters; and autobiographies and memoirs. Where we could, we identified these in our own histories and brought in sample documents. At the same time I brought in published examples from several fields of study, presented as whole books or periodicals, that is, in the context in which educated readers find them. I also brought in similar writing of my own.

I wanted students' artifacts of personal culture and development to have authority within the community of the class in the same way that artifacts generally have for scholars, and I wanted students' research to contribute genuinely to our knowledge. With private writing, this goal seems possible; class members did make connections between their letters and notebooks and those of other writers, whether local or remote. In particular, from their own past writing class members observed several times that private writing may be time-bound; for example, there are diaries for once-in-a-lifetime trips, and there are flurries of letters connected with certain periods of one's life. The following excerpt, the opening of a reflection by a student whom I shall call Terry, states that emphatically:

> I am not a letter writer. Letters are too personal, too intimate and too permanent. However, there have been times in my life when letter writing was a must. One of these times was from February to May of 1982 when I was a Marine Corps Recruit at Parris Island, South Carolina. Recruits are not allowed to use the telephone or have visitors, and for three months letters were my only method of communication with the outside world.

Terry, a junior majoring in political science, had never heard of psychologist Anna Freud and was only beginning to become aware of traditions of private writing, but his reflection on the spring of 1982 compares with her reminiscence of 1943, both cued by examining personal correspondence:

> I know from memory, as well as from notes of mine and letters I received and answered, what a dark year that was. The war seemed endless. . . . It took a special person to be hopeful that year. (Coles 3)

Having considered their own reasons for voluntary writing, class members were able to assess the generalizations of other investigators, such as Thomas Mallon, who also details a rich set of purposes for private writing in *A Book of One's Own: People and Their Diaries* (5).

Although I stressed private writing, any documents produced by class members were fair game. Berthoff's analyses of lists and other informal, often schematic writing gave method to our reflections on a wide variety of items (56-62). The goal was to make connections among some of the items. A writer could also compare his or her productions with others', and some students did so, as in comparing a set of course notes with those of a former classmate.

Focused on specific texts and their settings, class members did not recreate childhoods or otherwise write extended autobiographical narratives. Examining the texts in their lives prompted reminiscence, but also analysis. Because there was no requirement to write an essay, a number of students chose to take up different items in a series of observations, sometimes ending in a generalization. Likewise, there was no need to examine intensely personal material; choices depended on interest and the availability of their previous writing. Writers were free to find the private and personal in any text of their own making.

Students who looked only at graded school papers were more judgmental and dissatisfied with their writing than students who looked at any type of voluntary writing, even if it were a calendar, course notebook, or check register. This was true regardless of the student's academic success with writing. For example, Mark was accustomed to earning A's and B's on his papers, but he said of them, "They are like barroom chats: pleasant, fun, but speckled with flaws and very, very indulgent—superficial in their simulated passion." He went on: "Though they were written at different times, the same errors in the first are the same errors present in the last. I was very persistent in my ignorance." Dennis, whose academic writing had received a number of C's, began in the same vein, dissatisfied with his school writing; yet, he wrote this of his voluntary productions:

> In the drawer at home where my coin collection sits are countless papers with records of how many, how much, and when. The lists were constantly updated to keep up with a growing collection. Often the lists were rewritten for the sole purpose of neatness. The coins were always something that interested me and that's why I enjoyed doing the writing that went along with the collection. I was also proud of the collection which is why I kept all the writings neat.

He noted that he continues to make precise lists for other collections, in particular his record albums and tapes. These lists not only aided his own searches but also let him keep track of borrowed works. Dennis's private writing is part of his identity within a discourse community that understands his interest and whose members seek him out. Most important, his reflection in writing began to make him aware of that identity, by using some of the discursive practices of the academic community. For Mark, who had no choice but to take the role of the usual teacher-reader as he examined his papers, these discursive practices remained largely unhelpful in constructing any positive sense of identity from texts.

Several students examined their course notebooks, marginal notes in textbooks, desk calendars, or check registers. Class members who had been mediocre academic writers sometimes had only these types of voluntary writing to examine because they wrote little outside of school. But in spite of stated doubts and criticism, everyone noted definite habits and made specific comparisons either with their previous writing or other students' similar writing. All took credit for discovering patterns, even a writer who learned from her calendars that she was now less organized than she had been as a high school senior. Humor also crept in: a check register reminded John of "the countless numbers of pizzas" that he had eaten. Observations were not limited to what is usually called writing, or to examination of the text itself. One class member was struck by the graphic sense of her voluntary writing—scrapbooks, coloring books, and drawings; yet another speculated about the conditions that preserved a piece of his childhood writing that he had found taped to the underside of a dresser drawer.

Nor is the commonplace book dead. Two class members observed that they routinely copied quotations or pasted clippings, poems, and other texts into their journals or diaries. Louise also kept her school papers in her journal. Rod observed that he sometimes wrote about items after copying or pasting, and he related quoted texts to his own development:

> Amidst this character change, smaller but significant changes also occurred. A quote from *The Sound and the Fury* by Faulkner states that "a nigger is not a person, so much as a form of behavior; a sort of obverse reflection of the white people he lives among." This came at a time when I often pondered my bigotry and racism and struck me as an appropriate definition to a word I then used often and wanted to erase from my vocabulary.

For these writers, like those of an earlier time, the object character of personal books testifies to the important parts of life. Commonplace books also provide connections to a self conceived by reference to wider communities, implicitly through the selection of items and explicitly by writing about them.

Two class members revealed themselves as "impelled" writers, in Britton's sense (218). Their journals were self-initiated, as several others were, but these students wrote nearly every day and at length. Both wrote their entries with the ultimate purpose of shaping imaginative works, either short stories or poems; they regarded the journal work as preparatory. Neither had published any of their creative work so far, and although they had friends with whom they shared some writing, the journals were private. The sheer effort, as well as the voluntary nature of their writing, made them very conscious of their habits. Both wrote detailed observations of working habits. Daniel's reflection began, "My writing is a very important personal tool." Beth's journals were separate, validated artifacts, which she called "this book" or "this collection."

The impelled writers made extended connections between writing and self; in fact, they identified strongly with their writing, but this was not news to them. In the course of this reflection, two other class members made sustained intellectual and emotional discoveries in connecting writing and self. Terry, whose piece about boot camp I mentioned earlier, went on to describe differences between letters to his mother, which he named "eyes only" letters, and those to his family as a whole. Each feature of the letters, such as the lack of dates or the presence of postscripts, was interpreted to create a portrait of a young man who did not know how deeply his facade of bravado was cracked or how much his cryptic explanations worried the very person he wanted most to reassure. It was a moving but analytic examination of intensely personal materials.

In a different type of reflection, Marie traced a broad pattern of intellectual change in her life by examining several pieces of writing since eighth grade: a diary, a copy of *Walden* with passages that she had underlined, and a required journal from a women's studies course. She noted that underlining, a habit from high school, had carried over to college, particularly to her women's studies course the semester before she enrolled in advanced writing. While reading Dale Spender's *Man-Made Language*, she began to respond to the writer's powerful argument, and her underlining became annotations, at first one word and then a passage "at the end of one chapter that is not connected to any one thing, but is indirectly connected to the whole chapter." She wrote, "This writing and underlining became a major force in the journal that I was required to keep for the same class. My margin writing expanded into page after page of journal entries" and "sparked" personal revelations. She ended, "While I didn't change the world with that entry and although my thoughts were incomplete and underdeveloped, I did show myself that I do have the ability to be an independent thinker." She saw herself developing over the whole set of writings presented, from selfish interests in the diary to "social consciousness" in *Walden* to writing as "an active thought process" in her journal. Marie's and Terry's pieces sustained and built up a related series of discoveries that others also made more briefly. Their works were also autobiographical essays in the literary and textbook sense.

These pieces were read by other class members, and for some this was their most valued writing. The students treated this assignment with care and enthusiasm. Why? In part, because the investigation was real and enabled each writer to contribute new, analytic knowledge to the class; but I think there is another reason. No one, not even the impelled writers, had anyone publicly recognize the existence of their private writing. Students' and indeed most adults' private writing is rarely acknowledged, except for its being instrumental to public writing. There is no place for students to learn why private writing is valued by a segment of the academic community (a segment to which college students might aspire to belong) because they have rarely had the chance to reflect in an academic way about it. School is geared to weeks and months, not years, and that also works against recognition of sustained private writing, whether by students or writers held up as models. It is ironic that such writing is a primary source of document-based inquiry in the humanities. In a classroom, two or three isolated journal entries or letters must usually stand for the slow accumulation of trials, *essais*, repetitions, dead ends, renewed efforts, compelled and impelled thinking within the intellectual life of one person.

Afterthoughts

The course suggested several insights and many questions about the relations between private and public writing. Judging from writing over the term, I found that class members did not easily construct selves from texts, but insofar as they did, voluntary writing had a compelling part. More often than not, they related voluntary writing to actions outside school or formal preparation for a career. And voluntary writing often arose from and led to action rather than more writing. Class members regarded graded academic writing, even in a major subject chosen for its interest, as having a different, more tenuous relation to what some called their "true selves." In making this distinction, a number seemed to suffer that "diminished sense of private individuality" which Rodriguez has called the price of assimilation, in this case into the public communities of professional life (26). These writers had not achieved "public individuality," although several may have been on the brink. Researchers like Lucille Parkinson McCarthy have begun to study college writers over a period of a year or more (234). Voluntary writing might also enter into such research.

As writing teachers, we can examine our assumptions about disciplinary knowledge. If as scholars we value life study, we can make writing sustained over time part of classroom investigation of texts and treat students' texts with the same seriousness and persistence that we accord others' texts. By asking writers to reflect on it, we can encourage voluntary writing in whatever settings it occurs. By employing the idea of a private self that adapts in different settings but endures nonetheless, we can show that texts construct us and impel not only further writing but action. That is, we can help our students construct a sense of public individuality. To reconceive the metaphor of the novice from the standpoint of inquiry in the humanities, the writer's identity from and in texts is important. In this re-conception, the writer is not a humble aspirant to a cloister who must renounce his or her past, but an authentic voice, prepared to reflect on his or her history and the ways in which it relates to a community. It should be possible to make the classroom a place for such reflection.

Works Cited

Bartholomae, David, and Anthony R. Petrosky. *Facts, Artifacts, and Counterfacts: Theory and Method for a Reading and Writing Course*. Upper Montclair, NJ: Boynton, 1986.

Beach, Richard. "Differences in Autobiographical Narratives of English Teachers, College Freshmen, and Seventh Graders." *College Composition and Communication* 38 (1987): 56-69.

Berthoff, Ann E. *Forming/Thinking/Writing: The Composing Imagination*. Portsmouth, NH: Boynton, 1982.

Bizzell, Patricia. "Arguing About Literacy." *College English* 50 (1988): 141-53.

Bloom, Lynn Z. "Life Studies: Interpreting Autobiography." *College English* 49 (1987): 345-52.

Britton, James, et al. *The Development of Writing Abilities* (11-18). London: Macmillan Education, 1975.

Coles, Robert. *Simone Weil: A Modern Pilgrimage*. Radcliffe Biography Series. Reading, MA: Addison-Wesley, 1987.

Faigley, Lester. "Competing Theories of Process: A Critique and a Proposal." *College English* 48 (1986): 527-42.

Florio, Susan, and Christopher M. Clark. "The Functions of Writing in an Elementary Classroom." *Research in the Teaching of English* 16 (1982): 115-30.

Goswami, Dixie, and Peter R. Stillman, eds. *Reclaiming the Classroom: Teacher Research as an Agency for Change*. Upper Montclair, NJ: Boynton, 1987.

Graff, Gerald. *Professing Literature: An Institutional History*. Chicago: U of Chicago P, 1987.

Maimon, Elaine P. "Some Uses of Autobiography: Private Writing in Public Places." *Journal of Advanced Composition* 5 (1984): 131-38.

Mallon, Thomas. *A Book of One's Own: People and Their Diaries*. New York: Ticknor, 1984.

McCarthy, Lucille Parkinson. "A Stranger in Strange Lands: A College Student Writing Across the Curriculum." *Research in the Teaching of English* 21 (1987): 233-65.

Rodriguez, Richard. *Hunger of Memory: The Education of Richard Rodriguez*. New York: Bantam, 1983.

Part 4:
Theoretical and Political Issues

Recent Research in Reading and Its Implications for the College Composition Curriculum

by Joseph J. Comprone

Articles by Richard Fulkerson, Karen Pelz, and Michael Hogan in the first issue of the *Journal of Advanced Composition* (Spring 1980) all pointed to a serious lack of consistency in the profession's conception of what should be covered in advanced composition courses in college. Professor Pelz, while arguing against what she perceives as another teacher's advocacy of media-centered rather than writing-centered advanced composition courses, advocates the development of a "personal style" in advanced writing courses, seemingly calling for an emphasis on expressive discourse and self-discovery ("A Reply to Medicott: Evaluating Writing," 7-9). Professor Fulkerson ("Some Theoretical Speculations on the Advanced Composition Curriculum," 9-12) uses Abrams' and Kinneavy's theories of literary criticism and the aims of discourse to construct two different curricular models for advanced composition programs—one suggesting courses based on the skills required of students as they produce discourse with different aims, the other suggesting synthesizing all four discourse aims in a single advanced composition course. Finally, Professor Hogan ("Advanced Composition: A Survey," 21-29) sent questionnaires to 374 advanced composition teachers at 311 schools and found an enormously diverse range of course objectives and plans among the responses that he received. Hogan also found that many advanced composition courses used the same books as freshman writing courses in the same schools. Although rhetoric, Hogan found, dominated the courses of instruction, there did not seem to be any clear or consistent pattern of rhetorical approach in the schools or teachers who reported. Very few respondents, in fact, reflected much attention to types or aims of discourse, as Fulkerson had suggested, in their assignments or plans.

Articles such as these reflect the composition profession's general lack of explanatory and theoretical models of the composing process. Without these models, neither beginning nor advanced writing teachers have a clear sense of where their students are or should be in their development as writers when they enter their classes. As a result, writing courses often seem to rely on a teacher's make-shift, last-minute plan, constructed on the spot to meet the needs of the students who show up the first day of class, or they follow a pattern which simply applies different

Reprinted from *Rhetoric Review* 1 (1983): 122-37. Reprinted with permission.

subject matter to the rhetorical/linguistic approaches that students have already experienced as freshmen.

To provide a basis for creating an explanatory model that might help teachers
develop an approach to both beginning and advanced writing courses, I shall first
review an area of recent research that has significance for the teaching of composition—psycholinguistics and reading.

Psycholinguistics, Reading, and Composing

In 1908 Edmund Burke Huey produced *The Psychology and Pedagogy of
Reading*, a book that served as a distant and relatively brilliant precursor to the recent work of psycholinguists who have studied the fluent reading process.[1]

Huey in 1908 posited the functional tenet of all psycholinguistic approaches to
reading: that fluent readers do *not* decode either to phonetic features or to spoken
language; rather, they use "cues" or dominant features of letter formation, word recognition, and syntax to trigger a larger comprehension of meaning. Cues or dominant features, says Huey, function automatically as we read across a line of print, but
"[w]hen . . . total recognition completes itself . . . we are apt to be conscious of these
dominant forms [cues] as the most prominent parts of the word."[2]

Fluent readers, in other words, are fluent guessers. They have internalized
certain dominant letter and word features and their eyes move across the page constructing mental patterns from these configurations of selected cues. The reading
process then continues as readers check their guesses at meaning against the
printed features that surround cues at those points in the reading process where the
density of texture might make meaning ambiguous. We read closely, in other
words, only when our selective perception of features does not seem to square with
our evolving sense of meaning.[3]

Current work in psycholinguistics and reading, then, has emphasized what laboratory research has shown us about the human mind as it processes bits of information—in reading the bits of information would be perceived features of letters and
words, selected and organized to produce a hypothesis on a passage's meaning—and
current work has linked this cognitive theory with a generative-transformational understanding of syntax as the bridge between the surface and deep structures of written language.[4] What the psycholinguists, and the practitioners who are beginning to

---

[1] Re-published in paperback in 1968 by the MIT Press, with a Foreword by John B. Carroll and an introduction by Paula A. Kolers; first published by Macmillan in 1908. Perhaps the most succinct general review of
psycholinguistic approaches to reading for teachers is Charles Cooper and Anthony Petrosky, "A
Psycholinguistic View of the Fluent Reading Process,"*Journal of Reading* (Dec. 1976), 184-207.

[2] Huey, pp. 109-10.

[3] Researchers and teachers of reading who wish to apply psycholinguistic theory to actual readers must
make careful distinctions between fluent and beginning readers, as Cooper and Petrosky do on p. 187 of
their article. Descriptions of how fluent readers select and use dominant features or cues may, of course,
not apply to the beginning reader, who may be less selective and less willing or able to hypothesize meaning.

[4] The following anthologies and books can provide basic introductions to the general theory behind
psycholinguistics and reading, the empirical research that produced that theory, and some of its implications
for teaching: Kenneth S. Goodman and James T. Fleming, eds.,*Psycholinguistics and the Teaching of*

base teaching methods on their theories, have developed seems almost too simple; yet, it is undoubtedly a far-reaching and seminal concept for any teacher of composing: reading is as much an act of composing as writing. The fluent reader recognizes dominant cues from among a large array of distinctive features that he or she knows but does not—indeed *cannot*, if we accept the conclusions of laboratory research on letter and word recognition—perceive as distinct features while reading. The reader constructs hypotheses about meaning by rescanning difficult or ambiguous combinations of cues and their surrounding features. As Charles Cooper and Anthony Petrosky point out in their review-article on psycholinguistics and reading, "one has to read, make mistakes, and test hypotheses in order to become a fluent reader."[5]

E.D. Hirsch, Jr. recently added social, historical, and stylistic implications to the findings of the linguistics.[6] He argues, first, that writing is not to be confused with speech, that it is an essentially different medium—a "grapholect"—rather than merely another dialect, comparable to oral dialects in general.[7] A grapholect includes grammatical conventions, for example, whose norms "are not only more certainly fixed than those of a dialect but are also more widely promulgated than the grammatical norms of any dialect," and its "stability through time" is potentially greater.[8] In Hirsch's early chapters these essentially conserving qualities of written speech are linked with the recognition, long-accepted by rhetoricians and stylists, that writers and readers must recreate the situation implied by the discourse: "The chief problem of written speech as a mode of communication is that a sufficient context for interpretation must be supplied in the absence of the many types of contextual clues found in ordinary speech . . . intonation, gesture . . . facial expression—most of all, for its lack of tacit situational understanding and active feedback between speaker and listener."[9]

In summary, Hirsch argues that writing is a more conservative and prescribed medium because it demands from both writer and reader a more creative use of shared psycholinguistic conventions. These conventions—whether lexical, syntactical, or semantic—become the writer's clues to the reader, helping her or him to fill in implied context, to follow the intricate tracking of ideas through a mosaic of syntactic forms, holding meaning as a whole in mind while simultaneously allowing for its revision as the act of reading continues. Just as the psycholinguists are establishing correlations between reading and creative processes that were previously thought to exist only in the more generative composing activities such as writing, so Hirsch is

---

Reading (Newark, Delaware: International Reading Association, 1969); Eleanor J. Gibson and Harry Levin, eds., *The Psychology of Reading* (Cambridge, Mass.: MIT Press, 1978); Frank Smith, *Psycholinguistics and Reading* (New York: Holt, 1973); Frank Smith, *Understanding Reading*, 2nd ed. (New York: Holt, 1978).

[5] p. 191.

[6] *The Philosophy of Composition* (Chicago: The University of Chicago Press, 1977), pp. 92-137. These pages cover Chapter Five of the book, where Hirsch relates his concept of "relative readability" to the function of short and long-term memory in the reading process.

[7] Hirsch takes the term "grapholect" from sociolinguist E. Haugen, "Linguistics and Language Planning," in *Sociolinguistics*, ed. W. Bright (The Hague, 1966), 50-71.

[8] *The Philosophy of Composition*, p. 44.

[9] *The Philosophy of Composition*, pp. 22-23.

telling us that both reading and writing demand, together, a control over psycholinguistic processes that are intrinsically different, by nature and medium, from everyday, oral uses of language.

Mina Shaughnessy, in another recent seminal work on composing, takes the writer's rather than the reader's perspective on composing. She, too, emphasizes the essentially conservative nature of the written medium:

> We see then that many syntactic difficulties are rooted in the differences between writing and speaking—in the fact that writing serves a different purpose from speech, that it tends to exploit syntactic possibilities in language that speech either need not or cannot exploit, that it demands coordinations of hand and eye that a speaker does not automatically control and that inhibit the production of grammatically sound sentences . . ., that it is created through a process that is both more extended and conscious than the process whereby speech is created. . ., that it removes the writer from the supports of dialogue and puts him on his own in ways that even experienced writers find formidable.[10]

In summary, both Hirsch and Shaughnessy—although working from very different pedagogical perspectives—are saying that the rules, conventions, and—most importantly—the basic cognitive operations required of writers are essentially different from those required of speakers, particularly in everyday talk.

Relying himself on psycholinguistic research, Hirsch goes on to establish the concept of "relative readability." Short-term memory in even fluent readers greatly limits their ability to store actual lexical and syntactic items and, in turn, limits to some degree the amount of time these items can be retained.[11] As a result, Hirsch explains, writers and readers must know whole meanings in at least hypothetical forms before they can either place or find clues to meaning in their texts. Long-term memory cannot store and retain more than a few words or phrases, especially over an extended period of time. What it can do, however, is store whole meanings that are not linguistic by picking up on essential clues, whether lexical, syntactical, or semantic. Written texts, then, contain semantic intentions that writers have had in mind as they wrote, and they contain degrees of readability that derive from the clues that writers place in their texts. These clues then allow readers to develop their own senses of a text's semantic intention, which, in turn, becomes a working semantic hypothesis as the reading process is completed. By picking up lexical, syntactic, and semantic clues as reading progresses, the reader either confirms or revises his or her hypothetical sense of semantic intention until it squares with the text. The

---

[10] *Errors and Expectations* (New York: Oxford, 1977), p. 87.

[11] George A. Miller, "The Magic Number Seven, Plus or Minus Two," in *The Psychology of Communication*, ed. by George A. Miller (New York, 1967). This is the seminal article on the capabilities of short-term memory. D.E. Broadbent, "The Magic Number Seven," *Studies in Long Term Memory*, ed. by A. Kennedy and A. Wilkes (London, 1975), suggests that the number of items capable of being stored is closer to five than seven. See, also, *The Philosophy of Composition*, p. 111. Some recent researchers are positing a theoretical distinction between sensory-based and abstract memory—see Endel Tulving, "Episodic and Semantic Memory," from *The Organization of Memory*, ed. by Tulving and Donaldson (New York: Academic Press, 1972), pp. 381-403.

reader, literally and cognitively, reconceives the author's meaning, following the empirically-defined processes of psycholinguistic theory.[12]

Perhaps a physical analogy, however imprecise, will help here. The reader follows a trail laid by a writer, picking up different kinds of clues along the way. Both reader and writer almost always have some very general idea of the trail's destination even as they begin. And they both have a working knowledge of how these verbal trails are made and marked. But within these shared general directions, the path could be remade in endless ways. Further, whatever changes in direction occur do not qualitatively change the pathmaker's and pathfinder's general sense of destination.

What do psycholinguistic explanations of reading, combined with Hirsch's and Shaughnessy's definitions of the differences between reading and writing, imply for teachers of composing, who must integrate the reading and writing processes in their classrooms?

1. It tells us that fluent writers are always making tentative hypotheses and confirming or revising them according to what they discover in the cues they place in their own writing. This is probably what E.M. Forster meant when he said that he could not tell what he meant until he had seen what he had written.

Writers, then, are always reading, discovering, and rewriting. Writers, however, must use psycholinguistic processes in two different ways while composing. First, they must employ their tacit knowledge of language and rhetoric expressively, composing rough drafts that will enable them to act as their own readers while revising and editing. Second, they must later use that same knowledge of language and rhetoric to produce a finished writing with dominant features, as defined by psycholinguists, serving as cues to the reader's evolving understanding of the piece's semantic intention. Writing works progressively through expressive to transactional stages. In the former stages, composing is the record of an idea developing; in the latter, composing becomes meaning objectified for an abstract audience of others. Writing teachers, recent psycholinguistic and composition theory suggests, must recognize the possibility that students in their classes may have to employ lexical, syntactic, and semantic cues differently during these two developmental stages of composing. See James Britton, *Language and Learning* (Coral Gables, Florida: University of Miami Press, 1970) for a more complete explanation of the function of expressive and transactional discourse in general language development.

2. Readers, in at least a restricted sense, are always writing; at least, they are following cognitive processes similar to those of the writers who

---

[12] E.D. Hirsch, Jr., *Validity in Interpretation* (New Haven: Yale, 1967), pp. 24-27. Here Hirsch explains the process of re-cognition as it applies to interpretation, which he borrowed from Emilio Betti,*Teoria generale della interpretazione*, 2 vols. (Milan: Giufre, 1955), 1, 343-432.

produced what they are reading. They make, test, and revise hypotheses, working with cues from the text. Teachers of composing must capitalize more than they have in the past on the concept of reading as an active cognitive process, as much a process of composing as is writing. This can be accomplished when writing teachers learn to show writers how readers actively create meaning from a text by combining cues into patterns of meaning and by testing implied meanings against one another.

3. If points one and two are valid, then the teacher must find, define, and exploit those points in this shared process that can be used to reinforce one another, and they must suggest to students cognitive operations that will help them develop and control the use of cues within defined frameworks of meaning. Composition teachers, for example, can begin to integrate the reading and writing processes by simply interspersing the two—having students read opening paragraphs of an assigned text aloud, focusing upon cues and propositions about meaning as they are developed in process, and then interrupting reading with practice writings that carry that evolving meaning off in either subjective or objective directions. If an entire composition course were organized to intersperse reading and writing in this way, students would come to understand how meaning is created from language rather than thought-out in one stage and communicated in another, separate stage.

Inner Speech, Expressive Discourse, and the Need to Integrate Reading and Writing

Why are these implications significant for college writing teachers, and how might they be translated into actual course plans and strategies?

Above all, these research implications suggest a totally different relationship between writing and reading than now exists at both the freshman and advanced levels. Freshmen, we have long known but seldom admitted, are not experts on their subjects. They are learners using writing as a means of expressing how and what they are learning. Research in reading suggests that teachers of freshman composition assign writing exercises in which students take on the learner-discoverer's role, and that they use expressive discourse, first, to structure their own learning experiences more objectively and, second, to provide the teacher as audience with a clear record of that learning experience.

Many freshman teachers avoid this emphasis on expressive discourse because they mistakenly make the word *expressive* a synonym for "free" or "personal" writing. Actually, much recent rhetorical research on expressive discourse has indicated that it can be as objectively structured as any form of discourse, and that it can communicate insights of social significance as effectively as any other form of discourse.[13] The distinctions between expressive and other discourse aims are rather

---

[13] See James Kinneavy's section on expressive discourse in *A Theory of Discourse* (New Jersey: Prentice

simple: expressive discourse places emphasis (within the writer's triad of speaker, subject, and audience) on the speaker, and objectifies the speaker's process of discovery as he or she works through a subject rather than the result or significance of that process *after* it has been experienced.

Early in the writing process, expressive writing is often a sketchy record of the responses of a reader. Words take on a personal color, influenced by the past experience of the reader and textual content. Syntax is often elliptical, with substantives referred to in vague pronouns or nouns, or omitted altogether because the writer assumes knowledge of the reading in his or her readers. As these early expressive responses are reread and revised, however, the writer begins to see a purpose in these early efforts. What, at first, was but dimly shadowed is seen in sharper relief as early drafts are revised into more detailed and objective responses to reading cues. Expressive writing becomes an organic record of an idea developing, moving the writer from a confused sense of initial response to a pointed understanding of the purpose of a final draft.

Expressive writing is capable of the same degree of objective precision as persuasive (which focuses upon audience), referential (which focuses upon subject), or literary discourse (which focuses upon the experience of reading and the literary world objectified in the literary work). It simply reports on the process rather than the products of discovery.

Expressive discourse, because it begins with subjective response and moves progressively toward more objective stances, is an ideal form of discourse for learners. It enables freshman writers to interact in much more honest and less abstract ways with what they read. It would, for example, encourage freshmen to objectify their own feelings and experience *before* they read; it would encourage freshmen to respond more systematically and objectively to textual focal points *as* they were reading; and it would allow freshmen to avoid taking on the more abstract poses of experts when they wrote about what a story, essay, or news article meant *after* they had finished reading it. The freshman writer, then, uses writing to express the process of reading itself, to articulate and objectify what Louise Rosenblatt calls the "transaction" between the text and its reader.[14]

How does this emphasis on expressive discourse synthesize with the thinking skills that are demanded in academic discourse? We can find our answer, I believe, in Lev Vygotsky's concept of inner speech.[15] Jean Piaget's earlier research had hypothesized a single period of egocentric thought ranging throughout childhood, diminishing gradually and eventually being replaced by adult logical thought. He based his belief in the existence of the child's cognitive egocentrism on his observance of egocentric speech, a kind of speech in which the points of view of

---

Hall, 1971) for a systematic analysis of the logic, style, and aims of expressive writing. My division of discourse aims into literary, expressive, persuasive, and referential is also taken from Kinneavy.

[14] *The Reader, the Text, and the Poem* (Carbondale, Ill.: Southern Illinois University Press, 1978), p. 16.

[15] Vygotsky's research and theory are described in *Thought and Language*, ed. and trans. by Eugenia Hanfmann and Gertrude Vakar (Cambridge, Mass.: MIT Press, 1962); James Britton's work with Piaget and Vygotsky is set forth in *Language and Learning* (Coral Gables, Florida: University of Miami Press, 1970).

other individuals were excluded and all objects, sayings, and ideas were related back to the speaker's perspective. Egocentric speech was to Piaget evidence of a stage in which the child moved from purely sensorimotor uses of language to the more abstract and decentered speech of adults. It was reflective of a mental development from simple object-oriented talk to mature thinking and speaking, as influenced by social interaction on one side and the logical structures of the mind on the other.[16]

Vygotsky turned this around and posited a process developing from purely sensorimotor manipulation of symbols very early in childhood followed by a branching off into social and inner speech thereafter. What Piaget called egocentric speech was, to Lev Vygotsky, not a simple transition from infantile autism to socialization, but a sign that the child's earliest object-bound speech was going partially underground and becoming a somewhat sophisticated form of interior monologue:

> Our findings indicate that egocentric speech does not long remain a mere accompaniment to the child's activity. Besides being a means of expression, and of release of tension, it soon becomes an instrument of thought in the proper sense—in seeking and planning the solution of a problem. (Vygotsky, p. 16)

Children talk to themselves not solely because they do not care about audiences and their viewpoints, but because they are giving themselves directions in developing integrated, conceptual solutions, to, first, situational and, then, abstract problems. Thus we have a developmental process in which a new type of semi-conscious autism follows rather than predates later forms of social speech and the early forms of thought.

James Britton best summarizes the general implications of Vygotsky's research when he describes the evolution of social and inner speech as simultaneously originating in the sensorimotor, egocentric thought and speech of infancy and, then, developing on two parallel but distinct tracks.[17] Social speech, from 3-7 years, works toward communication; it is more detailed and directed toward an audience, and it shares more completely in the linguistic cues and conventions of language as we use it in social contexts. Inner speech, from 3-7 years, works toward the solving of functional, then logical, problems for the individual; it is not directed toward an audience, but it more decidedly does include, even in its early developmental stages, most of the elements of mature, logical thought. Vygotsky defines its linguistic properties as ellipses (particularly the omission of those nouns and pronouns that are constant to the monologue), an emphasis on predication (on the propositional elements of language), a general emphasis on whole meanings rather than the specifics of lexicon and syntax, and the use of large numbers of word combinations that are understandable only to the speaker because they bring together word connotations

---

[16] Piaget's work is most easily accessible in *The Language and Thought of the Child* (New York: Harcourt and Brace, 1926), *The Construction of Reality in the Child*, trans. by Margaret Cook (New York: Basic Bks., 1954) and *Six Psychological Studies*, trans. and ed. by David Elkind and Anita Tenzer (New York: Random House, 1967).

[17] *Language and Learning* (Middlesex, England: Penguin Bks., 1970), pp. 59-64.

that are related to the speaker's mental processes rather than to external referents (Vygotsky, pp. 143-45).

James Moffett suggests many writing activities that can help students revise inner speech (*Active Voice*, New Haven, Boynton/Cook 1981). Free or associative writing helps students objectify their shorthand mental observations as they transfer them to written code; some free writings should be based, Moffett suggests, on first-hand observations of sensory experience, others on remembered events, still others on readings and other secondary sources. They should be assigned before, during, and after other learning activities. The imaginative teacher might have students make these free-responses into dialogues and monologues in which certain perspectives or positions control the rewriting—a past school experience, for example, is seen from the writer's perspective, then from a teacher's or other student's. These perspectives are developed into dialogue, with named speakers and careful scripting. When enough perspectives have been developed, the writer can write brief analyses of each perspective and follow with a synthesizing writing done first in chronological narrative—with thesis and support that has been drawn from the earlier stages of writing.

Staged writings of this sort help students use expressive discourse, in which they write for themselves in progressively more varied and abstract situations, to discover what they wish to say in exposition, and they help—in turn—to incorporate expository perspectives into the acts of perception and writing as expressive responses are developed. Throughout this entire process, inner speech becomes a conscious part of the composing process rather than an occasional interruption in the student's perceptual stream. Focusing on inner speech serves to turn the writer's attention to interior processing—not to distort perceptual processes that are based on the senses—but to clarify and control them. The inner voice becomes a sustained monologue. What the writer hears as he or she writes gradually becomes a voice with direction and purpose.

In secondary and college-level writing classrooms, then, teachers of reading and writing are faced with the problem of synthesizing three types of speech: the social speech defined by Vygotsky and Britton and distinguished as very different from written speech by Shaughnessy and Hirsch; the inner speech defined by Vygotsky and Piaget and correlated more closely with the development of thought by educational theorists such as James Moffett, Jerome Bruner, and James Britton; the early experiences with school writing, reading, and discourse.[18] This early school interaction of language in the spectator and participant roles (Britton's terms) combines in its most complex forms in writing, where the child is drawing on experience with both social speech as a participant and inner speech as a spectator. All three forms of speech are interdependent; all three have surface structures and conventions of their own; all three share universal cognitive structures. Just as all people use basic cognitive structures and operations to develop species-similar

---

[18] James Moffett, *Teaching the Universe of Discourse* (Boston: Houghton Mifflin Company, 1968); Jerome Bruner, *Studies in Cognitive Growth* (New York: John Wiley, 1966).

modes of thought, so teachers must search out the relationships between these forms of speech, the operations that are used to develop them, and the operations that can be developed to connect the effects of thinking in general with the specialized concerns of writing and reading, the media common to mature intellectual life. Reading becomes a means of "de-centering" student writing; writing becomes a means of "de-centering" student reading.

What does it mean to "de-center"? The student uses writing to move back from actual involvement in the experience itself. He or she sees, through the act of writing, an experience within a larger context. A story becomes a self-conscious part of a larger pattern of experience; an essay or news story becomes part of a larger system of values and current experience. With expressive writing, however, the students can create this distance without destroying clarity—the move from subjective or self-centered to objective and other-centered is accomplished through a gradual synthesis of both perspectives.

The inner speech of three- or four-year-olds, as reported in Piaget and Vygotsky's experiments, helps them talk their way through a recently learned activity. They literally talk to themselves to remind themselves of the steps and goal of a process. Without this verbal direction, they might not know where to go next, or they might get side tracked at a particular stage. Inner speech provides the three- or four-year-old with a transcription in narrative form of a procedural overview of an action.

At a much higher level of abstraction, college writers must cultivate inner speech—in the form of expressive discourse—so that it takes on a similar function, producing progressively more inclusive and abstract directional forms for more varied writing situations. The initial response to a particular piece of monologue in Joyce's "Araby" becomes, through de-centering, a part of a more abstract exposition on romantic and sexual maturity, addressed to readers who have shared the reading of "Araby" and are prepared to move to larger circles of meaning. Writers producing this type of abstract exposition will know better what they are doing if they have used expressive discourse to help them move gradually back from the experience of reading itself. Writing is self-discovery before it is interpretation. The move from a particular response to a part of "Araby" to a more general thematic perspective is then mapped in writing for writers to incorporate in their final drafts.

Applications to the College Writing Curriculum

More advanced college writers, having undergone practice in using expressive discourse to distance themselves from their writing and reading processes, can move on to develop inner speech that includes considerations of an outside audience's expectations. Freshman inner speech, bound as it should be to expressive self-discovery in objective form, poses and answers questions that are rooted in an understanding of what the student's transactions with a text have produced. Freshmen writers aim to accomplish self-understanding; they are not attempting an exhaustive or comprehensive understanding of the text itself and its general implications for an audience of specialists. The freshman's inner speech as he or she writes is a dialectic among personal response, textual features, and revised and more objective personal responses occasioned by the writing process itself.

Advanced writers, in contrast, must develop a more complex dialectic in their inner speech that more specifically includes the expectations of a defined and specialized group of readers. They, in contrast to freshmen, ought to be considering rhetorical effect and context much more explicitly, and they should be experimenting much more consciously than less developed writers with questions of the overall meaning and significance of what they read. They are closer to taking on, in other words, the pose of the expert speaking to a defined audience of experts or specialists; as such, they must ask themselves questions that move them from the text and their transactions with it to objective statements about the text's significance within a defined context. Their inner speech moves from personal expression to rhetorical statement much more rapidly than that of their freshman counterparts.

Linda Flower, in a recent article, effectively summarizes my argument concerning the function of expressive discourse in the process of learning to write by making two recommendations for teachers of composition: (1) teach writing as an activity that develops through stages, with the earlier stages directed toward the goal of objectified, structured self-discovery—in the forms of lists and subjective rough drafts; (2) teach writing as an activity that—later in the process of production—enables writers to look back on their prewritings from the perspectives of a defined group of readers.[19] I have tried to explain how these recommendations and the theory behind them might lead teachers to a restructuring of both freshman and advanced composition, with freshman writing courses given over to writing as self-discovery and advanced courses to writing for specific groups of readers. Individual teachers will not be able to follow the leads of composing-process researchers such as Flower until they have a curricular sequence that coincides with the developing skills of their students.

Before, however, a writing curriculum that follows this development can be constructed, teachers will need to re-define their concepts of expressive writing. Too many of us limit our uses of expressive discourse to free writing.

Expressive writing can, however, be more highly developed and objectively structured than free responses, notes, preliminary lists, and rough drafts. It can come to function as a careful record of an idea developing, much as we find in the best professional examples of expressive discourse, in autobiographies and personal essays. But these more highly developed expressive structures can be effectively taught only when we, as teachers, have developed a clear idea of how the inner speech of beginning writers can be focused on heuristics that will lead to systematically more objectified structures in student drafts. Also, our students' expressive writings will be more effectively read and evaluated by us when we learn how to respond to expressive discourse. Since expressive writing is written to and for the writer, we must learn to respond as trusted confidants to what we read, becoming extended selves for student writers, ready to help them clarify what they have tried to say rather than evaluating their writing as if it were actually written for an outside

---

[19] Linda Flower, "Writer-Based Prose: A Cognitive Basis for Problems in Writing,"*College English*, 41, 1 (September 1979), 36.

audience of experts or specialists. This article suggests that expressive responses to assigned readings might be the best place to begin—because teachers will have the assigned text in hand to use as a reference point while responding to student writings, and because the students would be able to track their discoveries of meaning while reading back through sequences of expressive responses.

A list of possible steps in controlling, through expressive writing, students' responses to a particular reading should help clarify this "reading back" process. This entire heuristic process is intended to help students use expressive writing to recognize, develop, and synthesize reading cues. This sequence supposes that students will be reading a modern short story. With slight changes, of course, it could be applied to any type of reading matter.

1. Students should make prereading notes on titles, on thematic discussions based upon subjects that are related to the reading, and on past experiences that the teacher knows will be relevant. These rough notes should originate in individual responses and be worked together into loose collections by workshop groups that are composed of students who will read the same text. Teachers should occasionally intervene in this process to assume that students pull together non-visual information from personal experience, from feelings and values, and from past reading of literature. These final lists or collections should then be categorized under headings such as "information on reading stories," "feelings I have experienced that are similar to those experienced by major characters in this story," and "associations I can make when considering the title and first paragraph of this story."

2. As they are reading, students should pause and look back at their collections of pre-reading responses. The pre-reading notes can then be rewritten as discursive entries in a reading journal. These discursive entries should explain how initial expectations, as captured in pre-reading notes, have been either confirmed or revised by subsequent reading in the text. Teachers should help inexperienced readers at this stage by pointing out significant cues in the text. These cues and their textual contexts can then become the catalysts of student entries in reading journals. Obviously, these points and their cues can also become useful starting points for subsequent class discussions.

3. Once students have finished reading, they should work through their notes and journal entries to produce a narrative that describes their reading experience. This narrative should become a written record of what the student felt and thought as he or she read the story, chronologically organized. It should not even pretend to be a finished expository/interpretive essay. It might, however, be considered a draft, or an initial effort in that direction.

This sequence could, of course, be expanded to meet the goals of different courses, audiences, and types of discourse. Whatever the goals, however, each stage of response should produce expressive responses in which students write to understand better their own reading and thinking processes.

Our advanced writing courses could then expand upon this beginning marriage of expressive writing and reading with practice in meeting the rhetorical needs of different audiences. But this expansion will, in turn, depend on our expanding our often simplistic notions of coherence into more sophisticated and precise accounts of how fluent readers are guided by an accomplished writer. No student, for example, can really know where he or she is going until having gotten there. Rough drafts, carefully structured to capture the contours of an idea developing, become the writer's means of mapping the reader's journey. That map, however, never simply reproduces the writer's journey; rather, it places old and new information, content and function words, and other significant cues to meaning into a pattern that is coherent to an audience made up of readers who are fluent with the language and knowledgeable of the specific context of the writing. By looking back over their own expressive writings, students learn to see through another person's eyes. In more advanced classes, this activity should be combined with student and professional writings within the same context. The result might well be the kind of de-centering writing teachers often call "effective rhetoric."

In other words, the advanced college writer uses expressive writings as records of ideas developing as they compose final drafts that are more directly related to the needs of a particular context. Aside from this different and more objective use of expressive writing, this revised sense of advanced composition would encourage the use of formal writers' plans as intermediate stages in the writing process. A writer's plan is simply a written analysis of what the writer believes his or her readers will know and will need to be told, and it often includes an explanation of why a particular form or structure would be effective for a particular audience. It is a refined form of rhetorical planning. The student, looking occasionally over his or her shoulder at rough drafts on the same subjects, looks forward to the needs of an assumed audience. The advanced composition teacher, with a complex concept of expressive discourse in mind, stands ready to help students look ahead to the needs of an audience from the base that has been created through systematic rereadings of expressive drafts.

A redefinition of expressive discourse might well produce a model for the first truly comprehensive college writing curriculum. Above all, however, it should assure that somewhere within a consistently planned college writing program students will, at the least, experience writing as a process of objectified self-discovery and, at the most, will put writing-as-discovery together with writing-for-readers. In that type of program, the advanced writer twice will have experienced the *whole* process of composing—first as a learner looking to writing as self-clarification in relation to personal experience and external subjects, and second as a communicator looking to writing as a means of sharing those clarified discoveries.[20]

---

[20] This type of advanced writing course has been described by Roberta Palumbo in "Writing for the Preprofessional within the Liberal Arts Tradition," *Journal of Advanced Composition* 1, (Spring 1980), 18-20.

Bringing Rhetorical Theory into the Advanced Composition Class

by Katherine H. Adams

"Advanced composition" is now taught in colleges throughout the country to students in a variety of majors. But, unlike freshman English where one finds similar curricula and texts, this course has not had a traditional structure. In some schools, it may even indicate technical writing or advanced grammar study.

In a 1979 survey, Michael Hogan discovered that at most colleges the course extended fundamentals learned in freshman English, with work on style and organization for argument, exposition, and other essay forms. Because few specialized texts were then available, teachers relied on books intended for freshmen, such as Hall's *Writing Well* and *The Norton Reader*, and thus repeated familiar advice on the modes of exposition, paragraphing and usage, with little attention given to research on composition.[1]

Since then, several texts have been published, such as Hairston's *Successful Writing* and Coe's *Form and Substance*, that are especially geared to this course. One of their primary differences from freshman readers and rhetorics is their inclusion of significant amounts of research. Into chapters on invention and organization, for example, Hairston incorporates Toulmin's logic, Christensen's downshifting, and problem solving. Coe has taken this tendency further with discussions of the Pentad, *topoi*, Rogerian argument, readability rates, and reader-based prose, lists of additional readings in theory, and authors' notes on the writing process.

This movement toward theory-based texts reflects the desire of writing specialists to teach composition in a way appropriate for the advanced group. With a majority of business, history, accounting, and sociology majors, we do have an audience capable of examining empirical data or testimony from experts. And a variety of such materials can have several positive effects on their work. Philosophical essays provide a forceful reminder of the importance of written or spoken dialectic, of the balances of responsibility, power and subterfuge a rhetor can obtain. Empirical research can immerse students in their importance as writers and in the career of writing. That students are analyzed at work surprises those who view their writing as trivial, as does reading about published authors who also can't produce, who also get mad, and who also must revise and revise. A writer's testimony or suggestions can give older students impetus for altering their ingrained writing habits. Without

Reprinted from *Rhetoric Review* 3 (1985): 184-89. Reprinted with permission.
[1] Michael P. Hogan, "Advanced Composition." *Journal of Advanced Composition* 1 (1980): 21-29.

such evidence, even the best advice on prewriting and revising can seem like undefended prescriptions of one more teacher.

Although advanced composition classes should concentrate on the student's own writing, actual research, including data and testimonies, can be a powerful addition to the curriculum. The advanced textbooks now provide some selections, but theory can also be used in its original form to extend the possible choices and to provide a realness not found in many interpretations. In my classes, I present this research briefly, perhaps for just ten minutes through short readings, graphs, and discussion. Whatever the other texts or teaching methods used, these selections will engage advanced students and sharpen their writing skills.

The Power of Rhetoric

Students now overwhelmed by computers and graphics need to see the importance of rhetoric in history—and thus their potential influence as skillful rhetors speaking to real audiences. Richard Weaver on the ethics of communication, I.A. Richards on significant symbols, Marshall McLuhan on the media, or Kenneth Burke on dramatism or Hitler's "Battle" could provide effective discussion of the importance of further training in rhetorical skills.[2]

In my classes, we use Plato's *Phaedrus* to analyze the ethics and power of rhetoric. Students can easily read the short dialogue, giving special attention to the three speeches. From Lysias' speech we examine pretended objectivity, "semantically purified" speech, and the abstractions of scientific notation.[3] We next move to Socrates' abuse of love, evil rhetoric blatantly subjecting the audience's will, denying fair definition, and employing impassioned language to work against true understanding. We also consider Socrates' third generous state, of ignoring the self while providing dialectic and an artful presentation of truth.

To work with these categories, we analyzed Knoxville's recent bid for the Miss USA pageant: "objective" cost statements by committees of businessmen, feminist pleas against this exploitation of women, advertising pamphlets, and a variety of editorials. Of course, we agreed on candidates for only the first two categories and saw the infrequency of Socrates' truth. We then experimented with writing for all three categories, carefully considering our generalizations and purposes.

Such study makes the students better critics of advertisements, the evening news, "objective" testing results, magazine articles, and even the teacher's rhetoric. It also extends their own intentions as writers: students who may have written only for a teacher—for a grade—need to see the possible effects of their persuasion on real audiences.

The Writing Process—What Writers Do

To introduce advice on invention and revision, I often discuss Janet Emig's interviews with Lynn in *The Composing Processes of Twelfth Graders*, showing the

---

[2] Selections from these authors can be found in *The Rhetoric of Western Thought*. James L. Golden, Goodwin Berquist and William Coleman, eds. (Dubuque, Iowa: Kendall Hunt, 1983).

[3] Richard M. Weaver, *Language is Sermonic* (Baton Rouge: La. State Univ. Press, 1970), p. 62. The chapter "The *Phaedrus* and the Nature of Rhetoric" provides a helpful guide for teachers and students.

class a typical student they have probably resembled in education and ability.[4] Like her, they may have avoided prewriting or planning and have seen revision as correcting errors, a form of punishment. If considering a school paper on an aging grandmother, relationships between boys and girls, or a cardboard Snoopy in the living room, they might also pick "the Snoopy thing" because writing extensively, non-personally, is safer and easier. Many also share her anxieties about spelling, handwriting, mechanics, and length, attitudes which must be discussed before I stress process as important—so that I am not just changing an ever-mystifying requirements game.

Lynn's case can be supplemented by later studies of more successful writing processes, from Linda Flower and John Hayes, Nancy Sommers or other researchers.[5] As we consider these experts, we talk about encouraging the reflective as well as the extensive voice in their class work; we add generating to each other's prewritten work; we try to make revision more than correction; and we compare our own average protocol segments to Hayes and Flower's results. Such data takes them beyond textbook advice such as "use an outline" or "be specific" and gives students a model for their work in progress—for removing the scary mystery and entering the real world of writing.

Testimony from writers can also aid in this effort: it can be taken from the *Writers at Work* series, from Donald Murray, Roger Garrison and other writers.[6] Connections can also be made to other creative processes in which students may participate. On the generating/planning stages, Mozart details mental processes similar to those of writing. Of particular interest to science majors is mathematician Henri Poincare description of incubation or "unconscious work."[7] These excerpts encourage students to see the relationship of their writing, as well as their architecture and engineering projects, to the best of creativity.

The Writing Process: Teaching Heuristics

Prewriting or freewriting will help students see possibilities for discovery, but the teacher may also want to introduce a more structured heuristic. Such invention aids lead to thorough prewriting, by revealing points of view and information that might be overlooked. They may be most needed by those students who require a specific structure or assignment to explore a subject fully. Especially for argumentation or report writing, a method that can be explained quickly and perhaps simplified

---

[4] Janet Emig, *The Composing Processes of Twelfth Graders.* (Champaign, IL.: NCTE, 1971), pp. 45-73.

[5] John R. Hayes and Linda S. Flower, "Identifying the Organization of Writing Processes," in *Cognitive Processes in Writing*, ed. Lee W. Gregg and Erwin R. Steinberg (Hillsdale, N.J.: Lawrence Erlbaum, 1980), pp. 3-30; Linda Flower, "Writer-Based Prose: A Cognitive Basis for Problems in Writing," *College English*, 41 (1979), 22-26; Nancy Sommers, "Revision Strategies of Student Writers and Experienced Adult Writers," *CCC*, 31 (1980), 387.

[6] *Writers at Work: The Paris Review Interviews*, 1st ser., ed. Malcolm Cowley (New York: Penguin, 1958). The second, third, fourth, and fifth series, edited by George Plimpton, appeared in 1963, 1967, 1976, and 1981; Donald M. Murray, "Listening to Writing," in *Learning by Teaching* (Montclair, N.J.: Boynton-Cook, 1982), pp. 54-57; Roger Garrison, *How a Writer Works* (New York: Harper Row, 1981), pp. 12-23.

[7] Wolfgang Amadeus Mozart, "A Letter," in *The Creative Process: A Symposium*, ed. Brewster Ghiselin (Berkeley: Univ. of Calif. Press, 1952), p. 34; Henri Poincare, *Science and Method*, trans. Francis Maitland (New York: Dover, 1952), pp. 52-53.

for immediate application can become a crucial tool. If such a heuristic is needed, teachers should rely on the actual researcher's documents, perhaps concerning Young, Becker, and Pike's nine-celled heuristic, or D'Angelo's or Larson's questions.[8]

Aristotle's *topoi* heuristic has proven excellent for my students.[9] Freshman readers are filled with organizational patterns for the modes of exposition, part of the current/traditional paradigm created by nineteenth century rhetoricians like A.S. Hill and John Genung. Whatever its effectiveness in freshman English, this adaptation is certainly stagnant for juniors. But Aristotle's original versions of comparison, causal analysis, and other *topoi* make a helpful invention aid. Students can read the section on *topoi* in Aristotle's *Rhetoric* and then create their own examples and notes about those "places" best suited to generate material on political questions, personal reflections, or other subjects. Here is part of one student's reminders:

> 1. Altered Choices: get reader to act consistently and make comparisons about decisions he made and might make. If he came to UT for an education—big decision—he should be willing to write letters for increased needed funding.
>
> 2. Cause to Effect—from fact to possible result. Bad attitude of day camp instructor may change summer for all. What will nuclear power do to East Tennessee? (Why did or will something happen? Who or what caused it?)

For a prewriting assignment done at home, students analyze their subjects by these categories. Then in brainstorming activities in class, they use *topoi* lists to quiz each other on their prewriting's thoroughness and logic. Instead of shackling the mind as set organizations, Ross Winterowd has asserted, the topoi can then liberate.[10]

On Style

For the argument, personal essay, review, or any other assignment, the class will also need to consider effective style. Although the advanced students rarely require extensive grammar help, they need to weed out wordy or plodding structures and extend their stylistic choices. As writers, they resemble their counterparts at other schools: "students who were dealing with sophisticated and syntactically complex material but who, in written interpretation of this material, reverted to a very elementary (S-V, S-V-O) style of discourse, characterized by a lack of sentence variety and by inadequate transitions."[11] For whatever method chosen, such as

[8] Richard E. Young, Alton L. Becker, and Kenneth Pike, *Rhetoric: Discovery and Change* (New York: Harcourt Brace, 1970), pp. 119-36; Frank D'Angelo, *Process and Thought in Composition*, 2nd ed. (Cambridge, Mass.: Winthrop, 1980), pp. 42-53; Richard L. Larson, "A Plan for Teaching Rhetorical Invention," in *Classical Rhetoric for the Modern Student*, Edward P.J. Corbett, 2nd ed. (New York: Oxford Univ. Press, 1971), pp. 163-67.

[9] Aristotle, *The Rhetoric*, ed. Lane Cooper (New York: Appleton-Century-Crofts, 1932), pp. 154-71.

[10] W. Ross Winterowd, "'Topics' and Levels in the Composing Process," *College English*, 34 (1973), 701-10.

[11] Jeannette Harris and Lil Brannon, "Sentence Analysis and Combining as a Means of Improving the Expository Style of Advanced College Students," in *Sentence Combining and the Teaching of Writing*, eds. Donald Daiker, Andrew Kerek, and Max Morenberg (Akron: L.&S. Books, 1979), pp. 170-77.

Christensen's downshifting or Walker Gibson's categories, students appreciate proof of its effectiveness.

For these students, sentence combining can be helpful out-of-class work for providing new syntactical choices. Before beginning Daiker, Kerek, and Morenberg's *Writer's Options* program in sentence combining, we take Kellogg Hunt's "Aluminum" test of T-units and compare our results to his averages for eighth and twelfth graders and professional journalists. I also review with them the Miami of Ohio study and Gary Olson's results in advanced college courses.[12] Once or twice during the quarter, we redo the "Aluminum" paragraph and examine our progress empirically.

Such quick reminders of our goals give students a sense of involvement in an ongoing project; examining researchers' results, writers' testimonies, and differences in prose style helps them form and achieve personal goals for improvement. A desire to widen their range of stylistic choices, to move beyond correctness, will then stem from their specific knowledge of what can be achieved.

In advanced classes, we don't have to avoid or reinterpret theory, but instead we should incorporate it into conferences, workshops, and discussions. Our students should be aware of working within a dynamic tradition, of contributing to research and creativity. And, to improve and grow in confidence, they should learn about the writing process, how writers write, not only by helping classmates in workshops but by reading and using research. Such materials provide much more helpful models than readers with finished products because they allow students to participate in work-in-progress, tested composing methods, the struggle and excitement of fellow writers and perhaps also the teacher's ongoing research projects. Whatever main texts and assignments chosen for the course, research should be included to influence the student's writing process, style, and commitment to a powerful discipline.

---

[12] Donald Daiker, Andrew Kerek, and Max Morenberg, "Sentence Combining and College Composition," *Perceptual and Motor Skills*, 51 (1980), 1059-1157; Gary Olson, "Incorporating Sentence Combining into the Advanced Composition Class," *Journal of Advanced Composition*, 2 (1981), 119-26.

The Politics of Teaching Professional Writing

by Kate Ronald

One of my colleagues remarked the other night at a party that he thought the subject matter of composition was essentially "personal and social change." I readily agreed and noted that our discipline came into its own again during the 1960s, an era devoted to those kinds of change, when students, not texts, became our subjects. Yet it could be argued that composition and rhetoric specialists have flourished not because of our culture's or our colleges' desire to spread "revolution," but largely because the corporate worlds of education and business ("ETS and Lockheed," my friend said) have given high schools and colleges a mandate to turn out "skilled" writers who understand the conventions and constraints of writing outside the academy. Those who employ our students are less interested in their personal growth than in their ability to fit in and obtain predetermined results. Despite this reality, composition theorists continue to describe writing as a way of "knowing," a way to help students learn about themselves, examine their own experience, and yes, change the world into a better place. In this essay, I want to explore these apparently contradictory purposes for writing instruction.

I have confronted this dilemma every Tuesday night for the past three semesters. Teaching an upper-level course in professional writing, I find myself questioning my colleague's statement more closely. This relatively new course works specifically with students as potential members of certain disciplines—the law, medicine, social sciences, and particular areas of business such as personnel or public relations. Despite the course's increasing popularity, the faculty does not seem exactly sure what a course in professional writing means. The students do, though. "Professional" means getting paid for what you do. And, put together with writing, it means mastering the kind of writing that will get you a job and then a promotion. The students want "in" to a certain group, and they believe that I can teach them the code that will unlock the door. This belief worries me; in fact, the whole idea of a course in professional writing worries me.

Professional writing classes are the most specialized incarnation of the current writing-across-the-curriculum movement. Here, the students do not survey the range of academic disciplines; rather, they concentrate on writing in the fields they have chosen to enter. Many of them are already working writers. They and I work together on projects that are often initiated by their employers or by their

Reprinted from the *Journal of Advanced Composition* 7 (1987): 23-30. Reprinted with permission.

imaginary visions of these employers. Consequently, we must maneuver through a complex rhetorical maze of several levels of audience at once: their classmates, their professional colleagues and clients, their superiors, their entire discipline, and me, their teacher. These students come into the course expecting to learn on-the-job writing, and they demand access to the codes, formats, and etiquette of specific fields. Already competent writers, they want "in" quickly. My dilemma results: am I helping students get jobs and promotions, or am I helping them become critical thinkers who can change and improve those professions? Do these need to be conflicting goals? And how can I achieve a synthesis that satisfies the university, the community, the students, and me? Should I even worry about such things? I am not certain that I have the answers to these questions, but I do want to offer some words of caution about professional writing courses and how they might connect or diverge from the other writing courses we teach in the English department.

This situation is a political one, first of all. English departments—under constant criticism from the community and from their colleagues across the university because students still "can't write" after completing the required composition sequence—have responded with writing-across-the-curriculum programs. Almost everyone agrees that encouraging our colleagues to incorporate writing into all disciplines is the ideal answer, and some programs have begun to work with teachers in other departments. But increasingly, English departments are taking on the complete burden of teaching students to write in their major field. Of course, this solution is attractive to university adminstrators, other departments, and community members who have often complained that English studies are not relevant, that they don't prepare students for their work life. And since almost everyone agrees that teaching writing is a most difficult chore, why not make the English department do it? And even within the English department, it is difficult to find instructors for courses like professional writing. It is a popular course; at Nebraska we could fill several sections of it each semester. But mine is the only one. None of my colleagues want to teach it, perhaps because they, too, are confused about exactly what the course should teach students, or whether we should be teaching it at all. As Lester Faigley and Kristine Hansen recently point out, such courses "challenge the old formalist assumption that 'good writing' is monolithic" (140). Our approaches to invention, arrangement, and style, and our beliefs about process, may not apply to these new courses. Perhaps, too, English teachers don't want to dirty their hands by exploring writing outside the academy. And even when they do, it seems to me that there is a serious question of whether we are going to study what executive officers of corporations say is good writing and try to imitate it, or whether we are going to look to research in our own field for approaches to teaching writing either inside or outside the classroom.

Faigley and Hansen, writing in *CCC*, warn that English teachers must first decide on the goals of these upper-level, discipline-specific courses. They focus on the writing-across-the-curriculum movement—helping students write for courses outside the English department—but their advice applies as well to professional writing classes. They describe two current approaches to these courses—the "professional" aim which trains students to imitate professional writing in the field, and the "liberal arts" aim which encourages students to explore issues in the subject matter of certain disciplines (141). Faigley and Hansen find problems in both strategies, and caution that both "pose major difficulties for a writing teacher outside the students' discipline" (141). They observed students who wrote flawless papers in terms of mechanics and format but who had not mastered the way a certain discipline transmits knowledge. Other students wrote papers that demonstrated a working knowledge of their fields, but were full of procedural or mechanical mistakes. I find the same discrepancy in my classes. One of my students this semester is working on the legality of policies regarding sexual harassment on the job. She is a legal secretary and is herself a victim of such harassment. Her papers are full of the appropriate "whereas's" and "thereto's," but she has yet to explore the implications of stated policies for women like herself. She sounds more like a lawyer than she did two months ago, but sounding like a lawyer is not the same as knowing the law or even knowing what she thinks of the way the law works. In other words, as Faigley and Hansen so clearly point out, style is not enough.

And a focus on style or format will certainly not lead to the kinds of personal response and change that I would like to see in that student. I want her to investigate what she thinks of the law as a profession while she has the freedom to do so. Faigley and Hansen say that if I really want to help this student understand the way the law defines such things as proof, knowledge, and relevancy, she and I will "have to internalize much more than the stipulations of the relevant style manual" (148). Yet so many of the more recent professional or writing-across-the-curriculum textbooks consider their nod to the *APA Publication Manual* a breakthrough in making composition studies truly cross-curricular. Nor do the readers that label themselves cross-curricular help me much by wrenching subjects out of context to represent specific disciplines; in my mind, an essay by Richard Selzer on the art of surgery does not present a science student with a model of how scientific knowledge is communicated. Subject matter, then, is not enough either. Perhaps the solution lies somewhere between these two poles, but we have not found it yet.

Nor is this dilemma a modern one, however tempting it may be to think it so. Plato, in a sense, was one of the first professional writing teachers, and he worried, as we should, about whether rhetoricians were instructing students in a method of intellectual inquiry or in tricks for persuading the crowds. In the *Gorgias* and the *Phaedrus*, Plato tries to move his students from a sophistic focus on style and sound, designed to dazzle the audience, toward a more personal dialogue that explores how knowledge comes to be knowledge. Aristotle's *Rhetoric* continued this work, attempting to show students that through careful analysis a speaker could "invent" an audience based on exploring how people come to believe. Both Plato and Aristotle wanted to teach their students a system of rhetoric that would be at the center of their intellectual learning. Perhaps we have forgotten this classical sense of a "professional" as one who is continually learning and exploring the boundaries of a discipline. Modern textbooks tend to over-simplify the process of knowing a subject or inventing an audience. My students are some of the worst culprits when they first come to my professional writing class. They have superficial notions of what a business executive wants in a piece of writing, for example, notions gleaned from their business textbooks, newspapers, and advertising. They start out writing, then, for an audience that they do not know.

Am I grappling, then, with an audience problem? The question "Who are my students writing for?" may illustrate the tension between what composition theory suggests teachers do and what the culture expects them to do, between teaching students to be perceptive or teaching them to be effective. In 1984, Lisa Ede and Andrea Lunsford summarized these two positions in their award-winning article "Audience Addressed/Audience Invoked." They define two basic attitudes toward teaching students a sense of readership, and they review theories that lead to two different teaching strategies. Audience "addressed," Ede and Lunsford maintain, has its roots in the influence of cognitive psychology, speech communications, and expectations from the world outside the academy. Teachers who subscribe to this model encourage students to write for actual readers, to engage in audience analysis, and to accommodate their writing to those readers in order to get results. Audience "invoked," on the other hand, finds its basis in textual analysis, usually from texts inside the academy, and argues that writers cannot know their readers in the same way speakers know their hearers. Teachers who use this model ask students to discover and define audiences through cues that other writers leave behind in texts. Following theorists such as Walter J. Ong, these teachers hope that by examining the way other writers have defined their audiences, students will come to internalize their own sense of "a reader." Ede and Lunsford conclude their review by advocating a synthesis of both approaches—since they consider each position an incomplete conception of the "rich" idea of audience (156).

Yet teachers tend to forget this "richness" when confronted with a class of students there to practice professional writing. It is tempting to revert completely to audience analysis, following the guidelines left for us by memos, sales presentations, and quarterly reports. No wonder the professional writing course isn't popular with the English faculty—there doesn't seem anything there worth knowing. But there can be if teachers strive for a balance between appealing to a preconceived notion of audience and carefully studying the texts from various disciplines. Such a blend seems particularly necessary in a professional writing class where developing a sense of audience is crucial but where students and teachers can come dangerously close to being satisfied with simple imitation or regurgitation, or where developing a sense of audience is crucial but where we can easily operate from wrong-headed or simplistic assumptions about audience.

Arthur Walzer argues recently in *CCC* that our methods for finding and analyzing audiences do not work for the new professional writing course. He suggests, as Faigley and Hansen do, that such courses need to return to a rhetorical approach through textual analysis of invention. Walzer borrows Douglas Park's theories of audience when he says that writers do not "adjust" their conclusions to "accommodate" a particular audience that they have analyzed demographically. Rather, they "discover" the significance of their conclusions by reflecting on their premises from the viewpoints of various "interpretive communities." For Walzer, what is important is not "what the audience already knows, but what kind of knowledge they expect to gain" (155). He suggests that we teach professional writing, then, by helping students analyze the places where writers from particular disciplines reveal their strategies for invention: "the manifest character of a particular audience is to be found in those statements in which writers cast . . . the importance of what they have done and of what they have to say" (156). In other words, we should be looking at how legal writers, for example, portray themselves in certain roles and how they justify taking up a certain topic at all. I am interested in Walzer's focus on the *topoi* of the professions—their implied justifications for their subjects and the roles they see themselves playing. This is where I'd like to see us place our emphasis in interdisciplinary classes—on rhetorical invention. Then, my legal secretary student might be able to "read" the research and memos from her attorney boss as the smokescreens they are. She would see the roles that this particular lawyer casts for himself and his profession—guardians of the *status quo* who find sexual harassment claims annoying at best but who can manipulate language to cover themselves.

I am worried, in a larger sense, about just this sort of adaptability to context and audience. I question one popular theme of professional writing-across-the-curriculum courses—that they will enable students to survey various fields and then maneuver through whatever situation presents itself. In one sense, of course, I want my students to have that kind of power. But I also want them to understand how such power works. Walzer says that if students analyze the rhetoric of various disciplines, they will then be able to find a "rhetorical home"—a community they feel comfortable addressing (159). I'd like to add that students should understand, first, what kind of home they are entering. This means getting below the surface of texts in the professions to the more difficult discovery of the relationships among writer, subject, and reader. My students have a very hard time with this sort of analysis; they constantly want to stay with the subject of a text and are quite stubborn about seeing the "audience" as actual, breathing readers rather than as an abstraction created by the interplay of voices and invitations within a piece of professional writing. For example, one of my students this semester is working on an assignment for the Nebraska Department of Revenue. He is redesigning their "Forms Management Program"—the controlling document that determines how all other forms will look and sound. He recognizes that the document desperately needs revision. It is full of jargon and in-house language, and it puts as much distance between itself and a reader as you would expect from a state tax agency. We have worked together on simplifying the language and changing the tone. But I also have encouraged him to investigate the rhetoric of such forms on a deeper level—the level of invention—to explore the kind of community the Nebraska Department of Revenue represents to itself and justifies to its outside readers. Through responding personally to the text, writing about its impact on him as a reader, my student is learning about the internal premises behind the rhetoric of distance and authority that operate in the discourse of his workplace. Then, perhaps, he will understand his place in that community more clearly, and decide whether he wants to use or change that kind of rhetoric. He will, on one level, be better able to revise the document to be more "readable"; on another, more important level, he will be able to "re-invent" its orientation, and his own.

In other words, I am arguing that we should be teaching expressive writing within the professional writing class itself, not only in courses that prepare students for more specialized tasks and audiences. Perhaps more than in any other kind of course, we should invite students to adopt what James Britton calls the "spectator's stance." Britton sees the spectator's role as that of evaluator, one who is free from the need to act and decide in response to social demands and is therefore able to evaluate more broadly, and at the same time, more personally. Britton calls this sort of discourse the "language of being and becoming," exactly the kind of language, it seems to me, that we need to use in writing classrooms (125). Particularly in professional writing classrooms, where it is tempting to select and order material according to demands from outside, the spectator's role would encourage looking at that material according to individual values. The spectator's role, manifested in expressive writing, demands relating the object of attention to the writer's system of values, an act which means exploring that system of values as well as analyzing one's own knowledge. I want to suggest that our students not try to write *in* the professions but *about* them. They should be encouraged to examine texts from particular disciplines and to write about what they find there. More importantly, we should explore with them the kinds of rhetoric that professionals from other disciplines use to characterize themselves and their purposes. If we do, we'll learn more about the subject we are teaching, and we will be engaging in the "search in common" that Plato argues is the foundation of learning (*Gorgias* 81).

But focusing on this kind of "invention" will not be politically popular, I suspect. Will corporate business, law, and government take kindly to our investigating what constitutes evidence in their fields, what underlying assumptions about clients and the public inform their communication, what their implied justifications and roles might be? Moreover, will the students and the professions like the idea of turning our focus away from style and format? It is easier to imitate the surface, as a recent piece from *CCC*'s "Staffroom Interchange" illustrates. Kathleen Kelly notes in "Professional Writing in the Humanities Course" that our courses in business and professional writing must also fulfill humanities requirements. She suggests, then, that we assign "writing about humanities *subjects* in professional writing *forms*" (235), so that students produce memos about works of art, for example. To me, this seems the worst sort of imitation and "flattery," as Plato called it. It suggests to students that form can somehow be separated from content, and it does fields outside of English the disservice of implying that they have no content worth exploring. I do not think we can teach the content of other disciplines, but I do think that we can teach students how to analyze the rhetoric of other fields.

Perhaps my worries and my proposals are too idealistic: like modern composition studies, I, too, am a child of the 60s. But I do believe that we have more to bring to professions outside the academy than training students in the textual etiquette of certain disciplines. Louise Wetherbee Phelps, writing in *Rhetoric Review*, explores the expanding "domain" of composition studies. She notes that we have discovered, "at the very moment of accepting a wider responsibility for facilitating the development of skill and power in written language, that we are not the only people, and school not the only context, to do so" (189). Certainly, we must learn about professional writing from people who aim their discourse beyond *College English* or *PMLA*. Recent articles like Tebeaux's "Redesigning Professional Writing

Courses to Meet the Communication Needs of Writers in Business and Industry" will help English teachers reevaluate how writing works and gets read outside our classrooms. However, as Phelps goes on to suggest, school is an ideal place for just the kind of learning I have been talking about; it provides students with their "only chance to experience the intensity of activity and discussion that seems to help people become expert in other kinds of skilled action" (189), the chance to write, in other words, as spectators. We should take the time, while we have it, to help professional writing students analyze their potential professions by focusing on the way writing invents those professions. I don't want us to forget all that we have learned about teaching writing in composition and literature courses once we walk into a course in scientific or legal writing. We do not work for corporations or governments, although at times it seems that way. And even when we do work with them and their employees, we must remember that our subject is our students, their learning, their opportunities fcr personal reflection, and maybe even social change.

Works Cited

Aristotle. *Rhetoric*. Trans. W. Phys Roberts and Ingram Bywater. New York: Modern Library-Random House, 1954.

Britton, James. *Language and Learning*. Coral Gables, FL: U of Miami P, 1970.

Ede, Lisa, and Andrea Lunsford. "Audience Addressed/Audience Invoked: The Role of Audience in Composition Theory and Pedagogy." *College Composition and Communication* 36 (1984): 155-72.

Faigley, Lester, and Kristine Hansen. "Learning to Write in the Social Sciences." *CCC* 36 (1985): 140-50.

Kelly, Kathleen. "Professional Writing in the Humanities Course." *CCC* 36 (1985): 234-37.

Park, Douglas. "The Meanings of 'Audience.'" *College English* 44 (1982): 247-58.

Phelps, Louise Wetherbee. "The Domain of Composition." *Rhetoric Review* 4 (1986): 182-98.

Plato. *Gorgias*. Trans. W.C. Helmbold. Indianapolis: The Library of Liberal-Arts-Bobbs-Merrill, 1977.

_____. *Phaedrus*. Trans. W.C. Helmbold. Indianapolis: The Library of Liberal-Arts-Bobbs-Merrill, 1981.

Tebeaux, Elizabeth. "Redesigning Professional Writing Courses to Meet the Communication Needs of Writers in Business and Industry." *CCC* 36 (1985): 419-29.

Walzer, Arthur. "Articles from 'The California Divorce Project': A Case Study of Audience." *CCC* 36 (1985): 150-59.

Toward an Ethics of Teaching Writing in a Hazardous Context: The University

by Sandy Moore and Michael Kleine

Prelude

The following essay is a collaborative effort by a writing teacher and a writing student to make sense out of a situation we experienced together when Sandy Moore, the writer, responded to an assignment given by Michael Kleine, the teacher. In an advanced persuasive writing course, Michael asked students to experiment with the major Aristotelian categories of persuasion: ceremonial, forensic, and deliberative discourse. For the ceremonial assignment, Sandy chose to write an essay of blame about patrons of her workplace, a restaurant/bar. Though ceremonial discourse aims to praise or blame its subject before a public audience, Sandy did not intend to publish the essay outside the context of the classroom. Aware of the charged nature of her essay, Sandy wanted to use the university classroom not as a place from which to launch a public attack on a private workplace; instead, she hoped that the classroom would provide a safe place in which to practice persuasive discourse and to develop her rhetorical skills.

A rumor that the essay had been written (true)—and that Sandy and another employee planned to publish it or something like it outside the classroom (false)—reached some of the patrons of the establishment where Sandy worked as a waiter and shift leader. Near the State Capitol of Arkansas, the restaurant and lounge was frequented by lobbyists and legislators. Although neither the legislators and lobbyists nor Sandy's boss ever read the written text, Sandy was fired.

Both of us were disturbed deeply by what happened to Sandy—for different reasons. Thus, we offer the following "Fugue" for two voices, a counterpoint that has helped us come to an understanding of the ethical problems Sandy's experience poses for writing students and teachers. We conclude with a "Coda" that considers how the experience affected the composition of our own essay.

Fugue

I Wrote a Paper for a Class and Lost My Job—Sandy Moore

For two and a half years I waited tables at a restaurant and bar across the street

Reprinted from the *Journal of Advanced Composition* 12 (1992): 383-94. Reprinted with permission.

from the Arkansas State Capitol. The restaurant was frequented by members of the General Assembly, State officers and employees, lawyers, lobbyists, and the political "in crowd." I regularly waited on a particular group of legislators and lobbyists. I knew their drinks, their districts, their special interests. We spoke on a first-name basis.

The tabs were large and my tips were good, but I was physically tired of making forty trips to the bar for this group over a two-hour period each night I worked. I was emotionally exhausted from holding my tongue after the nightly barrage of "Honeys," "Sugars," "Sweethearts," and drunken statements such as "Woman, fetch me another drink." I didn't like strange men's hands rubbing my leg, and I was offended by the cruel racist and sexist jokes I overheard at each table. One night a lobbyist was verbally abusive to me in front of the group because I would not date him. After three double scotches, he whined that I "didn't have time" for him. My employer would not have supported me if I had suggested that sexual harassment was taking place; he would have asked what I was doing to provoke the customer. I knew a public statement would put my job at risk, so I wrote a paper for a class as an outlet for my frustration; and I wrote it in a university writing situation, one I believed to be safe and benign.

When my paper was returned, I filed it with other writings I probably wouldn't read again. One month later the assistant manager at work called to inform me I had been suspended from my job; I was accused of planning to write a free-lance article for the *Arkansas Gazette* or *Arkansas Democrat* about the "goings on" of the legislators and lobbyists at the restaurant.

I admitted a paper existed, and my employer asked to see it. I refused. No one had seen it outside the classroom, and publication for a general audience was not my intent. I naively thought that my job was secure because I was a shift leader and the trainer at work, had been employed over two years, was always on time and rarely sick, and had told the truth. It never entered my mind that I could lose my job over a false rumor. Apparently, a co-worker had mentioned my paper and her own writing aspirations—possibly in the same sentence—at a private party for one of the senators. Within two days rumors were circulating that we planned to write a free-lance article for a local paper and that we were leaking conversations we overheard to the press.

I remember the owner's words two days later: "I cannot let you come back to work. After talking with numerous legislators and lobbyists it [the paper] has done some damage and has been a detriment to the business. You are fired because this paper that you have written . . . and some of the conversations that you had with [a female lobbyist], the lobbyists, and others about the goings on of their business has [sic] become a detriment to their business." The owner explained that my co-worker was fired because of what "could have or may have been written."

The co-worker and I had never discussed collaborating on anything beyond lunch. My accusers didn't even know what my paper said, and none of them had confronted me directly. I thought that people with power, money, and influence only preyed on other people with power, money, and influence. What did they have to fear from a writing student?

The ACLU couldn't help. Because I did not have an employment contract, I was employed "at will," and I could be fired for any reason. Two civil rights attorneys told me I had no legal recourse; my civil rights had not been violated. (In order for me to have any recourse in a civil suit, I needed proof that one of the legislators had made threats involving the publication of my paper.) I talked with an attorney friend who was willing to file a cause of action based on the tort of Outrage, but the restaurant filed for Chapter Eleven Bankruptcy the week after I was fired, listing the IRS as a creditor. My friend felt the chances of getting a judgment against my employer in a bankruptcy court were unlikely, and a bankruptcy judge would never give my claim priority over a claim by the federal government.

I talked to newspaper reporters. I collected articles related to my situation and did volunteer work for the ACLU. I learned how to use the law-school library as I investigated the legality of the action taken against me. I wrote summaries of law journal articles for a technical writing class I was taking. I warned my fellow creative-writing students to guard their papers. I wrote thirty letters to government officials, twenty-six of which remain unanswered. I tried to understand what had happened and blamed myself. I wrote again and again, wanting someone, anyone, to tell me they were sorry. I had been humiliated and abused. I didn't have a job. I had no money. I was in pain and no one seemed to care.

I conferenced with students in the writing center at my university, where I worked as an intern, about the content of their papers. I wondered if I needed to tell them not to name names, to be careful. Did I need to invite them to censor themselves because of my own fear? Never before had I worried about the content of school papers; I had believed that my academic writing was somehow protected. I thought I was safe so long as I chose not to take my writing outside the university. I was naive to think I could mention a paper about my workplace to a fellow employee. So, in a sense, it was my choice to take my paper out of the context of the persuasive writing class.

The week immediately after I was fired, I went out, rented movies, watched the television I rarely turn on, and did everything except write. The first time I did pick up my pen, I censored myself. I backtracked and read over my writing to make sure I didn't say anything that could be used against me. I added disclaimers to charged or questionable statements. I was miserable.

In retrospect, to say I lost my job because I wrote a paper for a class now seems too simplistic. There are several questions I must ask now:

- Is freedom of speech a right *given* by the Constitution, or is it a basic human right that *should be protected* by the Constitution? Currently, the First Amendment only protects us against governmental interference. Should private citizens, specifically employers, be allowed to encroach on the freedoms of private-sector employees as they desire? Should government employees be able to rob me of my civil rights when they are backed by a powerful lobby who will lie on their behalf?

- The Employment at Will Doctrine, which has been upheld by the courts since late in the nineteenth century, states that absent a fixed-term contract of employment, employers "may dismiss their employees at will . . . for good cause, for no cause or even for cause morally wrong" (*Payne v. Western A.R.R.*, 81 Tenn. 507, 519-20, 1884). As long as states lack Wrongful Discharge Legislation, will at-will employees continue to risk the loss of their civil rights?

• The courts have carved out a few protections by ruling that employers cannot discriminate for reasons based on race, religion, gender, disability, or for a reason that goes against public policy. (The public policy exception is vague, differs from state to state, and is decided on a case-by-case basis.) If the physical differences and belief systems of employees are protected, why isn't the freedom to express an opinion protected?

• Does a waiter break an implied confidence if he or she discusses a customer's purchases or actions? Would public consumers lose their right to privacy if an employee's free speech were protected from the employer?

• Is my situation a sign of a politically corrupt system, one in which a coercive lobby enjoys the right to squelch individual liberty in order to preserve its own special interest? Should lobbyists be made more accountable? According to Arkansas Law, a lobbyist is not required to name a recipient of a favor unless more than $24.99 is spent. If the host's group is large, the average spent on each individual might be less than the maximum allowed by law, but the total might be far more than $24.99. This loophole allows many legislators to go unnamed in the lobbyist's reports to the Secretary of State.

• Was the action the legislators, the lobbyists, and my employer took against me consistent with the action they would have taken against a man? My situation might be one that rarely occurs, but it seems to represent an abuse of power that my own political representatives are at least capable of.

• Is freedom of speech in jeopardy in the university as well as in the workplace? Should universities be allowed or forced to control a student's oral or written expression? Or should the university protect students from "outside" interference? Freedom of speech is fundamental in a free society. Without it, students and millions of at-will employees are not free to speak. We have a Constitutional amendment that guarantees our right to express ourselves, but we are not necessarily protected against the consequences of exercising that right if someone is offended by our actions, even if we tell the truth and, sometimes, especially if we do.

Throughout my life I have been told not to break rules, that I am somehow responsible if others are bad or mean or if things go wrong. I felt I had broken a rule—one I was not aware existed—and my hand was slapped. Now I realize that when I went to work I did not take any kind of loyalty oath or vow of secrecy. I am not responsible for the public actions of the men and women about whom I wrote. I wrote about adults who are responsible for their own actions, and it cost me dearly. I did not write with spite or malice. I expressed an opinion, an expression that is my Constitutional right. I have the right to write. I do not have the right to slander or abuse, but I have the right to express my opinion in writing. I also have the right to feel secure in my job and the right to due process.

It was not just that I wrote critically about patrons of my workplace; it was that I wrote about the wrong people—people lacking in principle. I was honest, and now I believe my subjects feared that the average person, their constituents, would be appalled at the behavior I observed. I got too close to the truth, and I was expendable. The legislators' and lobbyists' right to privacy in a public place was more important than my right to earn a living.

When I lost my job, I lost my seniority, and, for awhile, my self-esteem and my belief in my ability to make sound decisions. Now when I look in the mirror each morning I see an intelligent, strong, and independent thirty-six-year-old woman who has the right to demand that she not be referred to as "girl" or "honey." I am not afraid to be called a "bitch" because I show my outrage and ask that I be treated with courtesy and respect. My belief in the fairness and intelligence of Arkansas' legislators is lost forever. Much of the lobbying effort is corrupt. Although I have no recourse through the courts, and no way to recover my financial losses, I am determined to be heard. I will continue to seek recourse through my writing. Employers should not be allowed to fire someone indiscriminately, nor should legislators be allowed to infringe on the rights of their constituents. Legislators should not be allowed to abuse the system they themselves created. I have a responsibility to my fellow students and at-will employees to speak out against such abuses of power.

Four pieces of unseen typewritten paper, filled with the words of a student, created havoc among powerful lobbyists and legislators in Arkansas. Clearly, writing is powerful, and a voice keeps screaming in my ear, "Don't stop. Keep writing. Become their greatest nightmare!"

Arrested Without Charge—Michael Kleine

When Sandy called to tell me that she had been fired over the essay she had written for class, I felt like Joseph K. in Kafka's *The Trial*—arrested without charge, guilty of something, but uncertain of what. I had been teaching writing since 1971, and to my knowledge a student had never before been fired for writing an essay for class. After the phone call, I tried to convince myself that I had done nothing wrong, merely given an open-ended writing assignment. I wanted to believe that my sense of having been arrested was caused more by moral outrage over an abuse of political and economic power than by anything for which I personally could be held responsible. Now, nearly a year after Sandy's phone call, I still feel a sense of outrage; but I also recognize that I was culpable, that in my teaching I had perhaps not committed a crime of commission, but that certainly I deserved to be charged with a crime of omission: in my naivety, I had failed to tell students the whole truth about writing.

Like many contemporary writing teachers, the belief system underlying my pedagogical theory and practice was influenced from early on by the work of people like James Britton and Peter Elbow, compositionists who advise us to tap the expressive energy of our students and to encourage students to write without fear, to play the "believing game." Although my later reading of ethnographers and social activists—people like Shirley Brice Heath and Paulo Freire—may have caused me to shift my perspective and language (from a focus on *developing* the "voice" and "confidence" of the individual writer to a focus on *empowering* the writer in various "discourses," "communities," and "ideologies"), my teaching goals have remained relatively constant. I want written discourse to be available and meaningful to my students. I want them to make a personal commitment to their written expression, to write freely about their experiences, their visions of reality, their reading. Most of all, I want them to be empowered to participate in the construction of knowledge and the shaping of the world.

For the past twenty years or so, I have done my best to celebrate empowered writing with my students and with other writing teachers across the country. Because I encourage students to import their own discourses into my writing class and to shape those discourses there, I count myself participant in a pedagogy of "liberation" and permission, an advocate of free speech in writing. In technical writing courses, I have asked students to address problems from their workplaces and institutional worlds, to use the class as a place to practice acts of proposing and reporting that might in fact make a difference in those places and worlds. In persuasive writing courses, I have always directed students to write to "real audiences" about "real-world problems," and I have always encouraged them to find their own personal space in persuasive discourse.

But now I reread the two paragraphs above and discover that linguistically they embarrass themselves—and me. I notice the repetition of "I want" and the avoidance of "they want." I notice that words like "liberation," "permission," and "free" are mixed with words like "asked" and "directed"—that the notion of empowerment is problematized by the fact that it is more or less required by an agent of power, by the teacher, by me. My written celebration of empowered writing deconstructs. In the context of what happened to Sandy, it rings false—or at least oxymoronic: I celebrate "mandated empowerment"; I contradict myself.

When Sandy was fired, I was forced to confront the rationalizations that had enabled me to celebrate the freedom I had imposed on my students. Because I never forced students to disclose expressively when they were uncomfortable, never forced them to submit proposals and reports they wrote in class to supervisors at their workplaces, never forced them to publish the persuasive pieces they wrote outside the classroom, I felt rather smug. In that smugness, I believed that I had helped create a kind of sanctuary, a safe writing context where one could more or less import external contexts and write freely, not having to worry about the repercussions of external publication. I believed that my students were protected from the outside, that they could take risks with their writing, that they could experience the power of writing without having to deal with the possibility that power flows two ways: that it is capable of flowing outward and changing the world, but that it is also capable of flowing back toward the writer and doing harm.

What happened to Sandy changed everything for me, destroyed my pedagogical illusions and forced me to come to terms with my own power, my own responsibility. There is no sanctuary, no protected context. Writing is potentially harmful, both to the world and to the writer. Teaching writing is more problematical than I ever knew: when we give a writing assignment, we do more than ask students to take linguistic risks; we may in fact be asking them to take personal risks and job risks. Indeed, the more we ask students to invest in writing about non-academic contexts, the greater the risk we ask them to take.

Shortly after Sandy's phone call, I asked her whether she would like to discuss what had happened with the rest of the class. I assumed that the class, which was comprised of many older and non-traditional students, would be sympathetic and supportive. Sandy thought the same thing and agreed to lead a discussion of what happened to her because of the paper she had written. Although some of the students shared our outrage, others, especially several older male students, sympathized with the employer who fired Sandy. Some believed that a kind of implicit contract between employer and employee had been violated when Sandy decided to write about her place of work. Even though her writing was not read in final form by anyone besides me, and not at all by her accusers, they argued that Sandy had entered into a fiduciary relationship with the employer when she accepted money for her work, and that outside disclosure of insider conversation and activity constituted a breach of such a relationship. Others questioned the protected status of discourse within the university and even between teacher and student. They argued that a text, once written, can easily be dislocated from its context, and that once it is dislocated it can become a kind of unguided missile, capable of exploding and doing damage wherever it lands.

I will never forget a story that one of the students told me after class. She had written a report for a technical writing course concerning a problem at her workplace. She said that she wrote the report with full knowledge that if it had been read accidentally by the "wrong people" (meaning the ostensible audience for the report) she herself would have been fired. She went on to explain that at one point she had been writing part of the report at her word processor at work when she was called away from her desk. When she returned to her desk and reread on her screen what she had just written, she came to a dark realization: even though she was writing the report for class, the text itself, if read in the workplace, might lead to her dismissal. I asked her how a report written with the intention of improving the workplace might lead to her dismissal. She said, "Oh, it wouldn't be because I was writing a report about work, but because I was writing a report about work for somebody who didn't work there: my teacher."

The classroom discussion surprised me. Apparently some of my students had known all along that what writing teachers want for them and request of them may not be safe. Especially those students who had experienced the politics of workplace writing understood that certain contexts and subjects are best avoided—even in the "freedom" of the classroom. Before Sandy's experience and the classroom discussion of it, I probably would have rationalized most of my writing assignments in this way: "I ask students to bring their own worlds of experience and feeling, their own discourses, into the classroom, and there we work on translating those discourses into writing that would be effective if it were read by audiences outside of the classroom." Now, in my darker moments, I want to say, "I pay students with grades to import and disclose discourses that are none of my business and in so doing force them to betray the private discourse communities of friends, families, workplaces, and various institutions."

I asked myself why Sandy's experience surprised me so much. In order to come to terms with this question, I was forced to meditate on my own status as a tenured academic writer—a privileged status, I understand now, that had led me to believe in the university as a sanctuary, as a protector of free speech. Before I was tenured, I probably was just as wary of speaking freely about my own workplace, the university, as any other untenured assistant professor. Aware of the political realities of a multi-leveled tenuring process, I believed I was free to talk and write about ideas without fear of job retaliation, but only insofar as those ideas were safely dislocated from the interests and ideologies of those who had the power to judge my case after six years of speaking softly.

However, as I approached tenure time several years before Sandy was fired, I coauthored a risky article with a colleague about problems with corporate writing. The article was published and later read by executives at a local corporation. Although my colleague and I had not identified the specific corporation we had studied in order to write the article (we had called it "Corporation X"), some of the corporate executives suspected that their corporation was the subject of the article. They telephoned us several times, first to express their anger and then to persuade us to disclose the true identity of the corporation we had studied. Not knowing why the corporation wanted us to make such a disclosure, we refused. The executives then complained to the university and requested that our administrators pressure us to disclose the corporation's true identity. I was up for tenure at exactly this time and, needless to say, worried that the university might apply such pressure and deny me tenure. But administrators at my university politely refused to comply with the corporation's request and explained that such compliance would undermine academic freedom. I was later given tenure. In other words, I was not fired and to this day I receive a paycheck from the university.

In part because of my experience, I came to trust the university as a force of protection, as a kind of sanctuary. After all, it had risked alienating a powerful local corporation to protect the academic freedom of two of its professors. And because the university had protected me and my job, I over-generalized that it functioned as a protector of the academic freedom of all within, of each member of the "academic community." Although I still believe that the university should strive to protect the speech and writing of those within, at least from its own institutional power, Sandy's experience now forces me to question my belief that the university is capable of protecting the discourse of faculty and students equally. It is true that the university is *capable* of protecting the discourse that transpires therein from itself, from its own power to monitor, control, and retaliate. And it is also true that the university is *capable* of protecting the jobs of its employees, its professors, when they speak or write freely. However, Sandy's experience demonstrates clearly that despite such capability, students are inevitably vulnerable—that their jobs and personal lives are at risk every time they write for us: even if a professor doesn't retaliate powerfully and harmfully for a student's expression of value, belief, or knowledge, some outside force might retaliate. Thus, student discourse is in no way protected. For students, the university is not a sanctuary.

I see, now, that I am situated in an institution that both empowers me and expects me, because I am a writing specialist, to require that students express themselves in writing. Ironically, it is my effort to erase my own institutional position and power that puts students most at risk in external institutions and constructions of power. When they cease speaking and writing the discourse of the classroom and begin importing the discourses of "outside," they are no longer securely situated in either discourse. What they write within the university context, if discovered outside of that context, might be perceived as a kind of disclosure, or even betrayal, of a private discourse. In fact, my power is never really erased. Indeed, it now seems a kind of originating power, a force of exigence, that requires students to speak and write and that potentially complicates their relationships with other forces of power.

Perhaps my inability to connect with the experience of writing as a student in the 1990s can be explained further by reflecting on what it was like to write as a student in the 1960s. The rhetorical situation within the university was different back then—for me and, I suspect, for many others who now teach courses that focus on writing. Back then I did not take "writing courses." Most of the papers I wrote concerned dead literary figures and anthologized literary texts. The audience was clearly the professor. In fact, few of my papers were read by my peers. As long as I gave the professor what he wanted, writing was safe.

Since the Vietnam era, the writing revolution has resulted in a scrutiny of the school-writing rhetorical situation and a critique of a pedagogy that establishes the teacher as only audience and rewards the replication and perpetuation of a static academic discourse. Specialized writing courses require students to experiment with non-academic discourses. As they complete an English major at my university, upper-division students write literary nonfiction, technical and professional proposals and reports, expository pieces about themselves and their non-academic areas of knowledge, and persuasive pieces that aim to change the world outside the university. They are constantly encouraged to write for non-academic audiences, either to find or construct audiences other than the teacher. Thus, my own students experience a complicated rhetorical situation that I never had to face myself, a situation in which they must negotiate a text in and for two totally different worlds. Neither world, the classroom world or the one outside the classroom, is safe. Both worlds are capable of a response that may seem retaliatory to students. In my class, I tend to promote writing that evokes an external audience. If students do what I ask them to do, especially in a persuasive writing class, then they run the risk of offending the external audiences they evoke. What, then, am I to do?

Telling the Story

My familiarity with the schemas of academic discourse leads me to a superficial and easy answer to my own question: I must write a final "implications" section that will somehow make up for the unusual form of this essay. But this answer, by itself, does not suffice. Somehow what Sandy wrote, and what I am trying to write here, problematizes the ordinary discourse of composition theory. An implications section, by itself, is impossible to write. The implication is, at last, that I must write this essay with Sandy, that I must tell this story—to as many audiences as I can. And because my own understanding of the nature of the harm done by *not* telling such a story in the past is limited, because I cannot understand completely the feelings of my students, I must tell it collaboratively.

In my own classroom I must reiterate the tale told above. I must make space for honest discussion of the complex rhetorical situation that students face when they write to and for external audiences while at the same time they contend with the demands of the classroom context. Such discussion should not only help the students understand what they face, but it should also help me understand what it is I ask them to do when I request suasive writing, when I ask them to take rhetorical risks, when I encourage them to import discourses external to the classroom.

I will no doubt continue to encourage students to experiment with a variety of rhetorical contexts, but never again without warning and never again without vigilant protection of work in progress and of completed texts. Such protection would involve considering, with the student, the consequences of an actual reading by the intended audience. If such a reading would result in harm to the student, then I would need to suggest that any collaborative activity within the classroom be safeguarded. A student facing potential rhetorical risk should be allowed to decide whether to share his or her writing with a peer group. Upon request, I would need to pledge to the student that I would not show any given piece of writing to anyone else, including trusted colleagues.

Finally, I must problematize in this essay and in my classroom the notion of free speech and free writing. Writing students and teachers alike need to come to terms with the myth that free speech is protected as a right that can be exercised without fear of retaliation. Indeed, our speech is only protected by our government from the government itself. The government does not protect us from each other when we speak freely. Thus, free speech is not a given for the speaker or writer: it is more a process that begins in the knowledge that its use, its exercise, might bring harm to the user; at the same time, the exercise of free speech in the face of possible harm asserts the value of such exercise and works to promote that value universally.

It saddens me that my own future teaching of writing may involve not only the rhetorical action of encouraging free speech in writing, but also of warning about the possible consequences of such speech. Nevertheless, what happened to Sandy has persuaded me that such a warning is ethically requisite. At the same time, it seems ethically requisite that writing teachers encourage free speech among students and freely speak, ourselves, a discourse that celebrates its value.

Perhaps it is time for all of us who assign and supervise writing from positions of power to move away from the kind of "objective research" that tends to erase our presence and our ethical responsibility. If we told stories about ourselves and the consequences of what we do, and if we encouraged students to tell us stories about what happens to them because of what we do, then we could engage in a dialogue on the ethics of teaching writing, a dialogue that perhaps has been deferred for too long.

Coda

Michael—On Writing the Above Essay

Through our collaboration, Sandy and I learned more than what the text above tells: our process of exchanging and consolidating drafts helped us construct not only a shared understanding of the relationship between power and writing, but also a kind of reciprocal understanding of the position of the "other"—writer understanding teacher, teacher understanding writer. Moreover, the process of revising and editing this essay clearly revealed to us how much our mutual awareness of the possibility of retaliation affected, and infected, our composing process ("sanitizing process" might be a better phrase). For us, revising was mainly a process of deletion—deletion of any specific discussion that could possibly injure either or both of us, or even injure *JAC*, if it were read by the "wrong people"—powerful people external to the academic audience we *think* we address here. Editing was a process of erasure, erasure of the names of specific lobbyists and legislators, erasure of the name of the workplace, erasure, even, of the names of students in the classroom.

We wanted to write this "Coda" to make sense of our own writing, of our collaboration. But as I reread my part of the "Coda," I fear that it makes us seem paranoid. And this fear makes me want to gloss the gloss. The writing above is not only erasure. It is also iteration in writing of a story we both want to tell. In publishing the story, we want to change things, to make things better. At the same time, both of us have come to understand the necessity of self-protection. And so we engage in a rhetoric of cautious blame, of simultaneous iteration and erasure. Every future act of writing will seem to be an act of free expression and, at the same time, an act of discretion.

Sandy—On Writing the Above Essay

During one of our editing sessions, I wrote a note to Michael telling him I was not afraid of telling the truth and naming names if doing so would strengthen our paper. He said our audience wouldn't be familiar with local names and places, so specifics were not necessary. Something about this interaction made me uncomfortable.

After countless re-writes and hours of meditating on this piece, I realize that, again, my intentions do not match the reality of the writing situation. All writing is discretionary and potentially harmful, from papers I write for class to the journals that lay haphazardly around my house. I must protect what I put on paper, and, by doing so, perhaps I can protect myself. Outcomes, however, are unpredictable, and I do not have control over the reactions of unexpected audiences. Unless I intend to publish what I have written, I will guard my work with great care. Never again will

I write a paper for a class without first changing names and places. Nor will I discuss my ideas about work in progress.

I can honestly say that by naming my accusers in this paper I would intend to inflict harm. By censoring myself, I do not absolve them of responsibility for their actions. I believe that the individuals involved should be exposed to their constituents, but I will attempt to do that by writing to a different audience through another vehicle.

For now I must be satisfied with sharing my story in the hope that others will be aware of the risk involved in writing about real-life situations, even if that writing is done in the classroom. I also hope that this piece might stir up just a little trouble for the Employment-At-Will Doctrine and promote an awareness of the need for Wrongful Discharge Legislation to protect all citizens.

My sense of being a victim is slowly being replaced by the return of my sense of humor. Sometimes I sit back and think, "Hmmm. Isn't writing fun?"

Advanced Composition as Fishing Pole: Principles, Processes, Practices

by Richard M. Coe

Advanced Composition is an ambiguous title, affixed to a wide variety of courses—most of them useful, not all of them truly advanced. Indeed, "Advanced Composition" often serves students who, after completing two or three years at the university, have been sent back to the English department because professors in their majors judge that they did not master what "should" have been taught in freshman composition. Courses for such students are literally *re*-medial, for they reteach essentially the same material as regular composition, with perhaps some special emphasis on the particular tasks that face upper-level university students. One could quibble over titling such courses Advanced Composition—I am about to do so—but the courses do meet a real need. Because they cover essentially the same material as first-year composition courses (and often use textbooks written for first-year courses), however, such courses present few special pedagogical problems.

When you take a genuinely advanced course in anything, you do not expect it to be essentially the same as the regular course; after a brief review of basic principles and standard processes, you expect to learn sophisticated principles and subtle processes that advance you beyond ordinary competence. Insofar as Advanced Composition is advanced composition, our first, somewhat tautological axiom should be that it must advance beyond ordinary composition. At least in the United States, this means beyond freshman composition, the course that, in principle, brings everyone up to standard, up to minimal competence (if I may be excused the phrase), so that they can write what the university requires them to write.

If freshman composition is a preparation for writing at the university—and I think that is what it most commonly is, especially in its incarnation as a "service" course—then advanced composition should be for students already competent at such writing. What would you teach the students you gave A's in freshman composition for mastering most of what that course covers? What would you teach the students who already write well enough to get consistent A's on their term papers in their majors if they asked to learn whatever comes next in composition? Beyond traditional rules and precepts, beyond Strunk and White and the research paper, beyond "prewriting," free writing, and journals, beyond straightforward applications of rhetorical concepts like purpose and audience, what is there to teach?

Reprinted from *Teaching Advanced Composition: Why and How*, Ed. Katherine H. Adams and John Adams, Portsmouth, NH: Boynton/Cook, 1991. Reprinted with permission.

Defining advanced composition as a course for those who have mastered the standard writing curriculum does engender a few problems. For one, our discipline is far from unanimous about what should be taught in ordinary composition courses (and the majority of those who teach writing are not even part of our disciplinary community). And the law of uneven development most certainly applies to the development of writing abilities. Most advanced writers still retain a few elementary problems: one still dangles modifiers, another's "natural" voice sounds like gobbledygook, yet another punctuates by "breath pause" with idiosyncratic results—and many still suffer from overly self-critical, painfully inefficient writing processes. Still, the word *advanced* requires drawing a line somewhere somehow.

Very tentatively and minimally, let me suggest that those who have mastered regular composition:

1. Avoid most errors of spelling, grammar, and usage, especially what we might call the "mortal sins," (i.e., those errors that especially upset readers of job applications, proposals, term papers, and other such documents);[1]

2. Usually write reasonably clear, correct sentences and unified paragraphs and avoid "wrong words" and "awkward" sentences (at least when in good control of the subject matter);

3. Know, at least approximately, the conventional forms of academic discourse and follow the most important norms of academic discourse, especially the one that demands opinions be backed by reasons and evidence;

4. Have some strategies for discovering material (both in the library and in their minds); and

5. Have some sense of audience and how to write purposefully for the audiences they normally address.

My university's advanced composition course developed as it did partly because the preceding describes the students who first registered for it. And our noncredit writing courses developed similarly because they were aimed not at secretaries,

---

[1] Some conventions of grammar, punctuation, and usage are more important than others. The following is a short list of "mortal sins," which often lead readers to judge a writer illiterate, hence unintelligent and not worthy of their attention. Though this judgment may be unfair, it is real (see Hairston).

    Faulty agreement: subject-verb or pronoun-antecedent
    Unclear or ambiguous pronoun reference
    Ambiguous dangler
    Faulty and ambiguous parallelism
    Apostrophe errors
    Sentence fragment or comma splice (of the sort that indicates a lack of "sentence sense")
    Run-on (fused) sentence
    Blatantly unidiomatic expression (especially of the sort that indicates second-language or dialectic interference)
    An excessive number of errors that would otherwise be merely "venial sins."

entry-level professionals, and lower management, but at upper and middle management and professional writers, people who were already succeeding as writers. What should one teach such students?

The most common answer to this question brings us to specialized writing courses. These range from writing for science and technology (sometimes taught under the guise of writing-across-the-curriculum) to business writing, technical writing, proposal writing, and other such courses. These courses generally review the principles taught in regular composition and apply those principles to special writing tasks. Like remedial courses for advanced students, specialized writing courses are important and legitimate. Though these courses may not teach any advanced principles or processes of composition—indeed, they sometimes focus on writing tasks that are intellectually and rhetorically simpler than a term paper—these courses typically do teach students to handle writing tasks they will face in their majors and after graduation.

These courses, I should add, are most consistent with traditional assumptions. Traditional composition courses, though they dabble in process, essentially teach good form and the basic modes of discourse. Thus, it makes sense within the traditional framework to define advanced composition as instruction in special forms and modes. But this definition makes less sense within process assumptions. If one believes in a process approach, the key question should become, what is advanced process?[2]

Let me make a sharp distinction. I am not objecting to specialized writing courses. Indeed, our noncredit writing program at Simon Fraser offers many, from proposal writing to cookbook writing. We also offer, within our engineering department, a credit course in Engineering Communications. The issue is not whether, but how to teach such writing courses—how to create proper advanced university courses that develop students' understanding of "how words work in discourse" (Richards 8) while applying that understanding to a particular genre of writing.

By way of what Kenneth Burke might call a heuristic tour de force, let us ask what advanced composition might be if it were neither remedial composition for "advanced" students nor composition of specialized forms. What are advanced principles of composition? What is advanced process? What do advanced writers do that intermediate writers do not? What do those who write as professionals do that those who have just mastered freshman composition still do not know how to do? What should students be able to do before we may say they no longer need writing teachers?

---

[2] I do not use the terms *form* or *traditional* lightly. As Linda Robertson emphasizes (376-78), there is a sharp dichotomy between traditionalists, defined by their formalism, and those who have raised the banner of process. So sharp is this dichotomy, so clear is it to the advocates of process that formalism is the mark of the enemy, that it sometimes seems impossible to have a dispassionate discussion about form and structure in composition (though, obviously, almost all of us teach it, one way or another, from time to time). Indeed, I have been accused of giving succor to the enemy for trying to discuss how form, structure, and the modes of discourse might be reconceived and taught within the framework of a New Rhetorical process approach. For a fuller discussion of the distinctions between traditional and various process approaches to developing writing abilities, see Berlin, Faigley, and Coe, "Apology" 13-15.

A Prototype

As taught in philosophy and composition courses, definition is a negative process, a division between *A* and *not-A*, which may lead to invidious as well as useful distinctions. As performed outside philosophy and composition classes, definition ordinarily proceeds more by prototype (cf. Gardner, ch. 12, esp. 346), and that is what I proffer here. I certainly do not mean to suggest a prescription for what advanced composition should be—our courses were created in response to particular students and a particular departmental mandate—but I hope the following description of features of Simon Fraser University's advanced writing courses will be usefully suggestive.

The first time I taught advanced composition at SFU in 1980 I had a class of 17 students, almost all of whom were already good writers. Few had difficulty getting A's on term papers in other courses. Few made significant errors of spelling, grammar, or usage. Most already understood what can be learned from Strunk and White (and would also have been offended by Strunk and White, for the reasons articulated by Worby and Ohmann). Most had a good sense of their normal audience (i.e., of how professors read when they grade) and of conventional term paper form.

Five of the 17 (four women and a male Marxist) had some variation of this complaint/desire: "I know how to write to get A's on term papers, and I know how to write in my own voice to satisfy myself; what I want to learn is how to write in my own voice and still get A's on my papers." As I understood it, this was a statement about writing with contradictory purposes (to get A's, to learn, to feel good about what one has created) for contradictory audiences (the grader and oneself) on contradictory occasions (external evaluation and a learning experience).

Though many of my colleagues have significant doubts about Richards's literary criticism, our advanced composition course is founded on the assumption underlying his *Philosophy of Rhetoric*, that general principles of how words work in discourse can be learned and applied to particular writing tasks and problems. Our advanced composition course explicitly stresses theory—both because theory is useful (at least to those who know how to apply theory, which should include all university graduates) and because the belief that people should understand why they do what they do is a defining value of humanistic education. Only those who grasp theory, explicitly or intuitively, can adapt basic principles to new contexts.

Believing this, we go beyond regular composition by demanding more independence, which means both more theory and more self-help (including heuristics for self-help). We go beyond regular composition by covering advanced subject matter, such as paragraphs with two topics, contradictions of voice, collaborative writing, writing on non-"narrow" topics, writing for mixed audiences and "popular" audiences (hence issues of readability and techniques like appositional definition). We turn students inward to investigate their own writing processes, and we turn students outward to investigate specific discourse communities. Though pedagogy varies from course to course and instructor to instructor, we share the following defining goals:

1. We want students to come to understand their own creative writing processes—
   and how to intervene in their own processes to improve the quality of both

process and product. They should acquire techniques for dealing with process problems (e.g., procrastination).

2. We want students to understand writing as a social, communicative process that takes place in discourse communities. They should learn to deal with complex rhetorical contexts (e.g., contradictory purposes, multiple and/or hostile audiences). They should come to understand the implications of rhetorical contexts by writing for widely divergent purposes, audiences, and occasions (including nonspecialist audiences with no better than average—say, grade 10—reading abilities: the public).

3. We want students to understand the relationship between form and process, structure and strategy. Thus, they should learn how to initiate themselves into new discourse communities by analyzing discourses to reveal the functions of formal continuities. Ideally, they should also learn how to invent new forms for new purposes.

For both humanistic and practical reasons, students in their *last* writing course should learn how to help themselves thereafter. Our typical opening set of activities and assignments, therefore, helps students examine their own processes, describe their own problems, define their own goals, and monitor their own progress. Our typical closing assignment helps students learn how to teach themselves any particular type of writing they may later need to master. In between, the course confronts students with writing tasks that involve realistically complex (even contradictory) purposes, audiences, and occasions. It embodies both *generative rhetoric* and a New Rhetorical understanding of form-in-process.

Process Analysis

Our advanced composition instruction typically begins by focusing students' attention on their own motives, goals, and writing processes. This may be good pedagogy in any writing course, but it is especially important for advanced students. For one thing, many of their goals turn out to be process goals: to produce writing with less pain and/or procrastination; to manage their writing time more efficiently; to produce more per hour, day, or week. For another thing, when they run into writing blocks or other problems after they have left our course, they should know how to deal with them—and that means knowing how to intervene in their own writing processes. As Linda Flower has written, "Good writers . . . guide their own creative process[es]" (45).

This principle underlies not only our four-credit advanced composition course, but also our noncredit, special genre Writing Program courses. Our proposal-writing course, for instance, is a two-day intensive, which costs $275 and is taken by people who already write proposals at work, who know perfectly well what a proposal is and what proposals look like in their specialties. What they want to learn is how to write more effective proposals—without wasting time. Aside from examples (all of which have to do with proposals), the first day (the first half) of the course is indistinguishable from any of our advanced writing courses in its focus on teaching students to guide their own writing processes.

We teach students, when they have problems, to pay attention to their writing processes, to look at the relationship between process and product (cf. Della-Piana, Coe and Gutierrez, and Coe, *Process* ch. 1). We teach many standard process techniques—freewriting, heuristics, audience analysis, cut-and-paste revision, and so on—but always urge individual students to adopt particular techniques in relation to self-defined goals. We also teach new applications of standard technique (e.g., overcoming a writing problem by free writing not on the topic, but about the problem; see Hungerford 23-27).

A first assignment might ask students to write about their own motives, strengths, weaknesses, problems, and goals as writers. Here is one such assignment:

> Describe as specifically as you can the strong and weak points of your writing. Wherever you can, give concrete examples.
>
> Be sure to list strengths as well as weaknesses. Be sure to consider not only sentence-level strengths and weaknesses, but also strengths and weaknesses in such areas as finding good material, insight, organization, and adapting to particular audiences.
>
> A good way to approach this assignment is to review 10 or 12 fairly recent writings. If you are a student, it might be particularly useful to use papers written for courses you took from several different instructors in the past year or two. If you write at work, try to choose writing that has been edited or commented upon by several different supervisors. Then generalize any feedback you received and any insights you now have about the strong points and flaws of those writings.

Commenting on an early version of this assignment, which asked students to "describe your main writing problems," Richard Adler said his first response was, "Good gravy, I hope this assignment didn't work."

> . . . I immediately scanned the next two paragraphs for the results. I was greatly relieved to find the statement, " . . . this assignment confused my students. In the first place, most of them did not know what their main writing problems were." My past experience was once again borne out. If the students *knew* what their problems were, the odds are high that they would have corrected them.

I do believe that defining a problem precisely improves the odds of devising a solution, but I am not quite so sanguine as Adler that knowing what a problem is leads so frequently to solving it. I therefore ask each student, after doing the assignment, to reduce it to two lists: major strengths and main problems (in rough order of priority). Each student then rephrases each problem positively as a *goal* (and also adds forward-looking goals, based on their motives for taking the course, such as mastering a new type of writing). Then, in class and in conference, I help students flesh out each goal with (1) a plan for achieving it without undermining strengths, (2) a time limit or schedule, and (3) criteria for judging to what extent the goal has been achieved. The plan must say how the new ability will be integrated in the student's writing process.

While this is going on, the students are also—perhaps more importantly—analyzing their own individual writing processes. The day they turn in their first assignment— and it could be any first assignment, not necessarily the one just explained—I ask them to freewrite at length about how they wrote it. I have them take that freewriting home and add two types of detail: (1) what they may view as "non-writing" behavior (e.g., washing the dishes before starting to draft) and (2) what happened on paper (e.g., if the freewriting says, "And then I read the draft over and fixed a few sentences," I want to know what sort of "fixing"). Finally, I have them turn this narrative into a process analysis by adding comments about whether what they did in this case is typical (and if not, about what does usually happen). The reason for this staged assignment is that, if simply asked to write an analysis of their own writing processes, students too often write about some ideal process (e.g., how they write the one time in ten when they manage to get started well in advance of the deadline).

When students hold their lists of problems next to their process analyses, they often have Eureka responses, for a weakness in the written product is often a direct and obvious consequence of some weakness in the process. At any event, the means for dealing with virtually any writing problem should include a decision about when during the writing process that writer will pay attention to that problem. Thus a problem like "I make too many unsupported generalizations" is transformed into:

> From now on I will underline each generalization in my draft. I will make sure I have qualified each and explained how I know it is true. And I will give an example. By next month I will no longer receive complaints about unsupported generalizations, and by the end of the year I will no longer need to use this underlining procedure.

The solution is precisely located—during early revision, just after drafting—and turns on adding an extra procedure to the student's writing process.

While the students are doing these analyses, they are learning, both in class and in their assigned readings, about the composing process. They are learning various techniques for invention, revision, audience analysis, and so forth. But they are not learning "the right way to write." The assumption is that they already have writing processes, and the first axiom is "if it ain't broke, don't fix it." They learn about the composing process so that they can decide how best to change whatever aspects of their existing processes are contributing to their problems.

Rhetorical Contexts

Although composition specialists routinely assert that students should learn to write for a wide variety of purposes and audiences (cf., for example, NCTE, "Standards"), most university composition courses teach, at best, a rather narrow range. Sometimes without any explicit discussion of the nature of academic audiences, we teach students structures appropriate for writing with intellectual rigor to well-educated audiences, most often specialists. At least in its incarnation as a service course, freshman composition is primarily instruction in academic writing. For all our references to "the general reader," we do not ordinarily teach students how to communicate technical subject matter to general readers of average education (which in North America these days means roughly grade 10 reading ability or lower). Both these types of writing are important and difficult, and involve drastically different applications of the general principles of composition.

One way to focus students' attention is to insist that each piece of writing have a specifically defined rhetorical context, and to respond and grade accordingly. This rhetorical context may be stipulated in the assignment or, more often, stipulated by the student. In either case, I insist that it be typed on the title page. Then I respond to (and grade) each piece of writing according to my estimate of how well it would achieve the stated purpose(s) with the stipulated reader(s) on the specific occasion(s). The ultimate criterion becomes Donald Murray's question: "Does it work?" If in my estimate the piece of writing would totally fail to achieve its purpose(s) in reality, then it fails in my course—which, as in a real writing situation, means not an F but a rewrite.

Significantly, the primary role of the instructor becomes not judge, not critic, not even reader—but editor. That is, the instructor evaluates each student's manuscript just as an editor does, by imagining how well it would work, how well it would achieve its purpose(s) with its intended readers on the likely occasion(s)—and then by giving advice about how it might be revised to work better. (To assure a wide range of rhetorical problem solving, I also insist each student write at least once with the purpose of presenting complex, specialized material to a nonspecialized audience that reads at or below the grade 10 level.)[3]

Imagining realistic rhetorical contexts usually means confronting contradictory purposes and audiences, which are quite common in real writing situations. Confronted, for instance, with this sentence from a government brochure on "conjugal violence," "Abused women can seek help from establishments in the health and social services network, namely the local community service centres and the social

---

[3] I started making this demand after reading a letter written to an adult basic literacy group by the Solicitor-General of Canada. His letter included sentences like these: "It seems clear to me, therefore, that if we are to address this problem, we must do much more to stimulate interest and, even more importantly, to allay the anxieties that now play a large part in deterring inmates from entering the school program. . . . The granting of privileges will not be denied to inmates not participating in Adult Basic Education, but participation would be a positive factor when the granting of such privileges is under consideration. . . . It is perfectly appropriate for literacy skills to be one of the factors considered in the granting of parole. . . . We now believe that the institutions should, wherever possible, ask for the same prerequisite skills that are demanded elsewhere, and we hope that this approach will not be seen as punitive, but rather, as an incentive to acquire the necessary education." Why, I wondered, would an intelligent, well-educated politician write such sentences to an adult basic literacy group. It occurred to me that he, and the staffer who presumably drafted the letter, may not know how to write sentences that can be understood by people who read well below university levels—that *they* are in this sense functionally illiterate (i.e., incapable of performing a literacy task required by their work). And then it occurred to me that they could have passed through my composition courses without necessarily acquiring this important ability. Since I regularly inveigh against gobbledygook and government documents addressed to the public in prose beyond the average person's reading ability, I decided I had to take more responsibility here.

service centres," students should be led to see the contradiction between the writer's overt purpose (encouraging battered women to seek help) and the writer's tacit purpose (satisfying a supervisor by emphasizing a verbose description of the department's network). Can we rewrite to achieve both purposes, or must this writer make the hard choice? Our textbooks talk about writing with *a* purpose, for *the* audience; they do not give much advice about multiple and conflicting purposes, audiences, occasions. Advanced composition courses should.

Generative Rhetoric

Most of our students at SFU have had considerable instruction on the level of words and sentences. They often say that what they want is to "improve my style," and much of their revising is defined by a desire to evade two marginal comments—"wrong word" and "awk"—but where they are weakest, where they need most help is "beyond the sentence" (and especially beyond the paragraph). I often suspect this is because form has been taught in traditional terms (that is, inaccurately and dogmatically) or not taught at all (because it is supposed to arise organically from subject matter or process).

Our approach to form, organization, arrangement, *dispositio* is not traditional (though it may be classical). It is rather in keeping with New Rhetorical conceptions put forth by Richards and Burke in the 1930s, more recently espoused by Christensen, Berthoff, and D'Angelo, and elegantly argued by Phelps just a few years ago (see Coe, *Toward a Grammar* 19-22). For all the ways in which these rhetoricians do not see eye to eye, they all see writing as a forming process, all put form in relation to function and process. Traditional composition instruction treated form as textual. Consequently, form became procrustean—matter that would not fit the standard structure was chopped off; other parts of a draft might be stretched absurdly to fill the form. Early process advocates objected to formalism because they remembered it was artificial, procrustean, even algorithmic (cf. Dixon). But the distinguishing feature of what one might call the new formalism is that it studies form in process, formal structures as they function in social and individual creative and communicative processes.

Burke, for instance, suggests a poem is what happens when an intuition (i.e., an inchoate insight, an unarticulated strategy for verbally encompassing a situation) is juxtaposed with an appropriate (poetic) form (*Language* 32-37). He argues that writers who deny this function are unconscious of their own process (or dishonest). If form is, as Burke asserts, "an arousing and fulfillment of desires" (*Counter-Statement* 124), it is not just textual but psychological. And if it is psychological, it is also social.

We assume that rhetorical structures are *pre-pared* ways of responding, that they embody a social memory of standard strategies for responding to types of situations the community encounters repeatedly. When writers see past the uniqueness of a particular situation and recognize it as familiar, they activate (at least provisionally) a structure they have previously decided is generally appropriate to that type of situation. New types of situations or purposes, of course, often call for new strategies, which may be embodied in new structures (cf. Coe, "Rhetoric 2001"; also Davis and other feminists).

We have various pedagogical strategies for helping students grasp this functional, contextual conception of form. One is to teach them several forms for the same general function (such as classical and Rogerian persuasion), thus confronting them with the implications of formal choices (cf. Coe, "Apology," esp. 24-26). Another is to help them analyze the functional implications of prescribed structures (e.g., the parts of a scientific report or of a proposal), to see form as heuristic. When this analysis leads to contradictions (e.g., between their communicative purposes and the standard structure of term papers in their majors), we try to help them understand and perhaps sublate those contradictions—as experienced writers often can (cf., for example, MacDougall).[4] Through the writing tasks we assign, we lead them to understand formal rhetorical structures in relation to rhetorical contexts and discourse communities.

Product Analysis

Instead of teaching paticular types of writing—there are, after all, so many, and the world is changing too quickly to allow us to predict accurately which our students will need five or ten years hence—we teach *METAHEUR*, a heuristic for analyzing any particular type of writing in order to learn it. This becomes something of a test: have students mastered the principles of composition well enough to use them independently to analyze new material? It is also a base: students should emerge with confidence that they can, in the future, teach themselves any new genre they need to write.

The crux of the assignment is the heuristic, which attempts to make conscious and explicit much of what freelance writers do before adapting a piece to a particular medium.[5] The assignment attempts also to concretize the concept of discourse community as both a generative and constraining context for writing. One reason this tends to be a final assignment is that the questions make more sense to

---

[4] Whenever I use the word *sublate* in a manuscript addressed to English teachers, some editor always asks me to define it. Why, I am not entirely sure, for the work appears in my *Webster's New Collegiate Dictionary*, and both editors and English teachers presumably own dictionaries. But I am convinced there is some significance in the pattern. *Sublate* is a key word, the English equivalent of the German *aufhebung*—except that *aufhebung* is a perfectly ordinary word, understood by ordinary Germans, whereas *sublate* is a somewhat technical, philosophical term. *Sublate* is a key word because it can open the door to dialectical thinking, something that English speakers, perhaps influenced by several centuries of Anglo-American empiricism and pragmatism, tend to find particularly difficult. Sublate means to conserve and to transcend at the same time. Linearly logical thinkers tend to find that a contradiction (which it is, logically), but this contradictory concept can help writers (and others) avoid reducing contradictions to simplistic either/or choices. Besides, just about every major change I can think of involved both a transcendence and a conservation of what existed before. Somehow I keep thinking that if people knew the word *sublate* they might stop being surprised by this fact about the nature of change.

[5] The undergraduate students on our main campus are often amazed to learn that freelance writers will prepare to write an article by researching not only their subject but also the magazine in which they intend to publish. The students who take our downtown, non credit writing courses—for the most part, people who already write successfully in their work—are quite the contrary of amazed. I think this contrast says something about how traditional composition instruction, though it may prepare students for academic writing, fails to prepare them to write in other contexts. Though it claims to teach the principles of good writing, traditional composition instruction actually teaches one particular type of discourse. Though one may argue that such instruction is appropriate in courses which prepare students to write at the university, it is not so clearly appropriate to more advanced writing courses.

students toward the end of the course, after they have met concepts like *cumulative sentence* and *level of generality*.

The students are told to choose a specific type of writing—feminist criticism of Shakespeare, storybooks for young children, feature articles for ski magazines, term papers that get A's from literature professors—and then to create a mini-manual for people who might want to do that type of writing. Although they may refer to published manuals as secondary sources, this writing must be empirical, based on the students' analyses of samples of the discourse—because one object of the assignment is to create self-reliance and self-confidence. (I also encourage students to do this assignment collaboratively.)

Thus METAHEUR guides writers to a description of the parameters within which a particular type of writing should be produced. (See Figure 1.) This heuristic helps generate a description of the constraints within which writers produce that type of writing. The assignment is based on the assumption that the nature of such constraints and their priority varies from one discourse set to another. And, paradoxically, because the immediate focus is on written products, the success of the assignment depends upon the students' prior understanding of writing as process as well as on their understanding of the practical relationship between structure and strategy, product and process.[6]

Figure 1
Metaheur

Subject Matter

1. What kind of material is usually treated? Does there seem to be a shared heuristic that some or all of the writers use to generate their material? Could you invent such a heuristic? Is there any sort of material that is noticeably avoided?

2. Do the writers seem to share approaches, methods, or techniques for handling the material? How are writings focused in this discourse? Are there certain key terms, root metaphors, or standard analogies that recur in this discourse? Are there "buzz words"?

---

[6] Just as the result of the opening process assignment was formally a proposal (encompassing both supralineal process analysis and a problem-solution structure), so the result of this assignment is formally causal explanation by analysis of contextual constraints (see Coe,*Process*, 359-70).

   The theoretical assumption is that writing is a stochastic, equifinal, and multifinal process. The writing process is always purposive, hence not random, but stochastic (from the Greek, to aim, to guess) because it is more often goal-seeking or goal oriented than goal-directed (i.e., stochastic as the term is used in system theory and cybernetics). There may be more than one satisfactory process for producing any particular type of writing (hence *equifinal*). And a variety of written texts may satisfactorily fulfill the same particular purpose (hence *multifinal*). This terminology comes from that attempt to model*organized complexity*—a good title for the writing process—which goes under the name of General System Theory.

   This theoretical tangent has multiple implications, a few of which I have discussed elsewhere. One key implication is that a complex stochastic process like writing is not best described by attempting to follow temporally as writers write—because the point is that, efficiency aside, a writer may work in*any* order as long as the final product is satisfactory. The process is best understood by describing not a writer's behavior, but the system within which that behavior makes sense (cf. Cooper), especially the parameters of the task and how various writers adapt to them. Though different writers may perform the process using various techniques in distinct sequences these parameters define and explain the limits to individual differences.

Rhetorical Context

3. What basic purposes does the writing serve? Is it primarily expressive, explanatory, persuasive, or literary? Is there a "hidden agenda" beyond the overt purposes? Are distinct purposes emphasized in different parts? What specific functions does this type of writing serve within its discourse community?

4. Who reads this type of writing? Why? What do you know—and what assumptions do the writers seem to be making—about the knowledge, attitudes, beliefs, and vested interests of the readers?

5. Where is this type of writing usually published? Is it likely to be read casually or seriously, for entertainment or for use? If the writing must be accepted by one or more editors before it reaches its readers, what can you surmise about these editors' motives and criteria? How would you name and describe the discourse community that reads this type of writing?

6. Is there a common persona that the writers adopt? Can you detect shared values? Do the writers take a particular stance and, if so, what does it imply about readers' expectations? How formal are the word choice and usage?

Structure and Style

7. Is there a standard format or typical structure for the whole writing or any part of it? Which of the basic patterns of development are used regularly? Are different patterns used in different parts? How do the writings begin? How do the writings end? What sorts of transitions predominate? How long are the paragraphs and how are they typically structured? Do most paragraphs have topic sentences (and if so, where)? What is the relationship among levels of generality within typical paragraphs and for whole pieces of writing?

8. How long are most of the writings in your sample? How long and difficult are the words and sentences? What is the level of readability? Do any particular sentence patterns stand out? How many sentences are ten or more words longer than the average sentence? How many are five or more words shorter than average? Is the style nominalized or is more meaning carried by verbs and adverbs? To what extent are there overt figures of speech? Is there a standard jargon? How would you rate this writing on a scale of abstraction? Does the text have texture (i.e., many cumulative or embedded modifiers)?

9. What is missing? Are there any structures that are noticeably avoided? What unique features does this discourse have that were not elicited by the preceding questions?

10. What other significant features characterize this type of writing?

In Sum

Through this prototype course description, I have tried to suggest some genuinely advanced directions a composition course might take. Amidst the pressures of the "eighties" to be pragmatic and provide students with immediately useful "job skills," I try to remember the old adage about the virtues of giving a hungry person a fishing pole instead of a fish. This advanced composition course—especially the opening and closing assignments—empowers students to learn without teachers. Although rigorous and demanding considerable discipline, although based on recent research and recent theory, this is in one critical sense a "sixties" course: it attempts to do what really ought to be done instead of settling, in the way of the "eighties," for what is "possible." It empowers students by helping them grasp principles and develop abilities that allow them to get beyond needing teachers to help them handle whatever comes next. It works well at Simon Fraser University. I hope it also suggests directions that might be usefully explored elsewhere.

Works   Cited

Adler, Richard R. "Response" to Richard M. Coe, "The Practicalities and Politics of Error." *Language, Culture and Curriculum.* Ed. Kenneth Reeder and Donald C. Wilson. Vancouver: Centre for the Study of Curriculum and Instruction Monograph (University of British Columbia), 1978. 20-22.

Berlin, James A. "Contemporary Composition: The Major Pedagogical Theories." *College English* 44 (1982): 765-77.

Berthoff, Ann E. *Forming/Thinking/Writing: The Composing Imagination.* Portsmouth, NH: Boynton/Cook, 1982.

Burke, Kenneth. *Counter-Statement.* 1931. Berkeley: U of California P, 1968.

_____. *Language as Symbolic Action.* Berkeley: U of California P, 1966.

Christensen, Frances. "A Generative Rhetoric of the Paragraph." *College Composition and Communication* 16 (1965): 144-56

Coe, Richard M. "An Apology for Form; or, Who Took the Form Out of the Process." *College English* 49 (1987): 13-28.

_____. *Process, Form, and Substance.* 2nd ed. Englewood Cliffs, NJ: Prentice, 1990.

_____. "Rhetoric 2001." *Freshman English News* 3 (1974): 1-13.

_____. *Toward a Grammar of Passages.* Carbondale, IL: Southern Illinois UP, 1988.

Coe, Richard M., and Kris Gutierrez. "Using Problem-Solving and Process Analysis to Help Students Solve Writing Problems." *College Composition and Communication* 32 (1981): 262-71.

Cooper, Marilyn M. "The Ecology of Writing." *College English* 48 (1986): 364-75.

D'Angelo, Frank. *A Conceptual Theory of Rhetoric.* Cambridge, MA: Winthrop, 1975.

Davis, Fran. "A Practical Assessment of Feminist Pedagogy: Work in Progress." *Inkshed* 7.5/8.1 (November 1988): 1-3.

Della-Piana, Gabriel. "Research Strategies for the Study of Revision Processes in Writing Poetry." *Research on Composing: Points of Departure.* Ed. Charles Cooper and Lee Odell. Urbana, IL: NCTE, 1978.

Dixon, John. "The Question of Genres." *The Place of Genre in Learning: Current Debates.* Ed. Ian Reid. Victoria, Australia: Deakin University Centre for Studies in Literary Education, Typereader Publication, no. 1, n.d. 9-21.

Faigley, Lester. "Competing Theories of Process: A Critique and a Proposal." *College English* 48 (1986): 527-42.

Flower, Linda. *Problem-Solving Strategies for Writing.* New York: Harcourt, 1981.

Gardner, Howard. *The Mind's New Science.* Rev. ed. New York: Basic, 1987.

Hairston, Maxine. "Not All Errors Are Created Equal: Non-Academic Readers in the Professions Respond to Errors in Usage." *College English* 43 (1981): 794-806.

Hungerford, Anne. *Advanced Study in Writing for Business and the Professions.* Vancouver, BC: Writing Program (SFU), 1989.

MacDougall, A. Kent. "Boring from within the Bourgeois Press." *Monthly Review* 40.6, 7 (November, December 1988): 13-24; 20-24.

National Council of Teachers of English. "Standards for Basic Skills Writing Programs." (March 1979).

Ohmann, Richard. "Use Definite, Specific, Concrete Language." *College English* 41 (1979): 390-97.

Phelps, Louise Wetherbee. "Dialectics of Coherence." *College English* 47 (1985): 12-29.

Richards, I.A. *The Philosophy of Rhetoric.* London: Oxford, 1936.

Robertson, Linda R. "Why Dionysius II Can't Write: Plato's Confessions of a Failed Teacher." *College English* 48 (1986): 376-84.

Worby, Diana Zacharia. "In Search of a Common Language." *College English* 42 (1979): 101-05.

The Collaborative Classroom
as a Site of Difference

by Julia M. Gergits and James J. Schramer

Haven't we all, at some time or another, sat in a beginning-of-the-year workshop on writing instruction, summer settling in our stomachs like a not-quite-digested meal, listening with at least some skepticism as colleagues painted glowing pictures of the flourishing collaborative environment they had cultivated in the classroom? We wisely nod to signal our agreement with our colleagues' findings, but out from the dark corners of our minds jump unsettling questions: What am I doing wrong? Where did my groups stray from the path? Why don't my students come away from collaborative assignments with that aura of success and good will that their students experienced? Although our students' experience of the collaborative process seems not to conform to what we have been assured are appropriate outcomes, we may be doing nothing wrong, nor have our groups necessarily chosen the wrong path. Our students' problems with collaboration may lie not so much in the way we facilitate the collaborative process but rather in the way we conceive of the methods and goals of that process. Predisposed to accept the team ethos of American sports and business as the paradigm for collaboration, we may be overlooking our students' day-to-day experience of collaboration. Conditioned to listen for consensus and monological agreement, we may not appreciate contending voices.

Collaboration is more than teamwork. Teamwork is primarily goal and success oriented. Few of us have ever heard a college coach explain a losing season by proclaiming, "It was teamwork that got us there." Although collaboration can have a goal and an outcome or product, it is, above all, a process. At its most effective and affective levels, collaboration is a process in which individual participants redefine themselves as a group, approximating what Victor Turner refers to as *communitas*.[1] For *communitas* to result, group members have to exchange the monologic discourse that so often marks negotiations between the powerful and the powerless (the discourse that often characterizes group decision-making in management—a language designed to negotiate *from* a position of strength, in which one party "compromises" by giving up what he or she can afford to lose) for a dialogic discourse that allows

Reprinted from the *Journal of Advanced Composition* 14 (1994): 187-202. Reprinted with permission.
[1] Turner defines *communitas* as "spontaneous, immediate, concrete," emphasizing that it "differs from the camaraderie found often in everyday life, which though informal and egalitarian, still falls within the domain of structure" (274). Although we do not claim that collaboration is directly equivalent to the liberating, ritual experience that, for Turner, constitutes *communitas*, we do see collaboration as an anti-structural process that can bring people together by levelling difference and, at the same time, preserving personal identities.

for co-existent, often conflicting voices. We should remember that "collaboration" can also refer to the act of siding with those to whom one was once opposed, as in "collaboration with the enemy." Despite, or perhaps because of, the tranformational nature of collaboration, it is often a messy process, marked by conflict, disagreement, and difference. Students know a lot about all three.

Students come to technical and professional writing courses with cooperative experiences that teachers often overlook.[2] Students cooperate every day in their family lives, marriages, personal and social relationships; they negotiate decisions with family, spouses, lovers, friends, neighbors, and colleagues. The goal of familial cooperation is much like that of academically manipulated collaboration: successful problem solving or decision making. It doesn't always work. Who among us has not claimed that those nearest us, those who should care the most about what we think, say, and feel, are not listening to us, not respecting our ideas? We put this knowledge aside when we walk into our technical writing classrooms, forgetting that the students in those rooms share our expectations of and frustrations with day-to-day relationships. They, too, have families, friends, lovers, and co-workers from whom they expect a lot and with whom they do not always get along. Most of us are introduced to social cooperation within our family units: fathers and mothers organize children to clean up their rooms, dress up for company, prepare for vacations, and so on. Family life is one long cooperative enterprise. Without substantial training in child-rearing or productive collaborative strategies, most families muddle along. Although parents establish guidelines that they hope will foster healthy children and promote socialization, rules and goals are often not clear, or they may change as circumstances intervene. Divorce, drinking problems, economic instability, and psychological or physical abuse undermine cooperation in over fifty percent of American families. Often, family life consists of acrimonious fights and irrational decisions. Students are the products of approximately twenty years of familial and social cooperation, albeit poorly developed, unfairly exercised, at times even dysfunctional.[3] The more dysfunctional the family, the less likely it is that students will arrive at college well prepared to learn about collaborating in the work place.

Even in a "normal" family, whatever that may be, giving or withholding signs of love and affection control cooperation. To punish a resistant family member (or friend, since the concept of family should be expanded to include the entire social circle), emotional recriminations are common, sometimes accompanied by tangible punishment, such as isolation, verbal conflict, even physical blows. Further, although violating social rules leads to punishment, seldom is one thrown out of a family for failure to cooperate. Unlike professional collaboration, which is usually a studied and deliberate action, familial cooperation is instinctive and non-reflective. We plan vacations or discuss professional goals with family and friends without

---

[2] For the sake of clarity, we will be using the term "cooperation" to describe social collaboration.
[3] We use the term "social cooperation" for the sake of simplicity, not to imply that professional collaboration is anti-social but to allow us to distinguish between the two. It is certainly true that all collaboration is social in nature; it is impossible for it not to be so by definition. Thralls and Blyler, Kogan, and Forman instruct readers about the need to understand social parameters to be a successful professional.

giving much thought to the process. Although we may hope for the perfect vacation or help in making the best career choice, we value the continuance of the relationship more than the outcome of the collaboration.

Professional writing courses (business and technical writing) usually proceed without accommodating students' experience with social cooperation. Neglecting this shared experience and underestimating its importance, teachers ask students to launch into collaborative assignments that supposedly represent situations students will encounter when they enter the "real world": the work place. Since the conventions of social cooperation are not identical with those of professional collaboration, teachers frustrate students by requesting they set aside personal strategies for getting along and participate in role playing based on corporate models. These frustrations became apparent to us when we asked our students to assess their writing groups in personnel memos. In this essay, we examine selected examples of these memos for what they tell us about the collaborative process. In analyzing our successes and failures with collaborative assignments, we let students speak for themselves. These voices reveal that student writers use negotiating skills that are closer to familial models of group decision making than they are to managerial models.[4]

The Classroom as a Site of Difference

That "real world" for which our courses are, hopefully, preparing students is far from just and equal. It is also not somewhere "out there" beyond the protective walls of the classroom. With our courses' orientation toward work place writing, we participate intimately in the process of acculturation. In very real ways, our classrooms are sites of difference: contact zones between often conflicting cultures.[5] There is, of course, quite a bit of work extant on the cultural and social impact of writing courses. Using Paulo Freire as a standard, cultural theorists argue for allowing students access to their culture, respecting their roots, and accepting their varied social and linguistic histories. Richard Rodriguez's *Hunger of Memory* and Mike Rose's *Lives on the Boundary* represent the core issue: how do educators enable students to succeed professionally while respecting their often non-standard social and linguistic backgrounds?[6]

Thus far, teachers of professional writing courses have not participated significantly in this debate, perhaps because the titles of our courses indicate a foregone conclusion: "Technical Writing" and "Professional Writing" proclaim that students must acclimatize to the business world to survive. What research that has been done

---

[4] We use our students' documents with their permission; we agreed to blind the excerpts to ensure privacy. All the names used in the text are fictitious.

[5] Pratt explains "contact zone" as "the space in which peoples geographically and historically separated come into contact with each other and establish ongoing relations, usually involving conditions of coercion, radical inequality, and intractable conflict" (6). She takes the term "contact" from linguistics, where contact languages are defined as improvisational adaptations that allow speakers of different native languages to communicate to conduct trade (6). We find this a useful term for discussing what happens to our students as they adjust to new cultural demands.

[6] The debate about multiculturalism is far from over, and legions of thoughtful writers have participated. Bizzell establishes the core issues. Harris, Dean, Brodkey, and Bazerman have contributed cogent arguments.

on collaboration within business and technical writing environments has emphasized managerial rather than interpersonal aspects of collaboration.[7] Although teaching students "survival skills" so that they can better negotiate non-academic writing situations has definite value, such instruction assumes that our students accept the behaviors, language strategies, formal structures, and interpersonal strategies required of a middle-level white-collar worker. If we were to judge from business and technical writing textbooks, our method of achieving this goal is to nod briefly to social interaction and then move ahead to describing ideal professional collaboration.[8] Our failure to bridge the gap between what happens in the classroom and what our students can expect to have happen in the work place, hurts our ongoing discussion of professional collaboration and seriously hampers our ability to teach our students to collaborate.[9] They are not "blank slates" with no experience; they are not open to any and all instruction on collaborating; their complex lives and beliefs color and sometimes impede whatever they learn.

Into this complex network of social, collegial, and professional cultures, we interject the professional writing classroom, with its unique guidelines for using, controlling, and assessing "correct" collaboration. Experienced in social and familial cooperation, students use their familiar interpersonal problem-solving skills to solve technical or managerial tasks, all the while coping with the conventions of college. Students' previous school experience conflicts with collaborative projects. Individual work and independence are ingrained; students have been trained to view learning as an uncompromisingly individual process, not something to be shared. Ideas "belong" to someone; writing style gets "ruined" by running through several writers. Despite the growing emphasis on collaborative work at both the high school and college levels, students perceive quickly that their teachers value individuality highly and reward it accordingly. Leaning across the aisle to glance at another's

---

[7] The publication of Lee Odell's and Dixie Goswami's *Writing in Nonacademic Settings* (1985) marked a shift in the direction of composition research as it applied to collaborative writing. The entire focus of the book is on helping teachers understand the business world and its needs and adjust accordingly. Recently, *Technical Communication*, the official journal of the Society for Technical Communication, dedicated an entire issue to collaboration (see volume 38.4). In technical and professional writing, research has usually focused on work place collaboration. In "Interpersonal Communication for the Technical Communicator," David M. Craig and Thomas M. Steinfatt remark that bibliographies on technical communications rarely cite works on interpersonal communication: *"An Annotated Bibliography on Technical Writing, Editing, Graphics, and Publishing* (Carlson et. al. 1983), lists, for example, just four items on interpersonal communication in its over 4,700 entries" (137). Craig and Steinfatt do not claim that research in technical writing ignores interpersonal communications; they note, however, that "when work is done on interpersonal communication within technical communications, it almost always has a skills orientation on the applicability of interpersonal skills within a business or industrial context" (158).

[8] Clearly, although all collaboration shares features, social and familial cooperation differ in some important ways from professional collaboration. Social cooperation relies on and rewards emotional bonds that are often de-emphasized in American business transactions. That American business undervalues personal and emotional attachment to the organization may in part explain why highly touted Japanese management techniques which conceive of the business as a social or family unit are so difficult to employ in this country.

[9] Studies of how to bridge the gap between academe and the work place have begun to appear. Morgan applies classroom strategies to industry, and Debs discusses collaborative writing in industry, citing studies based on theories of small-group behavior that may offer some insight into the kinds of problems students encounter in their collaborative projects. Because, as Debs points out, these studies "have focused on well-defined groups," we have to be careful in developing hypotheses based on their findings "since some may be applicable only to the groups studied" (37). Among the more promising of these is Forman and Katsky.

paper, even if it assists the student in understanding what he or she was too timid to ask of the teacher, means expulsion from the very group (the competent) the student was attempting to join.

Most teachers, whose promotions depend upon a record of individual scholarship, equate individuality with creativity. Even well-intentioned and useful advice about the composing process, such as telling students that writing will help them find their unique voices, undercuts subsequent efforts to get students to see the value of a collaborative identity. Small wonder that students have trouble navigating the rocks and shoals of collaborative work.

The classroom environment, then, is filled with conflicting messages about the nature and value of collaboration. Conflict and difference do not, however, mean collaboration is impossible. Indeed, fruitful collaboration often starts with the recognition that difference is essential if a group wishes to generate truly original ideas rather than to rely on made-to-order compromises that satisfy no one. The problem lies not so much in resolving conflicts when they arise as in getting students to express their conflicting views openly and then deal with them productively.

Introducing Students to Collaboration

Like many of our colleagues, we have used peer reading groups for rough drafts, group editing, and small writing projects in our technical writing courses. Three years ago, we decided to attempt a larger group project: a collaboratively planned, researched, and written proposal. Students identify a local or university problem that needs to be solved, research the problem, construct a viable solution, and write the proposal to the appropriate audience. We do not assign students to groups in this project. Through trial and error, we have determined that students are more satisfied with collaborative work if they can select fellow toilers. Although assigning students to work groups might be reasonable from a business standpoint, if we intervene, we complicate the group dynamics. Usually, we let shared interests in a proposal topic determine group membership; that is, after the class has collectively brainstormed a number of likely topics, they select three or four of the most promising ones and interest groups form around a topic, such as ways of streamlining procedures for student registration. Some students select groups according to their own criteria, sometimes seeking friends or fellow majors, sometimes simply looking around for non-threatening faces and gravitating to them. All students in a group receive the same grade for the proposal; if the final proposal receives a B, a limited participant receives a B, even if she or he did not do as much work as the rest of the group.

We spend a few class periods orienting the students to group projects, using a variety of standard exercises for improving group dynamics. We discuss problems common to group projects, conflict resolution, productivity measurements, and decision-making strategies. For most students, training in group dynamics is limited to our class, except for organizational communications students who take several courses in interpersonal dynamics and small group decision-making. We allow substantial in-class time for development of the projects, but students must arrange outside time for more in-depth collaboration, As one might expect, groups run into many problems, ranging from a paucity of information on their problems through motivating lazy or irresponsible colleagues. Teachers work as facilitators, advising and helping where we can but refusing to solve the groups' problems. Occasionally, problems become so severe that more serious intervention seems warranted, but our roles remain neutral, quite intentionally. This project is the group's responsibility, not ours. To provide students with the opportunity to assess the process, product, and participants, we implemented a personnel assessment memo, similar to evaluative memos used in industry.

Although we occasionally had students come to us during the writing process to air concerns they had about the project or their colleagues' participation, the evidence that our students were having problems with collaboration emerged most forcefully in their end-of-project "personnel assessment" memos. The memos reveal many, often conflicting, aspects of the collaborative process. We have isolated two aspects of their documents for detailed discussion here: their use and misuse of the rhetoric of collaboration, and their resistance to and accommodation of conflict. Through their often creative adaptations of collaborative terminology, students revealed their gradual adjustment to this venture that requires them to set aside individual goals. Their social and collegial cultures were in active conflict with the collaborative strategy discussed in this class. Their avowed (or denied) reactions to conflict hit at the very heart of collaboration: most students stay far away from conflict; they view disagreeing as a failure. Acknowledgements of conflict are usually confessional in tone.

The Rhetoric of Collaboration

The personnel assessment memo is the final word on a project that most students find difficult but rewarding; it allows students to vent frustration, analyze their experiences, and help future students. In a sense, it is practice at meta-discourse because students are discussing a discourse community, anatomizing its weaknesses and strengths.[10] Assessment memos reveal how some students not only test out what they perceive as the language of collaboration but also how they get stuck at the level of language. For these students, collaboration is more a rhetorical term than an operable reality. In the example below, the writer affirms belief in the collaborative process while, at the same time, expressing alienation from that process:

> If individually I would have written a proposal, I would have selected a topic of some familiarity or one that would have provided knowledge in an area of interest to me. In my overall opinion group collaboration is a useful and productive means in achieving a goal. However, in working on this particular task I experienced much ambiguity in regards to this topic and the group itself.

Trying to sound objective and distanced from a project that clearly bothered

---

[10] Beach provides some practical advice for encouraging students to assess one another, and Sommers outlines how response memos allow the teacher a window into students' thinking processes and encourage revision.

her, this student claims that collaboration is "a useful and productive means in achieving a goal"; this particular instance did not, however, work well. She saw the purpose of the memo as an affirmation of collaboration and used what she felt was appropriate rhetoric to achieve that purpose. This rhetorical affirmation only heightens the disparity between the student's claims and the reality of her experience. Grafting the rhetoric of collaboration to a message that reveals her deep misgivings about the collaborative process, this student produced a document that denies what it affirms.

Such grafted discourse is common. In students' attempts to use the rhetoric of collaboration to define what their groups were doing, students often import terms without fully understanding their contextual meanings:

> Our focus on Non-Traditional student housing and the need for daycare was chosen through *group consensus*. Although this decision *forced* the group to *discard* other ideas I was more in favor of, such as entertainment on campus, I gave my *consent*. I found that other members of the group were less interested in my ideas, and foresaw a *better working experience* if I agreed to their focus. (emphasis added)

Verbs such as "force" and "discard" indicate that this student perceived consensus, perhaps more correctly than we were willing to admit, as a coercive rather than a collaborative act. In this context, consent equals unwilling acquiescence. Clearly, this student did not like the decision but went along to avoid conflict. "Consensus," for this group, meant some form of voting, with dissenting members giving up their positions; they behaved as is socially appropriate. Consensus, of course, means far more than a grudging agreement, but it is messy and time-consuming.

The conflict avoidance present in this and other memos is closely tied to students' experiences of familial cooperation in which "peace keeping" is more important than conflict resolution. Although students went to the teachers with complaints about poorly performing peers and although the personnel evaluation did not affect the grades of individual participants, students were reluctant to critique the performance or the contribution of their peers in writing. This reluctance mirrors the desire on the part of family members to maintain social amity often at the expense of constructive criticism. One of the primary rules of familial and social collaboration is not to "rat" on colleagues: children hide misbehavior from parents; friends protect one another from authority figures; coworkers bury problems to avoid repercussions. Our students read this exercise as "ratting" on friends, and perhaps they are right. After all, teachers grade students; we wanted them to work hard on the assignment; and we want them to tell us, in confidence, how well their co-workers did. In industry, evaluation usually comes from above, not from co-workers; students are peers—they are "in it together."

Familial and social experiences not only affect students' reluctance to discuss conflict but also the rhetorical frame of their evaluation memos, particularly their desire to narrativize rather than analyze the collaborative process. As we often do within family situations, the students transformed their group experiences into anecdotal rehearsals of the collaborative process. Rather than focusing on group members' successes or failures at meeting expectations, students often told "stories" about how the group divided the tasks and worked sequentially to complete them. These "success stories" went something like this:

> John was appointed secretary and did the majority of the typing on his home computer. John also worked with me researching project costs and alternative types of funding. He was very cooperative and accessible for collaboration.

Although this example ends with an evaluative statement, most of the paragraph is constructed on a narrative framework. Chronologically arranged and task-focused narratives bury or obfuscate students' contributions to both the process and the product. Rather than evaluative terminology such as "John's contribution was minimal" or "his data were crucial," we often received quantitative valuations: John "did the majority of the typing on his home computer." We should not be too surprised that students want to narrativize their assessment memos rather than analyze each other's performance. For many students, narrative is both a way to personalize observations and to distance themselves from an evaluative task they perceive as difficult. They can fictionalize the process, make it just a story.

Students are, however, comfortable with critiquing (often very constructively) the process of writing a group proposal and the product they submitted. One particularly clear-thinking student wrote:

> Although none of the group members were well acquainted prior to this time, we quickly learned a lot about each other. Each person involved in the project is a very distinct individual, with widely varying ideas and writing styles. Learning to compromise and work cooperatively together was a necessity for completion of this venture.
>
> We experienced few *serious* problems. On all occasions we were able to resolve any disagreements we had concerning text content by rationally discussing each side of the conflict. While we were not always in total accord regarding writing styles and editing, we managed to arrive at acceptable compromises.

This student identified the primary goals of the project and then assessed her group's success at achieving a "good" group. She avoids becoming personal (she doesn't name any single student), yet she credits the group with being sensible and professional, quite an accomplishment for a nearly randomly selected group of students under severe time constraints. Further, she comfortably uses the language and rhetoric of group dynamics established in the early stages of the group project. In this fragment, for instance, she mentions acceptable compromises and notes that each individual has distinct voices and methods. This rhetorical modeling allows her to objectify the experience; it helps her discuss, in a non-threatening way, what she and her colleagues have achieved.

In a less successful group, another student (who called herself "stifled aggressor") deflected responsibility for the disastrous group process from the group to the teacher:

> I feel that putting this group together was the worst thing that could have happened. Everything was distributed unevenly, which left some of us feeling left out. The reason your project failed was because you said, "If one person doesn't agree, then you don't do it!" I feel that was unfair and a big mistake. *All the problems we had came from that one statement.*

As previously explained, we do not put students into groups; the groups are self-selected, with the open option of re-forming if necessary. This student misunderstood or, more correctly, revised what the instructor had actually said about the advisability of achieving consensus instead of simply voting for solutions. Part of the instruction on group dynamics includes decision-making strategies; consensus is by far the best way to achieve affiliation with group decisions. When things go wrong, as they most certainly did in this group, students can point to the process itself and the instructor's set up as the "real" problem. Again, evaluation moves away from fellow students and toward the teacher. The product becomes "your project," not theirs.

This preference for the textual over the personal, in addition to being "safer" and less threatening, is related to the fact that most students' previous experiences with collaboration have occurred within two distinct environments: the familial or social group, and the classroom group. Within the family group, while there are few opportunities (other than family gatherings with their tales of family triumphs or failures) to textualize experience, individual critique is often deflected in the interest of preserving the unit. Within the academic setting, most often the composition classroom, students' collaborative roles are more those of readers/editors than of fellow participants in a group project. Even when they have had some exposure to truly collaborative work, it has often been on an assignment that has been set by the teacher. Those few students who are willing to critique the work of their peers and call attention to another student's failure to match the group's expectations are more likely to be those who have had work place experience with collaboration and who know the consequences of managerial evaluations of group projects.

Difference and Dissent: Conflict Resolution

In their personnel assessment memos, students commonly insist that everyone in their group was truly cooperative. Because we have observed group dynamics through the three years of doing this project, we know that nearly all groups experience conflict of varying kinds, often very severe. Students neglected to mention conflict in these formal documents because teachers, much like parents, are perceived as authority figures who can hurt people. Students neither want to be "hurt" by a poor final grade nor want to hurt one another. The following memo clearly represents the ambiguous feelings students often have about the conflicts they suppress rather than redress. She begins with an insistence that they did not experience conflict:

> Conflict in the group was minimal. There was a point in the group process when I became very intimidated by Kelsey. I was responsible for obtaining certain information before the second progress report was due. I

reported my findings to Kelsey who in turn was to report them to Jean for inclusion in the progress report. The information was never used.

When she writes about Kelsey's editing of her work, she confesses that she had backed away from confrontation:

> Another issue was that of editing my written work. Kelsey had edited so much of my proposal draft that its intended purpose was lost. I did try to confront Kelsey on these situations but she became slightly defensive. I chose to drop the issues to avoid conflict.

> The negative side to this situation was the attitude I assumed. I allowed myself to pull away, indiscreetly, from the group. I only did what was asked of me and chose not to offer any suggestions for fear of confrontation. I realized that this was only "pretend" and didn't think the hassle was worth it. The way I handled this situation was not in the group's best interest. Confrontation should have been allowed to transpire. This could have led to more cohesiveness and openness while encouraging others to address any hidden issues.

This memo is an interesting example of a conflicted text in which the writer both denies and admits conflict. Although this student claims that "conflict in the group was minimal," conflict clearly surfaced at all points in the process, from information gathering to final editing. Her remark that "conflict was minimal" means, in this case, "we never faced our problems." The writer's comments pin down the reasons why students are reluctant to confront one another. Politeness strategies combine with extremely practical concerns (is it worth the effort?) to discourage students from resolving conflicts. Students have only familial/social conflict models: if you disagree, you will fight and the more powerful will win the fight. If you don't have strong emotional reasons to pursue resolution, don't bother. Students who feel they are being ignored or who note problems in the process avoid commenting for fear of disrupting a fragile illusion of collaboration. If someone speaks up, it is often a targeted complaint (why didn't *you* use my material?), resulting in defensiveness from the other students.

Since students have little or no professional experience resolving conflict, they don't believe that conflict might be good. Although the writer of the preceding memo knew that the group was masking its problems and concluded that "confrontation should have been allowed to transpire," the fictionality of the situation ("I realized this was only 'pretend'") is cited as the reason for the writer's and the group's unwillingness to express or deal with conflict. In avoiding conflict, students rush into decisions, force assent, and smother dissent. Their rushed decisions result in poorly done documents.

One student, familiar with the language of group decision-making assessed her own role in the group as follows: "I was not present for the decision as to what our proposal would be; therefore, I relinquished my right in negotiating a topic. . . . Where the process could [have] been stronger, I would say was related to our communication structure, collaboration, and lack of structured criticism." In a similar vein, another student cited the process of selecting a topic as the main impediment to successful collaboration:

> Because I was not in the group initially, I can not say how the topic was chosen. It appeared to be a unilateral decision to work on teacher effectiveness. . . . We didn't define the problem well enough in the initial meetings so it was hard to communicate with each other when we got together. There were major communication problems that we couldn't resolve. People were not focused on the task and talked about unrelated matters. Perhaps a general consensus about the subject chosen would have made people more open to the task we performed.

In each of these examples, the student did not participate in the initial selection of the proposal topic. Surprisingly, in light of the random assemblage of the groups, initial group affiliation seems to have been important. The student who missed the session in which the group chose its topic but who felt herself a member of the group from the start was more willing to relinquish her right to a voice in the process. The student who joined a group after it was formed felt that topic selection was a "unilateral decision" (although she did not say who had made that decision). In each case, however, the student's awareness of a language in which she could discuss the group's decision-making process or the lack of that process allowed her to bring the issue into her evaluation.

Time constraints were often cited as reasons for allowing group tensions to go unattended. A self-motivated student who frankly wrote, "I don't like working in groups and I respond to conflict by withdrawing," observed that the tensions in her group were left unresolved because there wasn't time to deal with them:

> The short duration of the project probably encouraged everyone to ignore the tensions in order to get the work done. Had the project lasted longer it would have been almost impossible to get anything done until the members brought the conflicts out in the open. In an actual job situation, I would suggest that the group have a meeting for the express purpose of discussing why we were having difficulty working together.

Ironically, although the short time available for completing the project hampered collaboration, it also allowed them to get the project done: "It would have been almost impossible to get anything done." Classroom constraints work against collaboration yet allow students to hide from true conflict, which might well be messy and unsettling.

In another case, what appeared to be a complete disaster became a more complex learning and collaborative venture than the instructor would have ever expected. Bonnie produced a diary of her experiences instead of the expected assessment, but she found it necessary to think through just what had happened, why her group project became such a grueling experience. She detailed her introduction to the group process:

> When we were told to get into small groups I was a little nervous. I looked around the room to see if anyone was feeling the same way. I

wanted to be with people who were interested in really doing a good job.
I thought Mark would be nice to work with because he seemed to be active
in class, so I motioned and asked if he would like to work with me.

Bonnie wanted to be in a good group, one with energetic and involved students; unlike many more passive students, she actively pursued group members. In
her diary she recalls one of the group's first meetings:

> We put our desks in a circle and began to talk about the topic I had
> suggested earlier. . . . Everyone seemed to be happy to have a topic to
> work on. I liked my idea, but I've worked in groups before and I wanted
> to give everyone a chance to offer suggestions. . . . Mark pulled out a
> piece of paper and wrote down the new topics that were mentioned. . . .
> Our first meeting ended with each of us exchanging full names and phone
> numbers. *Mark* was different. He gave us his work number and told us
> that if we needed to get in touch with him, just leave a message there. Mark
> was quite verbal and it was obvious that he was going to try to lead the
> group, but a leader needs followers and nobody was listening to Mark. I
> think part of the reason no one listened was that he had not earned the
> group's respect.

As the group puts together the final proposal, Bonnie fires a final salvo at Mark:
"Mark made no suggestions and kept saying he didn't have time to look at them.
We managed to pull it all together the last day and turn our group project in."
Clearly, things went wrong in this group almost from the start, but the conflicts between the group and Mark were not resolved during the project; instead, they were
written into Bonnie's narrative that documented his attempts to dominate the group
and his refusal to participate in the work of the group. Interestingly, Bonnie decided it was important enough to resolve the conflict that she pursued resolution well
after the end of the collaborative project: she met with Mark and hashed out their
differences. Conflict, in this case, was resolved after the project. For her, this
project was *not* "pretend."

When students did realize the value of debate and criticism and sought it out
during the process, they often focused, as would be common in familial or social
groups, on the actions of one member of the group:

> Tom's occasionally rigid skepticism served as the main point of debate
> at many of our meetings. Although some of the debates did not resolve
> themselves sufficiently, most of the argumentation was absolutely essential to
> the proposal's success. Without Tom as the catalyst to such discourse, I
> don't think we would have completed the project.

Although the group found Tom occasionally annoying, they saw that his input
made the document stronger than it would have been without it. Unlike many of the
other groups, they confronted the conflict and, while they did not resolve it completely, they did see value in it. In this case, conflict generated the energy that en-
hanced their final project.

When other groups discussed problems they had in making their collaboration work, they often focused on ways of making the process smoother. Students commonly lamented that they did not have enough free time outside of class to get together and discuss their projects. Conflicting schedules make out-of-class meetings difficult if not impossible. Students also stated that they wanted more intervention from the teacher. What they meant by this, usually, was that they wanted the teacher to step in and direct or redirect the group and often to bring a recalcitrant or non-participating group member into line—that is, to reduce the conflict. For instance, one student wrote:

> The strain of the project itself accompanied with uninvolved and unco-operative members resulted in more of a headache than a constructive learning experience. Methods of avoiding this may include forming smaller groups and possibly submitting a weekly or daily memo on each member's performance. It's difficult to leave it up to group members to keep on the others. As college students, it is surprising that this type of supervision is necessary.

They felt that the teacher's role, much like that of a parent, was to assure that "good" students were not harmed by the "bad" ones, clearly a misunderstanding of collaborative projects, albeit an understandable one.

The call for prescriptive or authoritative intervention is interesting in that, if followed, it would subvert the collaborative nature of the assignment by reestablishing the familial and social model of collaboration, with teacher as gatekeeper, time and task manager, and academic disciplinarian. In our classes, the teacher volunteers to help as a facilitator but avoids becoming the "repairer" of problems and "resolver" of conflicts. No matter how much teachers want to stay out of the collaborative process, students often want to pull them in and make them responsible for the texts coming out of the group.

Conclusion

As a forum in which students experiment with conflicting models of collaborative behavior, the writing classroom is truly a site of difference. It is the locus at which familial and social, academic and economic models of collaboration converge. If, as linguists assure us, the site of difference is also the point at which meaning is negotiated and understanding occurs, then we have a unique opportunity in our often conflicted classrooms. To make the most of this opportunity, to create an environment in which students feel that they can afford to take the risks of collaborating, we have to remember what initially motivates their response to even the best of collaborative assignments. Students are following our directions: we ask them to collaborate, so they do. We assure them that they will have to collaborate on the job; they believe us. We provide them with a language and rudimentary processes for successful collaboration; they use them. In most cases, however, they are doing what they believe minimizes personal conflict; they are performing and writing to please the teacher, a process strikingly similar to the performance models that worked for them in familial or social situations. Their cooperation, a term that appears and reappears in their memos, does not indicate that they have internalized collaborative processes or converted from individual strategies for problem solving to group strategies. They are primarily concerned with their individual grades; they are universally grateful that their grades are not harmed by the project. We must not fool ourselves into believing that our brief courses will convert students from socially adroit team players and individual students to people for whom collaboration is empowering, perhaps even liberating. To borrow an analogy from linguistics, students' verbal comments about collaborative work and their frustration with collaborative tasks indicate that familial and social models still provide the deep structure for their emerging grammar of collaboration.

Surface features of that developing grammar that appear in their personnel memos are, however, important, as they indicate students' willingness to experiment with collaborative modes of discourse. Our task as teachers of professional writing is to bring the deeper issues to the surface, to allow our classrooms to become those sites of difference from which true collaboration emerges. We must not only teach what James Moffett has called the "universe of discourse," we must step out of the way and let that universe of discourse develop in which social and familial, academic and managerial worlds bump into each other, perhaps even collide. If things seem to be going wrong, if we don't see the facile teamwork that advertisers assure us is the hallmark of everything from the modern army to investment banking, we may be doing something right.

Works Cited

Bazerman, Charles. "Scientific Writing as a Social Act: A Review of the Sociology of Science." *New Essays in Technical and Scientific Communication: Research, Theory, Practice*. Ed. Paul V. Anderson, R. John Brockmann, Carolyn R. Miller. Farmingdale: Baywood, 1983.

Beach, Richard. "Showing Students How to Assess: Demonstrating Techniques for Response in the Writing Conference." *Writing and Response: Theory, Practice, and Research*. Ed. Chris Anson. Urbana, IL: NCTE, 1989.

Bizzell, Patricia. "Arguing About Literacy." *College English*. 50 (February 1988): 141-53.

Brodkey, Linda. "Transvaluing Difference." *College English* 51 (1989): 597-601.

Craig, David M., and Thomas M. Steinfatt. "Interpersonal Communication for the Technical Communicator." *Technical and Business Communication*. Ed. Charles H. Sides. Urbana, IL: NCTE, 1989.

Dean, Terry. "Multicultural Classrooms, Monocultural Teachers." *College Composition and Communication* 40 (1989): 23-37.

Debs, Mary Beth. "Recent Research on Collaborative Writing in Industry." *Technical Communication* 38 (1991): 476-94.

_____. "Collaborative Writing in Industry." *Technical Writing: Theory and Practice*. Ed. Bertie E. Fearing and W. Keats Sparrow. New York: MLA, 1989. 33-42.

Forman, Janis, ed. *New Visions of Collaborative Writing*. Portsmouth, NH: Boynton, 1992.

Forman, Janis, and Patricia Katsky. "The Group Report: A Problem in Small Group or Writing Processes." *Journal of Business Communication*. 23.4 (1986): 23-26.

Freire, Paulo. *Pedagogy of the Oppressed*. Intro. Richard Shoull. New York: Seabury, 1970.

Harris, Joseph. "The Idea of Community in the Study of Writing." *College Composition and Communication* 40 (1989): 11-22.

Kogan, Myra, ed. *Writing in the Business Professions*. Urbana, IL: NCTE, 1989.

Moffett, James. *Teaching the Universe of Discourse*. 1963. Boston: Houghton, 1983.

Morgan, Meg. "Patterns of Composing: Connections Between Classroom and Workplace Collaborations." *Technical Communication* 38 (1991): 540-45.

Odell, Lee, and Dixie Goswami, eds. *Writing in Nonacademic Settings*. New York: Guilford, 1985.

Pratt, Mary Louise. *Imperial Eyes: Travel Writing and Transculturation*. London: Routledge, 1992.

Rodriguez, Richard. *Hunger of Memory*. Boston: Bantam, 1982.

Rose, Mike. *Lives on the Boundary*. New York: Penguin, 1989.

Sommers, Jeffrey. "The Writer's Memo: Collaboration, Response, and Development." *Writing and Response*. Ed. Chris Anson. Urbana, IL: NCTE, 1989.

Thrall, Charlotte, and Nancy Blyler. *Professional Communication: The Social Perspective*. Newbury Park, CA: SAGE, 1992.

Turner, Victor. *Dramas, Fields, and Metaphors: Symbolic Action in Human Society*. Ithaca: Cornell UP, 1974.

Bibliography

Adams, Katherine H. "Bringing Rhetorical Theory into the Advanced Composition Class." *Rhetoric Review* 3 (1985): 184-89.

_____. *A History of Professional Writing Instruction in American Colleges: Years of Acceptance, Growth, and Doubt.* Dallas: Southern Methodist UP, 1993.

Adams, Katherine H., and John L. Adams. "Advanced Composition: Where Did It Come From? Where Is It Going?" Adams and Adams. 3-15.

_____, ed. *Teaching Advanced Composition: Why and How.* Portsmouth, NH: Boynton, 1991.

Allen, Virginia. "Some Implications of Kenneth Burke's 'Way of Knowing' for Composition Theory." *Journal of Advanced Composition* 3 (1982): 10-23.

Anderson, Chris. "Teaching Students What Not to Say: Iser, Didion, and the Rhetoric of Gaps." *Journal of Advanced Composition* 7 (1987): 10-22.

Anderson, Charles. "Coming into the Country . . . and Living There: Literary Nonfiction and Discourse Communities." Adams and Adams. 223-48.

Anderson, Laurie J. "A Sense of Audience or Conventional Wisdom?" *Journal of Advanced Composition* 7 (1987): 112-20.

Bank, Stanley. "Composition Aims in Advanced Writing Courses." *College Composition and Communication* 15 (1964): 190-91.

Beck, James P. "'Advanced Composition' and Occasion-Sensitivity." *Journal of Advanced Composition* 2 (1981): 79-87.

Behr, Robert. "Teaching Advanced Composition for Teachers." *College Composition and Communication* 13 (1962): 77-78.

Berg, Temma. "Marking the Differences: Teaching Freshman and Junior Comp." *Maryland Composition Review* 4.2 (1984): 2-9.

Berke, Jacqueline. "Invitational Workshop on Advanced Composition." *College Composition and Communication* 18 (1965): 199-200.

Bisson, Lillian M. "From Composition to Career: Sequential Assignments for Professional Writing." Conference on College Composition and Communication. Dallas, March 1981. ERIC, 1981. ED 202 026.

Bjork, Robert E. "When We Dead Awaken: Reviving Metaphor in Medical Writing." *Journal of Advanced Composition* 4 (1983): 139-46.

Bleich, David. "Genders of Writing." *Journal of Advanced Composition* 9 (1989): 10-25.

Bloom, Lynn Z. "Autobiography and Audience." *Journal of Advanced Composition* 4 (1983): 119-31.

_____. "Creative Nonfiction, Is There Any Other Kind?" Adams and Adams. 249-66.

_____. "Diving into the Mainstream: Configurations of Advanced Composition." Conference on College Composition and Communication. New York, March 1984. ERIC, 1984. ED 243 114.

_____. "Re-Creating Creators: Teaching Students to Edit Autobiographical Materials." *Journal of Advanced Composition* 3 (1982): 136-52.

_____. "Why Don't We Write What We Teach? And Publish It?" *Journal of Advanced Composition* 10 (1990): 87-100.

_____. "Why Graduate Students Can't Write: Implications of Research on Writing Anxiety for Graduate Education." *Journal of Advanced Composition* 2 (1981): 103-17.

Blyler, Nancy Roundy. "Purpose and Composition Theory: Issues in the Research." *Journal of Advanced Composition* 9 (1989): 97-111.

Boiarsky, Carolyn. "Fluency, Fluidity, and Word Processing." *Journal of Advanced Composition* 11 (1991): 123-33.

Brand, Alice G. "Hot Cognition: Emotions and Writing Behavior." *Journal of Advanced Composition* 6 (1985-86): 5-15.

_____. "Social Cognition, Emotions, and the Psychology of Writing." *Journal of Advanced Composition* 11 (1991): 395-407.

Brannon, Lil. "The Teacher as Philosopher: The Madness Behind Our Method." *Journal of Advanced Composition* 4 (1983): 25-32.

Briand, Paul. "Turned On: Multi-Media and Advanced Composition." *College Composition and Communication* 21 (1971): 267-69.

Burke, Virginia M. "The Advanced Course in Expository Writing: Aims, Texts, Methods." *College Composition and Communication* 9 (1958): 165-67.

Carter, Michael. "What is *Advanced* About Advanced Composition: A Theory of Expertise in Writing." Adams and Adams. 59-70.

CCCC. "Guidelines and Directions for College Courses in Advanced Composition." *College Composition and Communication* 28 (1967): 266-68.

Chapman, David W. "Forming and Meaning: Writing the Counterpoint Essay." *Journal of Advanced Composition* 11 (1991): 73-81.

Cherry, Roger D. "Fictional Scenarios and Rhetorical Specification in Writing Tasks: A Cautionary Note." *Journal of Advanced Composition* 9 (1989): 151-61.

Christensen, Francis. "The Course in Advanced Composition for Teachers." *College Composition and Communication* 24 (1973): 163-70.

Clark, Francelia. "Writing as Learning and the Superior Student." *Journal of Advanced Composition* 4 (1983): 147-60.

Clark, Wilma. "Writing for Publication in an Advanced Course for Undergraduates." *Journal of Advanced Composition* 3 (1982): 24-36.

Clifford, John. "Ideology into Discourse: A Historical Perspective." *Journal of Advanced Composition* 7 (1987): 121-30.

Coe, Richard M. "Advanced Composition as Fishing Pole: Principles, Processes, Practices." Adams and Adams. 71-88.

_____. "Defining Rhetoric—and Us." *Journal of Advanced Composition* 10 (1990): 39-52.

_____. *Form and Substance: An Advanced Rhetoric.* New York: Wiley, 1981.

_____. "Outline Later." *Journal of Advanced Composition* 1 (1980): 86-88.

_____. *Process, Form, and Substance: A Rhetoric for Advanced Writers.* Englewood Cliffs, NJ: Prentice, 1990.

Comprone, Joseph J. "Narrative Topic and the Contemporary Science Essay: A Lesson from Loren Eiseley's Notebooks." *Journal of Advanced Composition* 9 (1989): 112-22.

_____. "Reading Oliver Sacks in a Writing-Across-the-Curriculum Course." *Journal of Advanced Composition* 8 (1988): 158-66.

_____. Recent Research in Reading and Its Implications for the College Composition Curriculum." *Rhetoric Review* 1 (1983): 122-37.

Connery, Brian A. "Using Journals in the Cross-Curricular Course: Restoring Process." *Journal of Advanced Composition* 8 (1988): 97-104.

Cooper, Marilyn M. "Dialogic Learning Across Disciplines." *Journal of Advanced Composition* 14 (1994): 531-46.

Couture, Barbara. "Against Relativism: Restoring Truth in Writing." *Journal of Advanced Composition* 13 (1993): 111-34.

Covino, William L. "Defining Advanced Composition: Contributions from the History of Rhetoric." *Journal of Advanced Composition* 8 (1988): 113-22.

_____. "The Grammar of Advanced Writing." Adams and Adams. 31-42.

Crew, Louie. "The Style-Checker as Tonic, Not Tranquilizer." *Journal of Advanced Composition* 8 (1988): 66-70.

Crosswhite, James. "Authorship and Individuality: Heideggerian Angles." *Journal of Advanced Composition* 12 (1992): 91-109.

Crowley, Sharon. "Rhetoric, Literature, and the Dissociation of Invention." *Journal of Advanced Composition* 6 (1985-86): 17-32.

Crusius, Timothy W. "Reflections on *A Pragmatic Theory of Rhetoric.*" *Journal of Advanced Composition* 10 (1990): 53-72.

Daiker, Donald, and Nedra Grogan. "Selecting and Using Sample Papers in Holistic Evaluation." *Journal of Advanced Composition* 11 (1991): 159-71.

D'Angelo, Frank J. "Tropics of Arrangement: A Theory of *Dispositio.*" *Journal of Advanced Composition* 10 (1990): 101-09.

Dasenbrock, Reed Way. "Becoming Aware of the Myth of Presence." *Journal of Advanced Composition* 8 (1988): 1-11.

Dickerson, Mary Jane. "'Shades of Deeper Meaning': On Writing Autobiography." *Journal of Advanced Composition* 9 (1989): 123-50.

Dicks, Bernice W. "State of the Art in Advanced Expository Writing: One Genus, Many Species." *Journal of Advanced Composition* 3 (1982): 172-91.

Donovan, Timothy R., and Janet Carr. "'Real World' Research: Writing Beyond the Curriculum." Adams and Adams. 211-22.

Ervin, Elizabeth, and Dana L. Fox. "Collaboration as Political Action." *Journal of Advanced Composition* 14 (1994): 53-71.

Ewald, Helen Rothschild. "The Implied Reader in Persuasive Discourse." *Journal of Advanced Composition* 8 (1988): 167-78.

_____. "What We Could Tell Advanced Student Writers About Audience." *Journal of Advanced Composition* 11 (1991): 147-58.

Fahnestock, Jeanne. "Teaching Argumentation in the Junior-Level Course." Adams and Adams. 179-94.

Fey, Marion H. "Finding Voice through Computer Communication: A New Venue for Collaboration." *Journal of Advanced Composition* 14 (1994): 221-38.

Fishman, Judith. "Enclosures: The Narrative Within Autobiography." *Journal of Advanced Composition* 2 (1981): 23-30.

Fortune, Ronald J. "Problem-Solving and Autobiographical Writing." *Journal of Advanced Composition* 3 (1982): 153-71.

Foster, David. "What Are We Talking About When We Talk About Composition." *Journal of Advanced Composition* 8 (1988): 30-40.

Fox, Thomas. "Repositioning the Profession: Teaching Writing to African American Students." *Journal of Advanced Composition* 12 (1992): 291-303.

Freed, Richard C., and Glenn J. Broadhead. "Using High-Affect Goals in Teaching Proposal Writing." *Journal of Advanced Composition* 7 (1987): 131-38.

Frey, Olivia, and Mary Ellen Ross. "Writing Is More Than Words." Adams and Adams. 267-82.

Fulkerson, Richard. "Conjectures on (Advanced?) *Composition and Its Teaching.*" *Journal of Advanced Composition* 1 (1980): 30-34.

_____. "Some Theoretical Speculations on the Advanced Composition Curriculum." *Journal of Advanced Composition* 1 (1980): 9-12.

Fuller, David. "A Curious Case of Our Responding Habits: What Do We Respond to and Why?" *Journal of Advanced Composition* 8 (1988): 88-96.

Fuller, Mary. "Teaching Style in Advanced Composition Classes." Adams and Adams. 119-32.

Fulwiler, Toby. "A Personal Account of a Course Called *Personal Voice.*" Adams and Adams. 103-18.

Gage, John T. "A General Theory of the Enthymeme for Advanced Composition." Adams and Adams. 161-78.

_____. "Towards an Epistemology of Composition." *Journal of Advanced Composition* 2 (1981): 1-9.

Gaillet, Lynée Lewis. "An Historical Perspective on Collaborative Learning." *Journal of Advanced Composition* 14 (1994): 93-110.

Gale, Xin Liu. "Conversing Across Cultural Boundaries: Rewriting 'Self.'" *Journal of Advanced Composition* 14 (1994): 455-62.

Gates, Rosemary L. "Applying Martin Greenman's Concept of Insight to Composition Theory." *Journal of Advanced Composition* 9 (1989): 45-68.

_____. "Causality, Community, and the Canons of Reasoning: Classical Rhetoric and Writing Across the Curriculum." *Journal of Advanced Composition* 8 (1988): 137-45.

Gebhardt, Richard. "The Subject is Writing." *Journal of Advanced Composition* 1 (1980): 13-17.

Gergits, Julia M., and James J. Schramer. "The Collaborative Classroom as a Site of Difference." *Journal of Advanced Composition* 14 (1994): 187-202.

Golding, Alan, and John Mascaro. "A Survey of Graduate Writing Courses." *Journal of Advanced Composition* 6 (1985-86): 167-79.

Goodburn, Amy, and Beth Ina. "Collaboration, Critical Pedagogy, and Struggles Over Difference." *Journal of Advanced Composition* 14 (1994): 131-47.

Grady, Hugh H., and Susan Wells. "Toward a Rhetoric of Intersubjectivity: Introducing Jürgen Habermas." *Journal of Advanced Composition* 6 (1985-86): 33-47.

Greene, Stuart. "Mining Texts in Reading to Write." *Journal of Advanced Composition* 12 (1992): 151-70.

Griffin, C.W. "Writing-Across-the-Curriculum Programs, Theory and Practice: A Selected Bibliography." *Journal of Advanced Composition* 4 (1983): 161-71.

Hagaman, John. "A Comparative Analysis of Revisions Made by Advanced Composition Students in Expressive, Persuasive, and Information Discourse." *Journal of Advanced Composition* 3 (1982): 126-35.

_____. "Encouraging Thoughtful Revision in a Kinneavy-Framed Advanced Composition Course." Annual Meeting of the New York College English Association Conference. Saratoga Springs, NY, October 1980. ERIC, 1980. ED 196 040.

Hairston, Maxine C. *Successful Writing: A Rhetoric for Advanced Composition* New York: Norton, 1981.

_____. "Working with Advanced Writers." *College Composition and Communication* 35 (1984): 196-208.

Halio, Marcia Peoples. "Conferencing at the Advanced Composition Level." *ATAC Forum* 2.2 (1990): 11-13.

Halpern, Jeanne W. "The Structure of Advanced Composition." *Journal of Advanced Composition* 1 (1980): 45-52.

Hammond, Eugene. "Freshman Composition—Junior Composition: Does Co-ordination Mean Sub-ordination." *College Composition and Communication* 35 (1984): 217-21.

Haring-Smith, Tori. "The Role of Theory in Advanced Writing and Tutor Training Courses." Adams and Adams. 151-60.

Harris, Joseph. "The Other Reader." *Journal of Advanced Composition* 12 (1992): 27-37.

Hart, Edward L. "Advanced Composition: What Is It?" *College Composition and Communication* 22 (1971): 291-92.

Hesse, Douglas. "The Recent Rise of Literary Nonfiction: A Cautionary Assay." *Journal of Advanced Composition* 11 (1991): 323-33.

Hilligoss, Susan. "Preoccupations: Private Writing and Advanced Composition." *Journal of Advanced Composition* 9 (1989): 124-34.

Hoffman, Eleanor M., and Kenneth Risdon. "Managing Student Writing: A Cross-Disciplinary Venture." *Journal of Advanced Composition* 3 (1982): 37-47.

Hogan, Michael P. "Advanced Composition: A Survey." *Journal of Advanced Composition* 1 (1980): 21-29.

Horning, Alice S. "Propositional Analysis and the Teaching of Reading *with* Writing." *Journal of Advanced Composition* 6 (1985-86): 49-64.

_____. "Readability: Reading/Writing Tools for Measurement." *Journal of Advanced Composition* 7 (1987): 101-11.

_____. "Readable Writing: The Role of Cohesion and Redundancy." *Journal of Advanced Composition* 11 (1991): 135-45.

House, Elizabeth B., and William J. House. "Problem-Solving: The Debates in Composition and Psychology." *Journal of Advanced Composition* 7 (1987): 62-75.

Hubbuck, Susan M. "The Writer's Stance: An Exploration of Context in Invention and Critical Thinking." *Journal of Advanced Composition* 10 (1990): 73-86.

Huckin, Thomas, and Linda Flower. "Reading for Points and Purposes." *Journal of Advanced Composition* 11 (1991): 347-62.

Hult, Christine. "Advanced Composition and the Computerized Library." *Journal of Advanced Composition* 9 (1989): 174-80.

Hungerford, Anne. *Advanced Study in Writing for Business and the Professions* Vancouver, BC: Writing Program (SFU), 1989.

Jacobi, Martin J. "Using the Enthymeme as a Heuristic in Professional Writing Courses." *Journal of Advanced Composition* 7 (1987): 41-51.

Jenseth, Richard. "Assignment Sequencing in Advanced Composition." *ATAC Newsletter* 1 (1989): 10-11.

Johnson-Eilola, Johndan. "Control and the Cyborg: Writing and Being Written in Hypertext." *Journal of Advanced Composition* 13 (1993): 381-99.

Jones, Steven Jeffrey. "The Logic of Question and Answer and the Hermeneutics of Writing." *Journal of Advanced Composition* 8 (1988): 12-21.

Kaufer, David S., and Cheryl Geisler. "A Scheme for Representing Written Argument." *Journal of Advanced Composition* 11 (1991): 107-22.

Kaufer, David S., and Christine M. Neuwirth. "The Irony Game: Assessing a Writer's Adaptation to an Opponent." *Journal of Advanced Composition* 2 (1981): 89-101.

Keene, Michael L., and L. Bensel-Meyers. "The Establishment of Rhetoric: Developing a Sense of Community." *Journal of Advanced Composition* 8 (1988): 41-49.

Keene, Michael L., and Ray Wallace. "Advanced Writing Courses and Programs." Adams and Adams. 89-100.

Kent, Thomas. "Externalism and the Production of Discourse." *Journal of Advanced Composition* 12 (1992): 57-74.

Killingsworth, M. Jimmie. "Realism, Human Action, and Instrumental Discourse." *Journal of Advanced Composition* 12 (1992): 171-200.

Kinneavy, James L. "The Exile of Rhetoric from the Liberal Arts." *Journal of Advanced Composition* 8 (1988): 105-12.

———. "The Process of Writing: A Philosophical Base in Hermeneutics." *Journal of Advanced Composition* 7 (1987): 1-9.

Kirscht, Judith, and Emily Golson. "Essay Thinking: Empty and Chaotic." *Journal of Advanced Composition* 4 (1983): 13-23.

Knoblauch, C.H. "The Rhetoric of the Paragraph: A Reconsideration." *Journal of Advanced Composition* 2 (1981): 53-61.

———. "Some Observations on Freire's *Pedagogy of the Oppressed.*" *Journal of Advanced Composition* 8 (1988): 50-54.

Koch, Richard. "Conversations with the Oriental Man: An Approach to the Imagination in Writing Class." *Journal of Advanced Composition* 2 (1981): 31-44.

Kottler, Barnet. "The Composition/Communication Course for the Gifted Student." *College Composition and Communication* 11 (1960): 168-70.

Kraemer, Don. "No Exit: A Play of Literacy and Gender." *Journal of Advanced Composition* 10 (1990): 305-19.

Krupa, Gene H. "Between Writer and Text." *Journal of Advanced Composition* 3 (1982): 84-88.

———. "Invention and Metaphor." *Journal of Advanced Composition* 3 (1982): 79-83.

Kumar, Amitava. "Brecht and His Friends: Writing as Critique." *Journal of Advanced Composition* 11 (1991): 301-14.

Laditka, James N. "Semiology, Ideology, *Praxis*: Responsible Authority in the Composition Classroom." *Journal of Advanced Composition* 10 (1990): 357-73.

Larson, Gale K. "The Advanced Composition Course." *College Composition and Communication* 21 (1970): 289-90.

Larson, Richard. "A Special Course in Advanced Composition for Prospective Teachers." *Journal of Teacher Education* 20 (1969): 168-74.

LeFevre, Karen B., and T.J. Larkin. "Freud, Weber, Durkheim: A Philosophical Foundation for Writing in the Humanities and Social Sciences." *Journal of Advanced Composition* 4 (1983): 65-83.

Leverenz, Carrie Shively. "Peer Response in the Multicultural Composition Classroom: Dissensus—A Dream (Deferred)." *Journal of Advanced Composition* 14 (1994): 167-86.

Long, Richard. "The Role of Audience in Chaim Perelman's New Rhetoric." *Journal of Advanced Composition* 4 (1983): 107-17.

Loux, Ann Kimble, and Rebecca M. Stoddart. "Denial, Conflagration, Pride: Three Stages in the Development of an Advanced Writing Requirement." *College Composition and Communication* 45 (1994): 521-34.

Mathes, J.C. "A Taxonomy of Communication Acts for the Design of Advanced Writing Courses." *Journal of Advanced Composition* 1 (1980): 53-57.

Matott, Glenn. "Linear Composing, Discourse Analysis, and the Outline." *Journal of Advanced Composition* 4 (1983): 33-45.

McCullen, Maurice L. "Looking Backwards: Advanced Composition to Freshman English." *Freshman English News* 4.2 (1975): 1-2.

McDaniel, Ellen. "Bibliography of Text-Analysis and Writing-Instruction Software." *Journal of Advanced Composition* 7 (1987): 139-70.

McLeod, Susan H. "The Affective Domain and the Writing Process: Working Definitions." *Journal of Advanced Composition* 11 (1991): 95-105.

_____. "Evaluating Writing Programs: Paradigms, Problems, Possibilities." *Journal of Advanced Composition* 12 (1992): 373-82.

Medlicott, Alex. "Cassette Commentary: An Approach to the Teaching of Expository Writing." *Journal of Advanced Composition* 1 (1980): 4-6.

Mitchell, Felicia. "Balancing Individual Projects and Collaborative Learning in an Advanced Writing Class." *College Composition and Communication* 43 (1992): 393-400.

Moore, Leslie, and Linda Peterson. "Convention as Transition: Linking the Advanced Composition Course to the College Curriculum." *Journal of Advanced Composition* 4 (1983): 173-87.

Moore, Sandy, and Michael Kleine. "Toward an Ethics of Teaching Writing in a Hazardous Context: The University." *Journal of Advanced Composition* 12 (1992): 383-94.

Meyer, Charles F. "Teaching Punctuation to Advanced Writers." *Journal of Advanced Composition* 6 (1985-86): 117-29.

Meyer, Sam. "Prose by Any Other Name: A Context for Teaching the Rhetoric of Titles." *Journal of Advanced Composition* 8 (1988): 71-81.

Meyers, G. Douglas. "Teaching Critical Thinking in the Technical Writing Class." *Journal of Advanced Composition* 6 (1985-86): 97-103.

Miller, Thomas P. "Treating Professional Writing as Social *Praxis*." *Journal of Advanced Composition* 11 (1991): 57-72.

Moore, Leslie, and Linda Peterson. "Convention as Transition: Linking the Advanced Composition Course to the College Curriculum." *Journal of Advanced Composition* 4 (1983): 173-87.

"Motivating the Gifted Student in the Composition/Communication Program." *College Composition and Communication* 12 (1961): 149-51.

Nielsen, Elizabeth. "Linguistic Sexism in Business Writing Textbooks." *Journal of Advanced Composition* 8 (1988): 55-65.

Olson, Gary A. "Advanced Composition." *Encyclopedia of English Studies and Language Arts.* Urbana: NCTE: 1995. 25-26.

_____. "Afterword: Needed Scholarship in Advanced Composition." Adams and Adams. 283-88.

_____. "The Generational Cliché: Then You Saw It; Now They Don't." *Journal of Advanced Composition* 6 (1985-86): 105-15.

_____. "Incorporating Sentence Combining into the Advanced Composition Class." *Journal of Advanced Composition* 2 (1981): 119-26.

Olson, Gary A., and Evelyn Ashton-Jones. "From Artifact to Utterance: Toward a Revised Conception of Critical Thinking in Advanced Composition." Adams and Adams. 195-210.

Olson, Gary A., and Irene Gale. "Selected Bibliography of Rhetorics and Readers for Advanced Composition." *ATAC Forum* 4.1 (1992): 5-9.

Olson, Gary A., and Sidney I. Dobrin. *Composition Theory for the Postmodern Classroom.* Carbondale: Southern Illinois UP, 1994.

Orgelfinger, G. "Differences between Teaching Freshman and Junior Level Composition." *Maryland Composition Review* 4.1 (1983): 12-17.

Orth, Michael P. "An Advanced Composition Course Aimed at Publication." *College Composition and Communication* 17 (1976): 210-12.

Otte, George. "Why Read What?: The Politics of Composition Anthologies." *Journal of Advanced Composition* 12 (1992): 137-49.

Palumbo, Roberta M. "Advanced Composition: A Course for Students in All Disciplines." ERIC, 1977. ED 147 843.

———. "Writing for the Pre-Professional Within a Liberal Arts Curriculum." *Journal of Advanced Composition* 1 (1980): 18-20.

Pelz, Karen. "James Britton and the Pedagogy of Advanced Composition." *Journal of Advanced Composition* 3 (1982): 1-9.

Peritz, Janice H. "When Learning Is Not Enough: Writing Across the Curriculum and the (Re)turn to Rhetoric." *Journal of Advanced Composition* 14 (1994): 431-54.

———. "A Reply to Medlicott: Evaluating Writing." *Journal of Advanced Composition* 1 (1980): 7-8.

Penfield, Elizabeth. "Freshman English/Advanced Writing: How Do We Distinguish the Two?" Adams and Adams. 17-30.

Phillips, T.J. "Imaginative Writing in Advanced Composition." *College Composition and Communication* 6 (1955): 153-55.

Qualley, Donna J., and Elizabeth Chiseri-Strater. "Collaboration as Reflexive Dialogue: A Knowing 'Deeper Than Reason.'" *Journal of Advanced Composition* 14 (1994): 111-30.

Rankin, Elizabeth. "From Simple to Complex: Ideas of Order in Assignment Sequences." *Journal of Advanced Composition* 10 (1990): 126-34.

Reynolds, John F., and Lita Liwag-Sutcliffe. "Team Teaching and Grading in Advanced Composition." *ATAC Forum* 3.1 (1991): 11-13.

Ritchie, Joy S. "Resistance to Reading: Another View of the Minefield." *Journal of Advanced Composition* 12 (1992): 115-36.

Robbins, Harry W., and Roscoe Parker. *Advanced Exposition.* New York: Prentice, 1935.

Roberts, Patricia. "Habermas' Varieties of Communicative Action: Controversy Without Combat." *Journal of Advanced Composition* 11 (1991): 409-24.

Robertson, Linda R. "Assignments in the Humanities: Writing Intensive Course Design." *Journal of Advanced Composition* 3 (1982): 48-59.

Ronald, Kate. "The Politics of Teaching Professional Writing." *Journal of Advanced Composition* 7 (1987): 23-30.

Ronald, Kate, and Jon Volkmer. "Another Competing Theory of Process: The Student's." *Journal of Advanced Composition* 9 (1989): 83-96.

Russell, David R. "Vygotsky, Dewey, and Externalism: Beyond the Student/Discipline Dichotomy." *Journal of Advanced Composition* 13 (1993): 173-97.

Rutter, Russell. "Research Writing in Advanced Composition: An Essay in Definition." *Journal of Advanced Composition* 6 (1985-86): 131-38.

Salerno, Douglas. "An Interpersonal Approach to Writing Negative Messages." *Journal of Advanced Composition* 6 (1985-86): 139-49.

Satterfield, Leon. "'Myself Must I Remake': An Existentialist Philosophy of Composition." *Journal of Advanced Composition* 8 (1988): 82-87.

Schafer, John S. "Linguistic Descriptions of Speaking and Writing and Their Impact on Composition Pedagogy." *Journal of Advanced Composition* 4 (1983): 85-106.

Schilb, John. "Ideology and Composition Scholarship." *Journal of Advanced Composition* 8 (1988): 22-29.

Schmidt, Jan Z. "The Use and Value of the Meditation in an Advanced Composition Course: A Meditation on Meditations." *Journal of Advanced Composition* 6 (1985-86): 65-77.

Schroeder, Melvin W., and Kenneth M. Sroka. "The Canisus Project: From Field-Work to Classroom." *Journal of Advanced Composition* 2 (1981): 127-37.

Shelby, Annette N. "Developing Content for an M.B.A. Communication Class." *Journal of Advanced Composition* 4 (1983): 189-97.

Shoos, Diane, Diana George, and Joseph Comprone. "Twin Peaks and the Look of Television: Visual Literacy in the Writing Class." *Journal of Advanced Composition* 13 (1993): 459-75.

Shumaker, Arthur W. "How Can a Major in Composition be Established?" *Journal of Advanced Composition* 2 (1981): 139-46.

Shumaker, Ronald C., Larry Dennis, and Lois Green. "Advanced Exposition: A Survey of Patterns and Problems." *Journal of Advanced Composition* 10 (1990): 136-44.

Sledd, James. "Linguistics, Obeah, Acupuncture, and the Teaching of Composition by that Bastard Sledd." *Journal of Advanced Composition* 2 (1981): 147-52.

Snow, Joanne Erdman. "The Advanced Writing Requirement at Saint Mary's College." *Writing to Learn Mathematics and Science.* Ed. Paul Connolly and Teresa Vilardi. New York: Teachers College P. 1989. 193-97.

Snyder, Carol. "Analyzing Classifications: Foucault for Advanced Writers." *College Composition and Communication* 35 (1984): 209-16.

Sotirou, Peter. "Articulating a Hermeneutic Pedagogy: The Philosophy of Interpretation." *Journal of Advanced Composition* 13 (1993): 365-80.

Spear, Karen I. "Thinking and Writing: A Sequential Curriculum for Composition." *Journal of Advanced Composition* 4 (1983): 47-63.

Spellmeyer, Kurt. "Writing and Truth: The Decline of Expertise and the Rebirth of Philosophy." *Journal of Advanced Composition* 13 (1993): 97-110.

Spigelmire, Lynne. "The Best Stylists: A Survey of Editors and Implications for the Teaching of Style." *Journal of Advanced Composition* 1 (1980): 69-73.

Spretnak, Charlene M. "Reading and Writing for Engineering Students." *Journal of Advanced Composition* 4 (1983): 133-37.

Stephens, Rory D. "Variations in Composing Style." *Journal of Advanced Composition* 2 (1981): 45-52.

Sternglass, Marilyn. "School-Sponsored and Self-Sponsored at the Same Time." *Journal of Advanced Composition* 9 (1989): 162-73.

Stevenson, Dwight W. "Teaching Rhetoric to Students in Upper Division and Professional Degree Program Courses." *Journal of Advanced Composition* 1 (1980): 60-67.

Stewart, Donald C. "An Advanced Composition Course that Works." *College Composition and Communication* 25 (1974): 197-200.

_____. "Practical Work for Advanced Composition Students." *College Composition and Communication* 31 (1980): 81-83.

_____. "Some Thoughts on Arrangement." *Journal of Advanced Composition* 7 (1987): 92-100.

Stone, William B. "Rewriting in Advanced Composition." *Journal of Advanced Composition* 1 (1980): 74-77.

Sturm, Rita. "Advanced Composition, 1980: The State of the Art." *Journal of Advanced Composition* 1 (1980): 37-44.

Suchan, James, and Craig Hawbaker. "Online Bibliographic Searches in Report Writing Courses." *Journal of Advanced Composition* 3 (1982): 60-68.

Sullivan, Dale L. "Political-Ethical Implications of Defining Technical Writing as a Practice." *Journal of Advanced Composition* 10 (1990): 375-86.

Sullivan, Patricia. "Desktop Publishing: A Powerful Tool for Advanced Composition Courses." *College Composition and Communication* 39 (1988): 344-48.

Sullivan, Patricia A. "Writing in the Graduate Curriculum: Literary Criticism as Composition." *Journal of Advanced Composition* 11 (1991): 283-99.

Tate, Priscilla. "Survey of Advanced Writing Programs." Unpublished report, 1985.

Teich, Nathaniel. "Rogerian Problem-Solving and the Rhetoric of Argumentation." *Journal of Advanced Composition* 7 (1987): 52-61.

Tingle, Nick. "Self and Liberatory Pedagogy: Transforming Narcissism." *Journal of Advanced Composition* 12 (1992): 75-89.

Van Winckel, Nance, "The Role of Preconscious Thought in the Composing Process." *Journal of Advanced Composition* 3 (1982): 102-15.

Voss, Ralph F. "Calculators and Quality: A Paradox for Writing Teachers." *Journal of Advanced Composition* 2 (1981): 11-21.

_____. "Composition and the Empirical Imperative." *Journal of Advanced Composition* 4 (1983): 5-12.

Wall, Susan V. "The Languages of the Text: What Even Good Students Need to Know about Re-Writing." *Journal of Advanced Composition* 7 (1987): 23-40.

Walpole, Jane R. "Ramus Revisited: The Uses and Limits of Classical Rhetoric." *Journal of Advanced Composition* 2 (1981): 63-68.

Ward, Jay A. "Changes in the Training of Writing Teachers." *Journal of Advanced Composition* 2 (1981): 153-60.

Watson, Sam. "Letters on Writing—a Medium of Exchange with Students of Writing." Adams and Adams. 133-50.

Welch, Nancy. "One Student's Many Voices: Reading, Writing, and Responding with Bakhtin." *Journal of Advanced Composition* 13 (1993): 493-502.

White, Bernice W. "Looking for Books?: Two 'Advanced Composition' Texts and one Draftee." *Journal of Advanced Composition* 2 (1981): 171-83.

White, John O. "An Advanced Writing Program Across the Disciplines." *ATAC Newsletter* 2.1 (1990): 6-7.

Winsor, Dorothy A. "What Counts as Writing?: An Argument from Engineers' Practice." *Journal of Advanced Composition* 12 (1992): 337-47.

Winterowd, W. Ross. "'Chicken' and Poetry: The Unspeakable and the Unsayable." *Journal of Advanced Composition* 7 (1987): 76-80.

_____. "Rediscovering the Essay." *Journal of Advanced Composition* 8 (1988): 146-57.

_____. "Transferable and Local Writing Skills." *Journal of Advanced Composition* 1 (1980): 1-3.

Wolf, Thia, Lauren Wright, and Tom Imhoff. "Collaborative Role-Playing and Negotiation: A Cross-Disciplinary Endeavor." *Journal of Advanced Composition* 14 (1994): 149-66.

Wood, Robert G. "The Dialectic Suppression of Feminist Thought in Radical Pedagogy." *Journal of Advanced Composition* 13 (1993): 79-95.

Woodman, Leonora. "A Rhetorical Model of Prose Style: Notes Toward a Synthesis of Rhetoric and Poetics." *Journal of Advanced Composition* 2 (1981): 69-78.

_____. "Teaching Style: A Process-Centered View." *Journal of Advanced Composition* 3 (1982): 116-25.

Woolever, Kristen R. "Untangling the Law: Verbal Design in Legal Argument." *Journal of Advanced Composition* 6 (1985-86): 151-65.

Young, Richard E. "The Rhythm of Education and the Teaching of Writing." Adams and Adams. 43-58.

Index